Basic Interviewing Skills

Basic
Interviewing
Skills

RAYMOND L. GORDEN
PROFESSOR EMERITUS, ANTIOCH COLLEGE

F. E. PEACOCK PUBLISHERS, INC.
ITASCA, ILLINOIS

Contents

Preface

THIS BOOK PROVIDES a process model and a corresponding set of structured, classroom-tested exercises designed to improve basic interviewing skills. The model—called the Skill Learning Cycle—is intended not only as a learning procedure for a college course, but also as a valuable tool to use in the future for continued growth in interviewing skills and sensitivity.

For the purposes of this book, interviewing is defined as a particular form of conversation between two people in which one person tries to direct the conversation to obtain information relevant to some specified purpose. Although information gathering is not the only purpose of an interview, it is the essential characteristic that distinguishes interviewing from other forms of conversation. Speech in which no information is being sought may be a sales talk, sociable conversation, lecture, explanation, and so on, but it is not an interview.

In order to focus on the most *basic* interviewing skills, only the information-gathering function, which is common to all interviews, is discussed. To sharpen the focus even more, I have excluded those highly specialized information-gathering skills needed to carry out certain complicated tactics peculiar to a specific interview setting. For example, I do not deal with skills needed in certain police interrogation tactics or with the special skills needed by a child-abuse worker counseling a victim or by a lawyer cross-examining a hostile witness. Unless a person has the more fundamental, simple skills presented in this book, there is little point in trying to master the more complicated tactics of a specialized field.

Some skills that are not practiced within the give-and-take of the conversation defined as interviewing are described. These additional skills are needed in the *planning* and *analysis* phases of the Skill Learning Cycle. They are also the skills necessary for future self-directed learning.

Twelve basic interviewing skills fit into the three phases of the Skill Learning Cycle:

1. *Planning phase:* formulating relevant questions, designing motivating questions, and establishing a communicative atmosphere.
2. *Doing phase:* delivering the question, listening to the respondent, observing the respondent's nonverbal behavior, evaluating the response, probing the response, and recording the information.
3. *Analysis phase:* coding the relevant information, testing the reliability of the coding, and analyzing one's own interview behavior.

Most of the many books on interviewing skills omit all of the skills in the planning and analysis phases as well as some of those in the doing phase. It is my conviction that completing the whole Skill Learning Cycle is a more powerful learning experience. It makes the student responsible for planning something he or she is going to do, for doing it, and then for objectively analyzing the results.

This book is designed to be used as an auxiliary text in a variety of courses in communications, journalism, counseling, social work, personnel selection, market research, nursing, law enforcement, litigation, public opinion survey methods, community studies, oral history, education, anthropology, sociology, and social psychology. It can also be used as the main text in a course focused on interviewing if the instructor is willing to furnish supporting theory and the context for the particular application of interviewing in lectures or assigned readings. In this case, the bibliography at the end of the book could be useful.

The book can also be used by small teams of two or three persons who are working independently to improve their interviewing skills. In such situations, the team needs a copy of the *Instructor's Manual.*

An instructor who is using this book as an auxiliary text will not have enough time in a course to assign all the exercises. The instructor should select the most appropriate exercises in view of the objectives of the course and the background of the students. In any case, as a minimum the students should experience the complete Skill Learning Cycle by doing the field project that forms Chapter 11. The project integrates the whole process of planning, doing, and analyzing the interview. Conceivably, it is possible to read the whole text and do only the field project—without doing the preparatory exercises at the end of each chapter. This would be difficult, however, and is not recommended.

In deciding which exercises to omit, the instructor should read both the exercises themselves at the end of each chapter and the corresponding materials in the *Instructor's Manual.* This will provide a clear picture of the nature of the assignment, the materials needed, the amount of time required, and the kind of feedback and discussion to be provided by the instructor. Many exercises are structured in phases, so some parts of the procedure can be omitted while others are retained.

The *Instructor's Manual* is not merely an ancillary convenience; it is *absolutely essential* for teaching basic interviewing skills. The manual is designed to maximize student learning and to minimize the time spent on busywork by the student and instructor (or teaching assistant). When appropriate, the following materials are provided for each exercise:

- A list of materials and facilities needed to carry out the exercise
- Step-by-step procedures for doing the exercise or demonstration
- Feedback forms for the individual student's solution or performance
- Keys to multiple-choice answers
- Model essay answers
- Discussion guides for the instructor
- Discussion guides for student dyads
- Listening and observation guides
- Self-analysis guides for the student
- Forms for coding relevant information
- Forms for calculating reliability of coding

Although these aids are not perfect, they all have been tested in the classroom, and they present challenging problems with facilitating guidelines and materials.

The enterprising instructor may want to adapt some of the exercises to the special interests of students by introducing different interview content into the procedures and formats provided.

Interviewing skills are not simple motor skills like riding a bicycle. Rather, they involve a high-order combination of observation, empathic sensitivity, and intellectual judgment which is difficult to learn and teach. It is my conviction that the basic skills needed for the information-gathering function common to all interviews are rarely given the attention they deserve in either undergraduate or graduate courses dealing with human behavior. This is one social scientist's attempt to improve this situation.

Raymond L. Gorden
Yellow Springs, Ohio

Acknowledgments

I WISH TO THANK the undergraduate students at Antioch College and the members of the continuing education seminars at Ohio State University for their patience and suggestions during the classroom testing of the exercises in the Skill Learning Cycle.

For their many suggestions for improving the style and organization of the book, I thank Dan Duffee and my wife Charlotte Gilson Gorden.

Any imperfections remaining in the content or style are my own responsibility.

*Learning high-order interviewing
skills requires thoughtful planning,
self-controlled performance,
and critical analysis of one's
own interview.*

1

Overview

BEFORE WE BEGIN a series of activities aimed at learning basic interviewing skills, we need to examine the general nature of interviewing. Interviews vary infinitely in their purposes and settings; despite this variety however, all interviews involve some common basic skills.

THE NATURE OF INTERVIEWING

Interviewing—A Pervasive Activity

Many people have such a narrow conception of interviewing that they do not recognize the pervasiveness of interviewing in their everyday lives. The parent who tries to discover why the four-year-old is crying, the student who tries to get a professor to clarify a concept, and the voter who tries to determine a political candidate's opinion on a specific issue are all interviewing whether they realize it or not. Yet such interviews often fail to obtain the information desired. The voter, for example, faced with a political candidate's evasive tactics may end the interview more exasperated than enlightened.

Similarly, in their professional roles people frequently have to conduct interviews, but they rarely have the skills needed for a high rate of success. Consider the police officer talking to a motorist for an accident report, the business manager questioning an employee to discover the cause of a dispute, and the nurse taking a medical history from a patient. Rarely do such people think of themselves as interviewers, and usually they lack adequate training in the basic skills involved. Nevertheless, a high order of skill is needed for success in these and many similar situations.[1]

Interviewing Defined

For the purposes of this book, interviewing is defined broadly to include a wide variety of situations:

> Interviewing is conversation between two people in which one person tries to direct the conversation to obtain information for some specific purpose.

This definition focuses on the information-gathering function of the conversation, even though there are additional functions in various interview settings such as persuasion, instruction, or emotional support. Without the information-gathering function we may have a lecture or a sales pitch but not an interview.

This definition, though broad, excludes many forms of normal sociable conversation. For a number of reasons the word *conversation* is central to the definition and is more appropriate than a technical term such as *dyadic verbal interaction*. First, much of the relevant interaction in any interview is nonverbal. Second, a more technical phrase may suggest that an interview is an artificial form of communication that lacks the ordinary sound of conversation or that possesses the qualities of acting. Also, interviewing is intentionally defined as a form of conversation rather than a form of questioning, because many situations require the interviewer to use statements designed to provide a context for a question, to summarize a question, or to challenge the respondent.

Although the definition focuses on information gathering, other forms of conversation are often permitted within the interview for the sake of maintaining a good relationship with the respondent. These other forms should not, however, interfere with the information-gathering function.

If we want to concentrate on the most basic interviewing skills, we must focus on information gathering—the function common to all interviews.

Interviewing Learned

Several decades ago even many social scientists thought that good interviewers were born not made. Therefore, they believed, there was no value in trying to teach someone to interview. At that time researchers focused on how to *select* good interviewers, and very little literature was devoted to experiments in training people to interview. In support of this point of view, numerous attempts to improve interviewing ability through formal training proved unsuccessful. In recent decades, however, many experiments have demonstrated that a person's interviewing effectiveness can be greatly improved by guided learning experiences. A few of these studies are cited later in this chapter.

Figure 1.1   Skill Learning Cycle

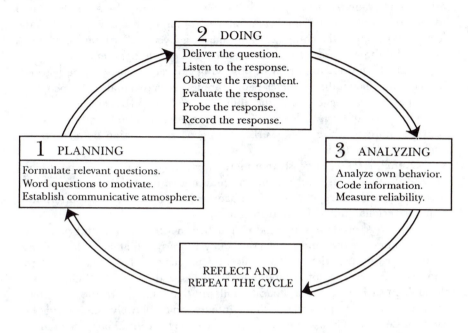

THE SKILL LEARNING CYCLE

The Skill Learning Cycle as shown in Figure 1.1 involves twelve skills. Three are used in planning the interview, six in doing the interview, and three in analyzing the interview. Then the learner reflects on all three phases of the experience before going on to plan, do, and analyze another interview. Such thoughtful, disciplined activity covering all three phases of the Skill Learning Cycle is more productive than spending dozens of hours in mindless interviewing activity.

The effectiveness of including the whole cycle in the learning process has been shown in several studies. For example, Parker and Meeks have found that in learning guidance interviewing it is important for the learner not only to do interviews but also to analyze them.[2] Studies have also shown that an important part of analyzing one's own interview is hearing a recording of the interview. A pioneering study demonstrated this when the tape recorder first became popular.[3] Some studies have even demonstrated that in learning certain types of interviewing it is more effective for the learner to analyze other people's interviews than to practice interviewing with no analysis.[4] In one case the analysis took the form of coding the relevant information from a tape-recorded interview as is done in Chapter 11. *Probably the most effective learning technique is to combine performance with analysis of one's own interview.*

The planning phase of the cycle is important because of its vital relationship to the doing and analyzing phases. For example, formulating relevant questions in the *planning* phase is clearly related to the mental process of evaluating the relevance of the response in the *doing* phase. It is also strongly related to the process of coding the relevant information in the *analyzing* phase. As the learner experiences the complete Skill Learning Cycle, other vital connections among the three phases of the experience will become apparent.

Even the more subtle skill of observing nonverbal cues can be learned. Studies have shown that younger people are less sensitive than older people to such cues, which suggests that the ability to read nonverbal cues comes with life experience and can be learned.[5] The same research also found that people who are more sensitive to nonverbal cues generally function better both socially and intellectually.

Overall, research suggests that mere repetitive performance without planning, critical analysis, and replanning may not result in improvement. Furthermore, uncritical repetition can fix bad habits into an inflexible pattern that requires serious remedial action to change.

This book presents a method of practice in which thoughtful planning, sensitive interviewing, and critical self-analysis are systematically blended into a vital learning experience. The following preview of the remainder of the book shows how the total experience is organized. Note that Chapters 2 through 10 each deal with a separate skill and that Chapter 11, the final chapter, provides a project that requires the integration of all twelve skills needed in the Skill Learning Cycle. At every step of the cycle the central purpose of maximizing the relevance, validity, and completeness of the information obtained from the respondent is kept clearly in view.

Planning

The planning phase assumes that the interviewer starts with nothing more than a problem or set of objectives; the interviewer does not depend on someone else to formulate the questions or set up the interview situation.

Formulating Relevant Questions (Chapter 2).   For a question to be useful in an interview it must first be relevant to the objectives of the interview. To arrive at relevant questions the interviewer must (1) clearly define the objectives of the interview, (2) translate each objective into specific points of information needed, and (3) translate those points into questions to be asked. The inexperienced interviewer tends to simply hand the objectives to the respondent in the guise of questions rather than breaking the objectives down into more concrete questions.

Formulating Motivating Questions (Chapter 3).   It is not enough for a question to be logically relevant to the objectives of the interview. The second quality of a useful question is that it helps to motivate by making the respondent either more willing or more able to answer the question.

Establishing a Communicative Atmosphere (Chapter 4).   Before the first question is asked the interviewer can increase the chances of obtaining the needed information by establishing a physical and verbal setting that helps the process. A poor setting can counteract the effects of the best questioning techniques.

Doing

The most frequently used interviewing skills are those in the *doing* phase of the Skill Learning Cycle, because in some interviewing situations someone other than the interviewer defines the problem and decides what questions are to be asked. However, for the purposes of learning interviewing skills, the planning and interviewing should be done by the same person. Defining the problem and formulating the questions in the planning phase will help sensitize the interviewer to what to listen for, to whether a response is relevant, to the need for further probing, and to what should be recorded. For these reasons, all of the doing skills described next assume that interviewer was also the planner.

Delivering the Question (Chapter 5).   If we assume that the exact wording of a question has been established in the planning phase, then the delivery of the question depends on nonverbal factors accompanying the question. These factors include the interviewer's body position, eye contact, facial expression, tone of voice, and pacing. All of these factors affect the respondent's ability or willingness to answer.

Listening to the Respondent (Chapter 6).   Listening is not something everyone does well, even in normal conversation. Listening is the active, intellectual process of seeking meaning in what another person says; it is hearing with a purpose. The good interviewer tries to understand what the words mean to the speaker as well as how this meaning is related to the objectives of the interview. The good interviewer listens to both the verbal and the audible nonverbal communication of the respondent. Audible nonverbal cues include the respondent's tone of voice, silences, intonation patterns, pacing, and so forth. They provide a context that completes the meaning of the verbal message.

Observing the Respondent (Chapter 7).   Just as the interviewer listens for the audible nonverbal cues, he or she *observes* the visual nonverbal cues or body language of the respondent. Cues such as body posture, movements of hands and feet, facial expression, and eye movement all constitute a nonverbal context that provides clues to the meaning and validity of the verbal message as well as to the energy level, mood, and attitude of the respondent. The interviewer should be aware of any discrepancies between the verbal and the nonverbal messages as clues to the meaning and validity of the response. The interviewer should also note *changes* in the predominant mood or attitude of the respondent as clues to the meaning of the response and to the respondent's changing need for encouragement, support, or challenge.

Evaluating the Response (Chapter 8).   After ascertaining the meaning of the response by careful listening and observation, the interviewer is ready to evaluate the response. There are three evaluative questions the interviewer must constantly keep in mind: Is the response relevant to the objective of the question? Is the information valid (true)? Is the information complete?

Probing the Response (Chapter 9).   If the interviewer's evaluation finds the response inadequate to meet the objectives of the question, then the interviewer must probe the response to improve its relevance, validity, or completeness. To probe effectively the interviewer needs to have command of a variety of probe forms that will encourage the respondent to elaborate and clarify without biasing the response with subtle suggestions or assumptions. About a dozen different probe forms will be provided for the interviewer's tool kit.

Recording the Response (Chapter 10).   Recording the response may be considered as part of the *doing* phase in the Skill Learning Cycle or as part of the *analysis* phase, depending on the particular method of recording that is used. For example, if the interviewer records a response by simply checking a predetermined category in order to classify a response into some analytical scheme, then recording and analyzing are being done simultaneously. On the other hand, if the interviewer writes verbatim quotes from a response or tape-records the interview, then recording the information is separate from the *analysis* phase of the Skill Learning Cycle.

Recording the response, then, may be part of either the doing or the analysis phases. To keep all of the choices of recording methods together, they will all be discussed in Chapter 10, Recording and Coding Information, which deals mainly with the analysis phase.

Analyzing

The analyzing phase is crucial to the process of learning those performance skills needed in the doing phase. By inserting the critical analysis phase into the Skill Learning Cycle we avoid mindless repetition of the interviewing process. Before conducting a second interview on a topic, the interviewer should critically analyze the results obtained in the first interview. This critical analysis has two main aspects: objectively analyzing one's own interviewing behavior and evaluating the total amount of relevant information obtained.

Without critical analysis the interviewer may remain unaware of mistakes and may optimistically assume that the information obtained was relevant, complete, and valid. Often interviewers are shocked the first time they hear their own interviewing on tape. This may be their first realization that they loaded the questions, accepted irrelevant answers, or failed to probe for relevance, completeness, and validity.

Recording and Coding Information (Chapter 10).   The interviewer needs to know how to select the most appropriate mode for recording information. Information may be recorded for two purposes: to help the interviewer remember points that need to be probed later and to store the responses.

Once the responses have been stored, the interviewer needs to know how to winnow out the relevant from the irrelevant and then how to classify (code) this relevant information into categories meaningful to the purposes of the interview. Classifying information into categories can make one acutely aware of missing information, of responses that are too vague to classify reliably, and of one's failure to persist in the pursuit of relevant, complete, and valid information. Often, after finishing the coding, an interviewer would like to have another opportunity to interview the same respondent.

Integrating the Major Skills (Chapter 11).   This final chapter provides an interview problem that requires integration of the skills covered in the Skill Learning Cycle. Students are assigned an information-gathering problem and are expected to plan, do, and analyze their own interviews aimed at solving the problem.

To accomplish this integration, the chapter provides the opportunity to use all of the skills covered in the first ten chapters and adds two activities: analyzing one's own interviewing behavior as revealed in a tape recording and testing the reliability of one's coding by comparing it with independent coding by another person.

SUMMARY

Interviewing is defined in this book as focusing on the most essential function common to the broadest range of interview situations: the information-gathering function. To learn basic information-gathering skills is to learn those skills that are useful for all types of interviews regardless of any additional functions they might have.

Interviewing skills are not simple motor skills like riding a bicycle; rather, they involve a high-order combination of observation, empathic sensitivity, and intellectual judgment. These skills can be learned by disciplined practice, particularly when learners assume responsibility for planning, doing, and analyzing their own interviews.

The Skill Learning Cycle provides an initial, guided experience for the complete interview-learning process. It also stands as a model for the learner to use in the future on a path of independent self-improvement. The potential rewards are considerable and the path can be exciting.

NOTES

1. For a more detailed analysis of interview dialogues in eight different professional settings, see Raymond L. Gorden, "Professional Settings of the Interview," in *Interviewing: Strategy, Techniques and Tactics,* 4th ed. (Chicago: Dorsey Press, 1987).

2. Aileen Parker and Clinton Meeks, "Problems in Learning to Interview," *Counselor Education and Supervision* 7 (1967): 54–59.

3. S. Womer and H. W. Boyd, Jr., "The Use of Voice Recorder in the Selection and Training of Interviewers," *Public Opinion Quarterly* 15 (Summer 1951): 358–63.

4. Lester Guest, "A New Training Method for Opinion Interviewers," *Public Opinion Quarterly* 18 (Fall 1954): 287–99.

5. Robert Rosenthal et al., "Body Talk and Tone of Voice—The Language without Words," *Psychology Today* (September 1974): 64–68.

*The beginning of interviewing
wisdom is appreciating the
difference between what you want
to know and how you should ask.*

2

Formulating Relevant
Questions

FORMULATING USEFUL QUESTIONS is critically important to meeting the
objectives of the interview. To be useful a question must have two characteristics: It must be relevant to the objectives of the interview, and it must be in a
form that maximizes the respondent's motivation to answer it. This chapter
examines the issue of relevance; the next chapter concerns putting relevant
questions in a motivating form.

WANTED—RELEVANT QUESTIONS

Often when an organization plans a study that involves interviewing, there is a
premature concern for training the interviewers in specific techniques. The focus is on how to get the information before the precise nature and purposes of
the information are clearly defined. Sometimes this error stems from a belief
that interviewers can formulate their own relevant questions if they are simply
told the general purpose of the interview.

Experience does not support this belief. For example, at the undergraduate level ten students were given thirty minutes to formulate questions relevant
to a general interview objective, and the objective was carefully defined in one
paragraph. Thirty minutes later, the group had produced ninety questions, but

there was not a single relevant question among them. This may seem incredible, as it did to the instructor, but the probability of such a result depends on the nature of the problem being investigated. Only a highly experienced person can quickly recognize the type of problem that might elude the attempt to formulate relevant questions.

Lack of relevance does not appear only in the attempts of undergraduates dealing with an elusive problem; it can also be found on a colossal scale in federal agencies. For example, in the early 1970s the federal Community Services Administration (CSA) proposed an information-gathering system to evaluate the effectiveness of the hundreds of local organizations using CSA funds in fifty states. The purpose of the system, mandated by Congress in the legislation that created the agency, was to safeguard against the waste of federal funds by ineffective local programs.

To achieve this purpose, the CSA planned to require that all local organizations submit quarterly reports providing "quantitative indicators of effectiveness" of those programs funded by CSA. In theory, this was a commendable attempt at evaluating the effectiveness of programs designed to help people out of poverty. Fortunately, before the plan was put into action, it was evaluated by a consultant who found that the plan was completely invalid: None of the 214 quantitative questions that were to be answered by the local agencies were relevant to the "effectiveness" of the programs in getting people out of poverty. To make matters worse, the time that would have been spent to gather, process, and report the data once every three months would have crippled the organizations' efforts on behalf of the poor.[1]

The consultant's critique, which was used by four national organizations lobbying in behalf of local community service organizations, was instrumental in scrapping all 214 irrelevant questions. Here are some of the questions typical of the CSA plan:

- How many explanatory pamphlets did you distribute in the last three months?
- How many community meetings did you have this quarter?
- How many professionals and volunteers are on your staff?
- In how many newspaper articles has your program been mentioned?

None of these questions or any of the remaining 210 dealt with the organizations' results or effects on poverty. Rather, all dealt with the amount of activity, personnel, money, and other resources that were part of the effort. The proposed evaluation questions would have encouraged the organizations to feel most effective when engaged in frenetic expenditure of resources regardless of their effects on the poverty rate. The proposed plan of evaluation would have been a colossal failure because the questions to be asked were irrelevant to the purpose of the study. The irrelevance of the questions was based on a failure to thoughtfully define the word *effectiveness*. Effectiveness concerns results not effort!

This example demonstrates the importance of defining a problem clearly before rushing in with questions which, on critical examination, are found to be irrelevant.

The important process of formulating relevant questions can be thought of as having three phases:

1. Clarifying the objectives of the interview
2. Specifying the information needed to achieve those objectives
3. Formulating concrete questions designed to obtain the information

CLARIFYING THE OBJECTIVES OF THE INTERVIEW

Only when objectives are clear is it possible to formulate relevant questions, evaluate the relevance of responses, or probe effectively for greater relevance. In some types of interviewing, objectives are simple and the relevance of questions is obvious. But in many cases seemingly simple objectives may not easily yield relevant questions, particularly when the objectives involve a social problem of community or organizational interest.

Consider this example. The faculty members of a small college came to an agreement that "we need to know more about why students do and do not come to our college." In effect, they wanted the answer to this basic question: Why do students come to College X rather than to some other college? An attempt to construct an interview guide with more specific questions quickly revealed that the agreement among the faculty members was more apparent than real. The interpretation of the purpose of the basic question varied widely. Some saw the study as an opportunity to test a few general hypotheses about the basic nature of human decision making, whereas others saw the study as a way of obtaining a practical understanding that would be immediately useful to the college. Even those who rallied around the second interpretation had little consensus among themselves.

Those who favored the second interpretation could not agree on whether the information should be useful in discovering how to increase the size of the student body or how to enhance the quality of the entering students. Those who agreed on the quality approach varied as to whether they wanted students with higher scores on college entrance exams or with stronger moral character or with interests in certain academic fields. After much discussion, the following consensus was achieved: the information should be useful to obtain more students with higher scores on entrance exams and predominantly those with a strong interest in general education as opposed to technical or vocational education.

Once the faculty agreed on the objectives and a tentative set of questions was devised, the administration noted that the college would not be interested in making every sort of change imaginable just to attract students. Discussions followed to determine whether the college was willing to change its geographical location, to remodel its dormitory facilities, to overhaul its curriculum, to raise its academic standards, to change the channels through which it sought publicity, and so on. These and other action-policy possibilities each required a different kind of information and a different set of questions. By deciding that the basic purpose was to do a study that was immediately applicable to the problems of the college, and by squarely facing the limitations in what the college was willing to change, it was possible both to reduce the number of questions needed and to demonstrate the relevance of each question.

In clarifying the objectives of any interview, avoid the extremes of including too many questions in a single interview and of conceiving the problem too narrowly. In the first instance, there may be little hope of collecting all of the relevant information within the limitations of time, money, and personnel to be devoted to the effort. In the second instance, the omission of certain related information may limit meaningful interpretation of the results.

SPECIFYING INFORMATION NEEDED

Two steps are important in determining the categories of information needed to reach the objectives of the interview. The first step is the usability test, that is, asking how the information is to be used in achieving the objectives of the interview. The interviewer must distinguish between information for curiosity's sake and information that is necessary. To apply the usability test, questions such as the following must be asked: Exactly how is this category of information to be used? Will different answers to this question matter to what we do? If the interviewer cannot clearly see how the information is to be used, either the question should be omitted or the objectives should be clarified. Putting questions to the usability test may save needless work in wording concrete questions, as well as in collecting and storing useless information.

The second step in determining the categories of information needed is to define precisely all of the important concepts in the statement of objectives. The Community Services Administration's failure to devise valid "quantitative indicators of effectiveness" illustrates a lack of usability testing and precise defining. Often the need for precise definition goes unappreciated until considerable irrelevant and confusing information has been collected. Remember that the need for precision in definition is present even when we are concerned with what appears to be an ordinary or obvious term like *family*.

To illustrate, assume that a community service organization is planning to help in the battle against crime by organizing a neighborhood watch system in which the residents of a neighborhood take turns watching the streets and monitoring a walkie-talkie network. The organization wants to begin with a neighborhood that has a high crime rate and to work through the heads of families, who will be invited to neighborhood meetings. To evaluate the effectiveness of the program, the organization wants to begin by measuring the rate of crime victims for families in different neighborhoods. Since only a small portion of crimes are reported to the police, the organizational committee decides to determine the crime rate by using a survey method. Thus, it would interview members of a random sample of households in each neighborhood to discover the types and number of crimes committed against each family in the past year. To obtain the rate for each neighborhood, the committee would then divide the total number of victimizations by the number of families in the neighborhood.

What categories of information need to be collected in these interviews? The crime rate depends on the number of crimes committed and the number of families in each neighborhood. To collect this information reliably so that the committee can compare one neighborhood with another and compare before-and-after crime rates to establish the effectiveness of the program, three concepts need precise definition: neighborhood, crime, and family.

Neighborhoods must be geographically defined so that they do not overlap or omit any territory. They must also be defined so that they are as socially and culturally homogeneous as possible because internal social cohesion is needed to facilitate cooperation in the neighborhood watch program.

Crime might be defined as any illegal act against persons or property that comes from outside the family. This definition would intentionally exclude child abuse and spouse abuse for several reasons. First, interviewers would have difficulty obtaining valid information on such acts of abuse from family members being interviewed at home. Second, the proposed type of street surveillance program would not be effective against internal family conflicts. Third, if a community organization first demonstrates effectiveness in combating street crime, it would then be in a position to design a second type of program aimed at the more difficult problem of family violence.

Family is the third concept that needs precise definition to establish an accurate before-and-after rate. It may seem that this everyday concept would need no special definition. Nothing could be further from the truth. Experience has shown that without a detailed definition of family, different interviewers' reports of the number of families in the same urban neighborhood can vary as much as 40 percent, a margin of error totally unacceptable either for a reliable ranking of neighborhoods according to crime rate or for a reliable measure of success in changing that rate.

A popular stereotype of the American family is a married couple with one or two children. This definition may do for an insurance company advertisement but it will be of little value in obtaining a reliable count of the number of families in a neighborhood. What if the mother in this stereotypical family dies in an accident and the daughter goes to live next door with her widowed grandmother—is the original family still a family? Are there now two families where there was once one? What if the daughter had stayed with her father and the grandmother adopted a Vietnamese orphan—then is each of these twosomes a family? What if the grandmother and the adopted child decide to live with the son and his daughter—does that household now have one family or two? Adding to the problem of definition is deciding whether a couple must be married to be a family, whether a single person acting as guardian of a child or a parent is a family, and so on.

Keep in mind that the definition of a family to be used in a neighborhood watch program need not agree with definitions used by the health department, the U.S. Census Bureau, or local social agencies (unless there are reasons to make the figures comparable). The definition should, like the definition of a neighborhood and a crime, fit the objectives of the interview.

To summarize, the principle of specifying the information needed in an interview requires subjecting each category of information to a usability test. It also requires giving each category a clear, logical definition in order to guide the construction of relevant, concrete questions.

FORMÚLATING CONCRETE QUESTIONS

After clarifying the objectives of the interview and specifying the types of information needed, the interviewer must formulate concrete questions designed to obtain the needed information.

An inexperienced interviewer tends simply to tell the respondent what information is wanted, but this practice will usually be unproductive. For example, in order to improve a social agency's efforts to get recipients into school a social worker wants to know how a particular welfare recipient decided to go to vocational school. Would it be a mistake simply to ask, "How did you decide to go into vocational training?" The beginning of interviewing wisdom is to appreciate the big difference between what you want to know and how you should ask. This general question should be treated as a topical area to be broken down into more specific, concrete questions.

In breaking the topic down, however, the interviewer must avoid missing the heart of the matter as stated in the general question. For example, the interviewer might mistakenly decide to start with the following series of concrete questions:

1. "How do you like vocational school?"
2. "Do you feel that you are learning?"
3. "Do you think that what you are learning will qualify you for a job?"
4. "What do you think of your fellow students?"

In a way, these questions are an improvement over the one general question in that they are easier to answer and they ask about matters both more concrete and narrower in scope than the general question. Nevertheless, they are all irrelevant because they focus on the respondent's experiences after going to school; they should be focusing on the decision-making process before starting school. Since cause precedes effect, the interviewer must discover what influenced the respondent to attend vocational school in the first place. The preceding four questions would be appropriate if the topical area were something like, What makes adults drop out of vocational school?

A more relevant line of questioning for the topic at hand would deal with the respondent's experiences before starting school; here are some examples:

1. "How did you first hear about vocational school?"
2. "When did you first hear about it?"
3. "What did you hear?"
4. "Did anyone try to encourage or discourage you from going to school?" "Who?" "What did they say?"
5. "At first, whose idea was it?"
6. "Did you have any doubts about it?" "What?"
7. "What finally made you decide to go?"

Even though these questions are all relevant, it might be necessary to use additional impromptu questions to elicit all of the relevant experiences affecting the final decision. The problem of follow-up questions, or probes, will be covered in a later chapter.

The foregoing example illustrated how concrete questions can be irrelevant to a topic when they deal with the wrong time period. Another common source of irrelevance is a question that does not fit the definition of the object (person, quality, event) to be studied. For example, an interviewer investigating child abuse allows the questions to drift out of bounds by focusing on arguments between parents and children. Or an interviewer trying to discover how many people have escaped poverty uses questions that elicit responses about the number of people who have gotten off welfare and have jobs, even though the minimum wage they receive is less than the value of the welfare benefits. Here "escape from poverty" is confused with "off welfare."

Another common source of irrelevance is a question aimed at the wrong dimension of human experience. Dimensions of experience include actions, thoughts, and feelings. The objective of an interview may be to discover what a person *did* on a certain occasion. If a respondent is not proud of what he or she did on that occasion, the response may tend to be subtly evasive by focusing on thoughts or feelings rather than actions. In this case the interviewer must use questions clearly focused on action and must be prepared to use probes designed to bring the respondent out of the feeling or thought dimension back to the action dimension. An excerpt from an interview with a Peace Corps volunteer in Bogotá, Colombia, illustrates the problem. The interviewer is trying to discover the respondent's typical daily activities on a community organization project in an Andean village.

I-1:   Bob, tell me about your work in your village.
R-1:   It is a very interesting place, no electricity—but that doesn't mean that they don't have radios. There are a lot of small battery radios that get only one station. There is no system of running water, no gas, no telephone. It is in the real boondocks.
I-2:   That's an interesting picture. Tell me what happens in the village?
R-2:   It is agricultural—some potatoes, yucas, sheep, and that sort of thing.
I-3:   Not too atypical for this area, but I am more interested in the specific project you were working on.
R-3:   Ah yes, the project. This is the most discouraging thing I have ever been involved in. Things move so slowly; people don't keep their promises, and

they are not interested in doing much except making demands on the federal government.

I-4: What do you do on the project?

R-4: I'm supposed to coordinate the activities of the Accion Comunal organization, the local village co-op, and the local priest.

The first three questions do not ask specifically what the respondent does, so not surprisingly he instead talks about the technological level of the village, its agricultural base, and his perceptions of the faults of the villagers. In response to the first direct question (I-4) he still avoids divulging his activities by talking about what he is *supposed* to do. If the respondent had been proud of what he was doing, the first question—"Tell me about your work in your village"—would have been sufficient to elicit information about his concrete activities.

From these types of experiences the interviewer learned that after a certain rapport had been developed, it was necessary to use concrete and pointed questions, such as:

1. "What time did you get up last Monday morning?"
2. "What was the first thing you did?"
3. "Then what did you do?"
4. "What was the first thing you did for the project last Monday?"

With such pointed questions, the interviewer discovered that the volunteer's morale was low and burdened by guilt feelings about being unable to do much of anything in community development.

In summary, the irrelevance of questions has three major sources: a focus on the wrong time period, a focus on the wrong (but related) topic, and a focus on the wrong dimension of human experience. Additional sources of irrelevance will be covered in Chapter 8 on evaluating responses.

SUMMARY

Formulating relevant questions is not as simple as it may first seem. And the failure to ask questions relevant to the purposes of the interview wastes valuable time while yielding no relevant information. In some instances the purpose of the interview is so simple and limited that the wording of relevant questions is easy. When the information needed is subtle or complex, or when the respondent tends to be evasive, the formulation of relevant questions must be done by a careful, logical procedure.

The first phase of the procedure is to clarify the objectives of the interview. This process is often difficult because the people involved in a particular setting have different ideas about the nature of the problem and the importance of various facets of the problem. The temptation may be to keep the problem broad and vague in order to achieve pseudo-agreement at the outset, only to create chaos later.

The second phase of formulating relevant questions is to specify information needed. The interviewer breaks the general topic down into specific categories of information that are needed to achieve the objectives of the interview. Each category must be clearly useful in terms of the purposes of the interview and must be clearly defined.

The third phase consists of formulating concrete questions to obtain information. The interviewer must formulate concrete questions that fit the purposes and definitions of the interview. Failure to do so is often the result of errors such as slipping into the wrong time period, falling outside the logical definition of the relevant concepts, or focusing on the wrong dimension (action, thought, or feeling) of human experience.

NOTES

1. Raymond L. Gorden, "A Critique and Suggestions Regarding the Proposed 'Standards of Evaluating the CSA-Administered Programs and Projects,'" Unpublished paper, May 1975.

EXERCISE 2-A
RECOGNIZING RELEVANT QUESTIONS

College X, founded in the middle 1800s, enjoyed over 100 years of growth. During this period it became coeducational and secular and made a strong effort to attract minority students. In the past decade it lost about 80 percent of its student body. It was recruiting fewer students each year although the drop-out rate remained at the same low level. The situation was desperate: a shrinking student body, a large deficit, and few financial resources beyond the tuition fees collected from students.

The president of the college ordered a survey of the student body to obtain information that could help reverse the shrinkage. Below are fourteen questions that could be included in the survey. Assume that you are to do the survey and can use only six questions. Indicate the six most relevant questions by listing the question numbers in numerical order.

1. Did your parents go to college?
2. Did you like high school? What did you like or dislike?
3. What courses are you currently taking?
4. What is your opinion of course X? What about courses Y and Z?
5. What do you think about the quality of the academic advising?
6. What are some of your favorite movies?
7. Do you expect to go to graduate school?
8. Do you know anyone planning to go to college next year? If so, who? Anyone else?
9. Have you corresponded with any of those you just mentioned?
10. Have you talked on the telephone with any of these people?
11. In your communication with them have you mentioned anything about College X? If so, what did you talk about?
12. Did any of these people ask any questions about College X or about your experiences here? What questions? What did you say?
13. Would you be willing to talk to prospective students on the phone to give your impressions of the college?
14. Are you tired today?

EXERCISE 2-B
DETECTING MISSING
RELEVANT QUESTIONS

The following interview guide is from a study to evaluate the effectiveness of Human Services Center (HSC). The center worked with single-parent welfare mothers to help them out of poverty by making them capable of earning an adequate living. The center claimed it was successful in getting people out of poverty. Independent Research Associates (IRA) was asked by the Department of Health and Human Services to objectively verify HSC's claim. IRA selected a random sample from the list of people the center claimed to have gotten out of poverty and asked the following set of questions of each member of the sample (in the privacy of their own homes).

Carefully evaluate each question of the interview guide as well as the combination of questions in order to answer these questions:

1. Would all of the information obtained by this interview, when compiled for the whole sample, be adequate to achieve the basic purpose of the study? Would you estimate the adequacy to be 0 percent, 25 percent, 50 percent, 75 percent, or 100 percent?
2. What questions, if any, are missing in the survey? Give the wording of two or three of the most important missing questions.

INTERVIEW GUIDE

1. Were you a participant in the program at HSC?
2. Which of the following services were available at HSC?
    _____ a. Child care
    _____ b. Courses leading to the GED certificate
    _____ c. Vocational training courses
    _____ d. Medicaid
    _____ e. Emergency rent and utility payments
    _____ f. Subsidized housing
    _____ g. Transportation vouchers
3. Which of these programs did you participate in yourself?
4. Did you feel the programs you were in were worthwhile? (Probe each.)

5. Are you currently working? IF YES, ASK:
   a. Where?
   b. Did HSC help you find this job?
   c. How long have you been working there?
   d. How much longer would you like to work there?
   e. How do you like working at _____ ?

IF NOT CURRENTLY WORKING, ASK QUESTIONS 6 THROUGH 10.

6. How long have you been out of work?
7. Did you have a job earlier after getting out of the HSC program?
   IF YES, ASK
   a. Did HSC find that job for you?
   b. What happened to that job?
8. Are you looking for a job now? Is HSC helping you find a job?
9. What do you feel about your chances of getting another job?
10. Are you back on welfare now?

Exercise 2-C
FORMULATING YOUR OWN
RELEVANT QUESTIONS

Exercises 2-A and 2-B allowed you to criticize someone else's attempt to formulate relevant questions. Now it is your turn to formulate questions. Carefully consider the objectives of the interview and the definitions given below, then formulate a set of questions to achieve the objectives of the interview.

OBJECTIVES OF THE INTERVIEW

Two basic types of groups are characterized by their relationship to an individual: membership groups and reference groups. Membership groups are those in which a person is a formal or informal member who encounters other members in direct communication. These groups have a powerful influence on the behavior of members.

The reference group is one to which the individual does not belong yet is influenced by. The group is used as a reference point to gauge one's position in society, one's self-perception, or one's success or failure. A person may aspire to belong but can't or may want to avoid being a member. The reference group may be a symbol of success or of failure.

The objective of this interview is to discover reference groups that are significant to the respondent.

DEFINITIONS

There are two concepts in the wording of the objective that need to be defined more clearly in order to formulate relevant questions. They are *reference group* and *significance*.

Reference Group.   For the purposes of this exercise, a reference group is a group to which the respondent does not belong yet uses as a standard of comparison or as a means of self-identification. The group may have positive associations (for example, when the person aspires to be like members of the group) or it may have negative associations (for example, when the person wants to avoid being like members of the group). This is the essence of the meaning of the word *reference* in the term *reference group*.

Now take a closer look at the definition of *group*. A broad definition is any set of people who informally interact with one another or who formally join and declare membership. For the purposes of this exercise, the definition is expanded to include categories or types of similar people who may not interact with one another but share certain characteristics symbolized by the category name. Thus, this expanded definition of *group* would include interacting sets of people like the Lion's Club as well as categories of people such as "liberals," "honest-but-poor," and "students."

Significance.   For the purposes of this interview, you do not want to list every reference group that might possibly have some meaning to the respondent. Instead, you want to discover those that are the most salient, most outstanding, or most important to the respondent. To be sure you are getting only the more important ones, you must avoid naming, listing, or otherwise suggesting any specific groups. Your questions must provide the stimulus to cause the respondent to demonstrate any strong associations with his or her most significant reference groups.

FORMULATING RELEVANT QUESTIONS

For the purposes of this exercise, you do not have to formulate all of the questions that would be needed for an interview of this type; but you must include the most important questions and be sure that they are all relevant.

When the questions are all worded to your satisfaction, arrange them in the best sequence to facilitate the interviewing process. In general, the questions with the broadest scope should come first.

SUMMARY OF STEPS

1. Review the objectives and definitions given.
2. Think of specific questions that are relevant to the objectives and that fit the definitions.
3. Formulate no more than eight questions.
4. Arrange the questions into what seems to be the most appropriate sequence to facilitate the natural flow of the interview.
5. Label this final revision "Exercise 2-C" and put your name at the top. Your instructor will advise you on the next step.

If we press people for information
before they are able and willing to
give it, the talking doesn't stop
but the misinformation begins.

3

Formulating Motivating Questions

F OR A QUESTION TO BE USEFUL it must first be logically relevant to the objectives of the interview. However, to be relevant is not enough; the question must also be formulated to motivate the respondent to give complete and accurate answers. Motivating means to make the respondent more willing and more able to give the information sought.

In the planning phase motivation is optimized by selecting the most appropriate verbal forms. In the doing phase motivation can be enhanced by proper nonverbal delivery of the question (shown in Chapter 5). This chapter deals only with the verbal forms. It will show that making proper decisions about verbal forms includes providing contextual statements preceding the question, selecting the most appropriate vocabulary for the question, and choosing between broad and narrow questions, between open-ended and closed answers, between direct and indirect questions, and between loaded and unloaded questions.

The respondent may be unwilling to give valid information and may lie or withhold certain information to avoid embarrassment. Perhaps the respondent may be willing but unable to give accurate information due to confusion, misunderstanding, faulty memory, or repression of unpleasant experiences. Whether the problem is the able-but-unwilling respondent or the willing-but-unable respondent, the result is a lack of valid and complete information.

Interviewing would be much simpler if respondents either told the truth or said nothing. Instead, they usually are cooperative or want to avoid the appearance of being uncooperative. Therefore, if we press people for information before they are able and willing to give it, the talking does not stop but the misinformation or disinformation begins.

MAXIMIZING FACILITATORS AND MINIMIZING INHIBITORS

A variety of social-psychological forces can permeate an interview either to facilitate or inhibit the flow of valid information. At least eight *inhibitors* and eight *facilitators* can be brought into play.[1] We will deal with only the two most common inhibitors (ego threat and forgetting) and with the two most useful facilitators (recognition and empathy) in order to focus on interviewing skills rather than theory.

Minimizing Ego Threat

Ego threat is commonly recognized as a major barrier to the flow of complete and valid information. Polansky[2] devotes most of his book to the various ego-defense mechanisms used by respondents in social work and therapeutic interviews.

We have all experienced times when we were asked a question we preferred not to answer candidly under the circumstances. What is not commonly recognized by the neophyte interviewer is that ego threat may lurk in unexpected places and in what may appear to be nonthreatening topics. To illustrate, let us return to the example of the interview to discover why the respondent matriculated at College X. Where is the potential ego threat in this topic? Most college students feel strongly that they should decide matters for themselves rather than being moved about like pawns. Furthermore, they feel their decisions should be based on a rational, logical assessment of evidence. Yet it is rare that an individual can select a college without any limitations other than the logical assessment of evidence. If the respondent feels that the interviewer approves only of fiercely independent and rational decision making, then the respondent would tend to repress any information about dependence or irrationality for fear of the interviewer's disapproval. So how can we reduce ego threat by the construction of the question?

First, we could avoid wording the question so that it seems to assume that the respondent made the decision *alone*. Instead of asking, for example, "How did *you* decide to come to College X?," a more neutral form of the question could be used: "How did you happen to come to College X rather than going to some other college?"

Second, the question could be prefaced with a contextual statement indicating that the interviewer is aware that the process of selecting a college is a complex one and that many factors other than the respondent's wishes might come into play. For example:

> We are trying to get a realistic picture of the sometimes complicated process by which a particular student arrives at a particular college. A student may or may not end up at the college that was a personal first choice because of things like distance, financial considerations, influence of parents or of peers, or simply because the first-choice college did not accept the application. So let me start by asking . . .

Such a contextual preface would indicate that the interviewer does not assume that the respondent is always independently rational.

All of the questions that follow the contextual preface should avoid the use of words like *choice, choosing,* and *selecting* as much as possible. Instead of what college did your friend *choose* we could ask, "Where did your friend go to college?"

Third, the interviewer could keep in reserve some intentionally *loaded* questions to use at points where the interviewer suspects that the respondent is fabricating too neat a picture of perfectly independent and rational thinking. For example, "So far you haven't mentioned any influence by high school friends, teachers, counselors, or parents. Were you completely isolated from any influences of others?" Such a loaded question may not be necessary if the interviewer first tried factual and neutral questions such as, "Did any of your high school friends have any ideas or information about colleges?" or "Did anyone who had come to College X talk to you during the time you were looking for a college?" Only if such questions receive a continued denial of any influence by others should the loaded question be used, and then it should be delivered in an amiable tone.

Minimizing Forgetting

Forgetting as a barrier to the flow of complete and valid information is just as common in many types of interviews as is ego threat, but it is less appreciated in actual practice. The natural tendency for memory to fade (for recall to become more difficult) makes it easier for the respondent's ego-defense system to reconstruct an image of the past by selective omission, distortion, and fictionalization to fill the blanks. This idea of the "reconstruction of one's own biography" is a recurring theme in the insightful writings of Schultz.[3]

Many interviews (such as the nurse trying to obtain a medical history, the market researcher asking why you bought a certain car, or the manager trying to discover why an employee came to work for her company) obtain a lot of invalid information because the interviewer fails to appreciate the respondent's need for help in recalling even personal experiences. Even the most simple and seemingly important personal experiences are often not accessible to the respondent without considerable help from the interviewer. This was convincingly demonstrated in a pioneer study by Moore[4] which showed that many employees who owned stock in the company where they worked did not recall the fact, even though it was recorded in the company records.

Such forgetting was mainly a function of elapsed time. Other studies have shown that not only the amount of elapsed time but also the nature of the information to be recalled has a strong influence on the respondent's ability to recall. For example, Dakin and Tennant[5] found that only 24 percent of the respondents could recall their salaries in a distant past year, but they could remember their street address for that same year.

To illustrate the importance of recognizing and dealing with the problem of forgetting, let's return to the interviews with college students to discover why they came to a particular college. The images of College X the freshman learned from the official orientation week and from upperclass students tend to crowd out the images and expectations they had of College X *before* they arrived. Yet it is essential to separate the two types of images and to revive the older ones since cause must precede effect. Correct wording of one particular question is not sufficient to help the respondent recall thoughts of College X during the college selection period. What is needed is a whole series of questions at the beginning of the interview to stir up associations that stimulate the respondent's memory and help him or her to relive the original experience. Thus the interview might begin with questions such as these: "When did you first think about going to college?" "What high school did you go to?" "What college did your best friends go to?" This line of questioning would help the respondent recall the earlier experiences and separate them from what was learned after arriving at college.

Now let's look at some examples of designing questions to maximize the two facilitators—recognition and empathy. To a great extent they are maximized by the interviewer's nonverbal communication, but they also can be maximized verbally to some extent.

Maximizing Recognition

Let us illustrate the process of maximizing recognition in the context of the same interview on college selection. One way to give the respondent recognition is to explain that the respondent has some unique qualifications that are needed to understand the college selection process. One place to do this is in the initial introduction to the set of questions. For example:

> There are many studies of the process of selecting colleges, but most of them get their ideas from talking to college admissions officers, high school counselors, college alumni, or college seniors . . . but none of these people can give as accurate an account of how it happens as *you* can. As a first-year student, you have just been through the process and know what it is all about, so I am very interested in *your* point of view.

This might be the first time anyone at the college has implied that the student is better qualified than a college senior or a high school counselor. Such recognition of the respondent's unique qualifications tends to increase the respondent's willingness to provide the needed information.

Another way the interviewer's verbal behavior may give recognition is simply to praise the response to a particular question. For example, any of the following remarks or questions could be used at an appropriate time: "I appreciate your taking time to be so thoughtful." "How do you remember so much detail?" "I appreciate your saying frankly that you don't know or can't remember rather than trying to bluff it through." "I know these are tough questions, but you are doing a terrific job." "Great! That's the kind of detail I want."

Maximizing Empathy

Expressions of empathy by the interviewer will help to overcome the effects of possible ego threat. Empathy can be expressed verbally at three levels.

First, empathy can be expressed by providing a contextual statement even before the interview formally begins. To some extent this can be achieved indirectly in the contextual statement quoted earlier to reduce ego threat. However, several additional statements could be made to more directly express empathy. For example:

> I know that some of the questions I am going to ask may be difficult to answer in detail after this length of time has passed. Just take your time and I'll assist you by helping you relive that period of time in which the college selection process was actually going on. Also, I am well aware that often we don't get exactly what we want in selecting a college or in life in general. So I am interested in any obstacles or problems—as well as in the triumphs—in your process of college selection.

Second, interviewers can show empathy by providing a sympathetic contextual statement as a preface to a single question. For example, the interviewer could show interest in obstacles or problems that may have interfered with the respondent's freedom in decision making:

> Sometimes parents feel that since they are putting up the money, they should make the decision or at least have a strong influence on the process. Some parents are qualified and some are not. What sort of influence did your parents try to exert?

Similar questions regarding the potential influence of high school teachers, counselors, and fellow students could be preceded by a contextual statement showing empathy with the respondent's point of view.

Third, the interviewer can give empathic responses to the respondent's remarks, such as:

> That must have been a confusing situation!
>
> How did that make you feel when they said that?
>
> Tell me more about the way they "meddled" in your selection of a college.

Up to this point we have seen in the case of a particular interview how the interviewer might try to minimize inhibitors and maximize facilitators of communication by designing certain verbal contexts, by using facilitating questions, and by making facilitating responses to the respondent's efforts. Now let us go beyond the limits of a particular interview and look at a more general treatment of the basic verbal forms of questions and their contexts. In the planning phase these are the verbal tools from which the interviewer can choose in order to communicate questions clearly, to minimize inhibitors, and to maximize facilitators.

BASIC VERBAL FORMS AND CONTEXTS OF THE QUESTION

There are six dimensions of verbal forms to be considered in designing a useful question. This section will provide examples of each.

Providing Verbal Contexts

The verbal context is a statement, as opposed to a question, that is used to put a series of questions or one particular question into a context in order to communicate the question more clearly or to motivate the respondent to answer it. In the college selection illustration, contexts were used mainly to motivate the respondent. Contextual statements can also be used to give more precise meaning to the question by supplying definitions, time perspective, spatial perspective, and facts needed for an informed judgment by the respondent.

Assume this basic question: "Do you think that children of common-law marriages should be entitled to the legal rights of inheritance?" Some respondents might not be familiar with the meaning of the term *common-law marriage* and would be too timid to ask, but they might take a guess and answer the question. The danger of guessing could be avoided by asking the same question *after* a contextual statement that gives a working definition of the term. For example:

> There are cases where a man and woman live together, set up housekeeping, have children, and take care of them, but do not get a marriage license or have a wedding ceremony of any kind. Do you think children of these common-law marriages should be entitled to the legal rights of inheritance?

Here, by using a *definition* in the contextual statement preceding the question, we increase the probability that the answer will be relevant to the purpose of the interview.

A second function of the contextual statement is to provide a *time perspective*. For example, if we want to discover whether people in business feel that economic conditions are getting better or worse, we should not simply ask, "Do you think business conditions are getting better or worse?" Two people in the same business might have precisely the same experience but give different answers because they were thinking about different time periods. One respondent, thinking about changes during the past month, could say that things are getting worse; the other respondent, thinking about trends in the past year, could say things are getting better. If, for example, the aim of the interview is to assess business trends during the past three years, the following contextual statement would be helpful to clarify the question:

> I would like to get your assessment of trends in your own business. As you know, business can fluctuate from week to week, month to month, and year to year, but what I would like to know is what you have found to be the basic trend, if any, in your business over the past *three* years. Also, try not to let your assessment be influenced by what you feel about the future. Would you say business has been better or worse this year than it was three years ago?

Note that the contextual statement takes care to avoid biasing the respondent's assessment of the past with expectations for the future.

A third function of the contextual statement is to provide a *spatial perspective* to the question that follows. In a sense, this is providing a special type of definition. For example, if an interviewer wants to know how a resident of the city feels about crime in the neighborhood, he or she could use one of two approaches depending on the information needed. The interviewer could ask the respondent first to define the boundaries of his or her own neighborhood. Or the interviewer could provide a spatial perspective by saying that the question is about the area within a certain number of blocks of the respondent's home or by providing the names of the boundary streets of the area of interest before asking the question, depending on the purpose of the interview.

A fourth function of contextual statements is to supply *facts* needed for an informed judgment from the respondent. In some cases we might want to know the relationship between a person's opinion on a topic and his or her knowledge of that topic. Suppose we were specifically trying to predict whether an information campaign would help a public school district pass a tax levy at the next election. We could ask one random sample from the community this simple question: "Do you feel the school district should pass a 5 mil tax levy for the schools at the next election?" For another random sample of the same community, we could precede the question with this contextual statement:

> As you may have heard if you were at the last school board meeting, the local schools are in financial difficulty mostly due to inflation. If they cannot get a 5 mil tax increase in May, next September they will have to lay off about 20 percent of the teachers and cut out most of the extracurricular activities such as football, basketball, drama club, and band. Also, they will have to use out-of-date textbooks and will not have enough of them to go around. With the situation as it is, do you think people should vote for the 5 mil levy in the upcoming election?

If the second sample showed a significantly larger proportion willing to vote for the levy, it would indicate that an information campaign would be useful. Respondents who say they would not vote for the levy, even after they heard the contextual facts, could be probed for reasons. Probing might discover, for example, that a respondent does not believe these "facts" or that a respondent feels it's a great idea to cut out all those extracurricular activities because they "distract from the main purpose of school" or that a respondent thinks the school district should not be given the money until certain policy reforms are made and efficiency is improved. Such insights could help in the design of a more effective information campaign.

Selecting Appropriate Vocabulary

The same question may be asked in many ways using different vocabularies. Each form of the question may be logically relevant to the purpose of the interview, but one may be superior to the other for communicating the question or for motivating the respondent to answer.

Four basic criteria can help determine the best vocabulary to use in wording the question: (1) the words should be clearly understood by the respondent; (2) the words should help establish the optimum role relationship between the interviewer and respondent; (3) the words should be selected to supply the vocabulary needed for the respondent to answer without violating the etiquette of the situation; and (4) words that would unintentionally load the question should be avoided.

To successfully select an appropriate vocabulary the interviewer must be familiar with both the topic at hand and the type of respondent involved.

Using Words That Are Clearly Understood.   If the interviewer uses words that are not clearly understood, the respondent may be too embarrassed to ask for clarification and may guess at the meaning. An incorrect guess is not always obvious in the respondent's answer, so the interviewer may be unaware of the misinterpretation and accept an invalid response.

Generally, the solution to this problem is to use the most simple, direct, and commonly understood vocabulary. Appropriate vocabulary can be a problem if the interviewer is highly educated and the respondent has little formal education. Also, regardless of education, technical jargon can create problems. To keep the language universally understandable, we would want to use "brothers and sisters" instead of "siblings," the "commanding officer" instead of the "CO," and "small farm where people raise their own food" instead of "subsistence farm."

The approach of using the simplest language is certainly appropriate when interviewing a random sample of the population. It would be more effective, however, to use a highly specialized vocabulary when interviewing members of one group with a common ethnic, religious, vocational, professional, or other background. In this case, the interviewer must learn the specialized vocabulary in order to establish rapport and to facilitate understanding.

Using Words That Establish a Proper Role Relationship.   The vocabulary used may mark the interviewer as either an insider or outsider in the eyes of the respondent. If the topic of the interview is one that the respondent feels freer to discuss with insiders, then insider vocabulary should be used. But if the respondent would feel freer in discussing the topic with an outsider, then outsider vocabulary should be used.

For example, if the interviewer is talking to a prostitute to discover the extent to which prostitutes contribute to the spread of disease, then it would be appropriate to use insider vocabulary. Instead of "prostitutes" the interviewer should say "working girls," instead of "male clients" say "Johns," and instead of "sexual intercourse" say "trick." Such insider vocabulary puts the respondent more at ease, since the interviewer seems acquainted with the life and so will not be shocked by an honest answer.

There is danger in trying to use insider vocabulary when the interviewer is really not familiar with the respondent's situation. The respondent may detect the superficiality and label the interviewer as an imposter, or the respondent may respond spontaneously with additional insider language not understood by the interviewer.

In some situations outsider vocabulary can be more effective, for example, a patient discussing health problems with a doctor. In this case the doctor, acting as interviewer, should use enough technical medical terminology to make it credible that he or she is a doctor. Using the appropriate vocabulary has the same effect as wearing a white coat; it is an indicator of the role of doctor. Often the doctor has to translate technical terminology so that the patient will both understand and be impressed. For example:

> We have found that you have an *asymptomatic cardiac arrhythmia* which sometimes goes into *atrial fibrillation*. In other words, you have an irregular heart beat which at times takes the form of rapid fluttering of the upper part of the heart which receives the blood that has circulated through the body. This does not hurt and it is not dangerous, but it may make you feel tired.

Technical vocabulary plus a white coat has been demonstrated by fraudulent practitioners to be enough to allow a person who has never attended medical school to persuade a respondent to answer questions for a detailed medical history.

Providing Words Needed for the Answer. In some interview situations the respondent recognizes that the interviewer is from a different social group and thinks he or she might be shocked by the language the respondent's peers use in discussing a topic like sex. The interviewer may provide an acceptable vocabulary in the wording of the questions which the respondent is happy to use on this occasion. For example:

> We are studying the trends in heterosexual sexual activity among high school students and their potential relationship to the spread of AIDS. We need to know how many students start having sexual intercourse at what age, how often they have it, with how many different partners, and whether condoms, IUDs, diaphrams, spermicide jelly, or other forms of birth control are used. Let's start with...

The principle of providing vocabulary could also take the form of asking multiple-choice questions with the vocabulary for each form of behavior supplied as the choices. To further reduce the potential barriers of etiquette or ego threat, the respondent could be handed a card with the multiple-choice responses on it and then be asked, "Which is most true of your case: A, B, C, or D?" Then the respondent can respond by merely saying "B." Of course, to know whether such precautions are necessary, the interviewer must be closely acquainted with the cultural background of the people from whom he or she is trying to obtain information.

Avoiding Unintentionally Loading the Question.   Loaded questions are not always prohibited. Research shows that there are circumstances under which loaded or leading questions are more likely to obtain the truth than the unloaded questions.[6] Most of the time when a leading question is used inappropriately, the interviewer does not recognize that it is loaded. So it is important to recognize the different ways of loading a question.

Perhaps the most obvious way of loading a question is using *emotional words* with either positive or negative connotations, for example, "What do you think of this tax mess?" Referring to the tax situation as a "mess" loads the question in a negative direction more than if the interviewer asked: "What is your opinion of the tax controversy now in the news?" It is not necessary to use words such as *mess, scandal,* or *fiasco* which are obviously pejorative in connotation.

As shown by Inbau and Reid,[7] even when interrogating crime suspects, where "anything you say may be held against you in court," the interrogator gets better results by using words that are less negatively loaded. For example, the police interrogator says "shoot" instead of "kill," "take" instead of "steal," or "tell the truth" instead of "confess."

Similar leading questions result from attaching a famous person's name as originating or agreeing with an idea or action. The response will then be biased in proportion to the strength of the respondent's positive or negative feeling toward that person. For example, in Democratic territory it would make a considerable difference whether the interviewer asks, "What do you think of President Bush's new tax law?" or "What do you think of the new tax law just passed by Congress?" To construct a valid question on this topic we must be sure we are getting opinions on a specific tax law undistorted by attitudes toward President Bush.

A second way that questions can be loaded is by mentioning only *one side* or *one direction* when there are actually two or more sides or directions that a response might take. For example, "Do you think your wife's attending night school is a good idea?" is more loaded than asking, "Do you think your wife's attending night school is a *good* or *bad* idea?" Even the latter form implies that it is either good or bad and that the respondent must make a choice and then justify this choice. So it would be even less leading to ask, "How do you, personally, feel about the idea of your wife attending night school?" This form is most appropriate since it allows the respondent the choice of being for, against, or ambivalent.

A third way that questions can be loaded is by suggesting one among many possible *specific answers*. For example, "Did you come to college because of the work-study program?" is much more loaded than, "What features of college sounded attractive to you before you came here?" The latter form of the question does not specifically suggest one particular reason.

A fourth way to load a question is to provide a *hidden argument*, either in a contextual statement or in the question itself, that supports one of the possible answers. For example, a social worker may want to know how a woman on welfare feels about going to vocational school as a means of getting out of poverty. This information is needed to anticipate the woman's need for support and encouragement. The interviewer might use an unintentionally loaded question by asking, "Do you feel that it is all right for you to go to vocational school for six months so that you can earn more money and give your child a better life?" This question contains an argument about why the respondent should say yes to vocational school and it represses any doubts, fears, or worries that would predict the need for support to help her start school or to prevent her from dropping out. A less loaded question would be, "How do you feel about the idea of going to vocational school?" The idea of a better life might well be used later in attempting to persuade a wavering mother that she should not drop out two-thirds of the way through the course, but it does not help to discover the possible fears or anxieties that might be aroused by the idea of returning to school.

Although there may be other ways of loading questions, in the author's experience these four ways are the most prevalent. The same four ways can be used legitimately when intentional loading of a question is needed as discussed later.

Choosing Between Broad and Narrow Questions

Questions do not simply fall into two extreme categories of narrow and broad: they actually fall on a continuum. A detailed description of how different degrees and dimensions of *scope* can be incorporated into the design of any question is given elsewhere.[8] In general, there are four dimensions in which the scope of a question can be narrowed or broadened: the *actor*, the *action*, relevant *relationships*, and the *scene* (site, setting, occasion).

For example, in the actor dimension the question could be either "Did John do it?" or "Who did it?" The second question is broader in scope. In the action dimension a question could be either "Did the driver leave the scene of the accident?" or "What did the driver do immediately after the accident?" In the relationship dimension a question could be either "Is Myra Mr. Johnson's ex-wife?" or "What is Myra's relationship to Mr. Johnson?" In the scene dimension a question could be either "Did anyone give a computer program to Margaret at the office this week?" or "Did anyone give a computer program to Margaret this week?"

It is important that we do not unnecessarily restrict the scope of a question when we don't know in advance all of the possibilities in each dimension of the question. For example, if the intent of the two questions regarding the computer program is to discover whether Margaret, who is absent from work, might have a missing computer program, then the first version of the question is too narrow in scope to get the needed information. The answer might simply be "no" because the program was not given to her at the office but was delivered to her home. Even though the respondent may give relevant information in spite of the wording of the question, we cannot depend on it. So we must be careful to avoid building restrictive assumptions into a question which might prevent discovering what actually happened.

Legitimate uses exist for both the narrowest and broadest of questions depending on their function in the interview. Let's look at some of the most important reasons and conditions for using questions that are broad in scope.

Value and Limitations of Broad Questions.   In general, broad questions are most useful in the *exploratory* phase when the interviewer may not know the kinds of specific narrow questions appropriate for the particular respondent's experiences. A whole study or a single interview must sometimes begin with an exploratory phase.

Say we want to discover what the respondent feels is most important about a situation. We may not know all of the possible *criteria* of importance that could be used by different respondents regarding the same situation, so we must leave this open. On the other hand, if for the purposes of the interview the respondents' criteria are not important and we have clearly specified our own, then the broad exploratory questions are not needed.

If we are trying to map out the respondent's paths of *association* regarding a certain topic, it is important to avoid narrow questions that are liable to impose a path of association that is not the respondent's.

If we are trying to discover the respondent's own *vocabulary* for discussing a certain topic, it is better to use an encompassing question. This broad introductory question can cover the whole topic rather than breaking it down into a series of narrow questions. Narrow questions choose a vocabulary in advance and impose it on the respondent.

If we need to discover the *chronological order* of the respondent's actions in a given situation, it is better to begin the discussion with one broad question. A series of narrow questions might incorrectly assume a certain chronology of action.

These conditions for the use of the broad question deal mainly with the types of data the interviewer is seeking. We can also view the value of the broad question in regard to how it motivates the respondent. If the topic is very real and important to the respondent who thus has a lot to say about it, broad questions should be used at least at the beginning of the interview or at the beginning of each subtopic.

The broad question has several advantages for motivation. First, it allows respondents to follow their own path of *free association* without being interrupted by specific questions in an arbitrary order. Second, it encourages the respondent to talk freely because the interviewer is implicitly recognizing that the respondent has much to contribute if given the opportunity to talk. Third, it allows the respondent the opportunity to obtain some *catharsis* by having the freedom (uninhibited by specific narrow questions) to talk about certain emotional experiences. Perhaps not all of this cathartic reaction will be directly relevant to the objectives of the interview, but it provides the interviewer the opportunity to demonstrate understanding, lets the respondent feel sympathetic support, and encourages spontaneous, truthful responses.

Fourth, the broad question can be tactically useful when the interview calls for specific facts that might be ego threatening for the respondent to admit. In such a case, if the specific fact is asked about directly, the respondent often becomes aware of its significance and may withhold or fabricate an answer. If the same information can be given indirectly as part of a broad question that does not call attention to the specific point, the respondent does not feel threatened. For example, in interviews with survivors in a community struck by a tornado, we already knew that most of the people who died had bled to death. We wanted to know how many of the survivors had tried to prevent someone from bleeding to death. Instead of asking, "Did you do anything to stop anyone's bleeding?" we began by asking, "Did you do anything to help any of the victims of the tornado?" This question was followed by probes to obtain a detailed chronological order of what each survivor did. The major discovery was that *no one* had done anything to control bleeding. The typical response was to help victims out from under the rubble and, if the victims were incapacitated or unconscious, carry them to the side of the road, cover them with a blanket, and wait for an ambulance to come and pick them up. Since the tornado had blocked the highways with trees and utility poles, the ambulances arrived after the victims bled to death. It would be a tremendous ego threat for the respondents to admit that they allowed this to happen to their friends, neighbors, and relatives.

Similarly, a police interrogator may be looking for specific clues that would link the respondent to a crime. The interrogator must, however, avoid pointing out these potential links, and mentioning them in specific questions would do so. Instead, broader questions that include the time and place of the crime must be used.

Clearly there are appropriate times to use broad questions. Broad questions are useful when the purpose of the interview is exploratory or when the emphasis is on discovering the respondent's perspective on events. Also, the broad question can motivate by allowing free association, giving recognition, allowing the interviewer to be a sympathetic listener, and avoiding more specific questions that might alert the respondent to ego-threatening information.

The principal disadvantage of broad questions is that they are liable to result in a larger proportion of *irrelevant* information than narrower questions.

Nevertheless, it is often wise to permit some irrelevancies in exchange for greater validity or truthfulness in the responses. Another disadvantage is that broad questions may fail to obtain the specific relevant items of information if they are not followed by skillful probing.

Value and Limitations of Narrow Questions.   In general, specific narrow-scope questions (if they are appropriate) will be more efficient than broad questions. Narrow questions avoid the tedious process of sifting out the relevant from the irrelevant portions of the responses. Because of this labor-saving aspect, narrow questions are often used in questionnaires and interviews even in situations in which they may seriously damage the validity of the information.

Several important conditions must be fulfilled before specific narrow questions can be legitimately used. First, we must know in advance exactly what information we need to meet the objectives of the interview. We must also know enough about the topic under investigation and the respondent's relationship to it to realize that a particular specific question is applicable to a particular respondent. Often the use of more broad, exploratory questions at the beginning establishes a background that indicates whether a specific narrow question is applicable. If it is not necessary to help the respondent recall events by following his or her own free association pattern, if chronological order of information is not important or is already known by the interviewer, and if the specific narrow questions do not alert the respondent to ego-threatening implications, then it is probably appropriate to use narrow questions.

When the narrow question is appropriate, it has several advantages. First, for reticent respondents or for respondents giving information not particularly important to them, it is easier to answer specific questions than to tell a story. Second, it is easier to prevent omissions of relevant information if we can use a specific question to obtain each relevant bit. Third, narrow questions allow very specific cross-checks to verify the accuracy of the information given. Fourth, narrow questions make it much easier to obtain quantitative data, particularly when a multiple-choice question can be legitimately used, as will be described in a following section.

Most interviews are a *combination* of broad and narrow questions. If many interviews are to be done on the same topic, good strategy calls for a series of exploratory interviews all of which begin with very broad questions. Then as the interviewer becomes more familiar with the range of possible answers and the kinds of inhibitors that may arise, he or she will be able to see more clearly where the broad questions are most fruitful and where the narrow ones can be used to increase validity, efficiency, or quantitative precision.

Exploratory field testing may result in a set of questions that are all broad or all narrow. More typical, however, is a combination in which a broad question introduces the whole interview and each subtopic of the interview and then a set of specific questions follow. In some types of interviews one broad opening question will yield the answers to 90 percent of the specific questions, leaving only 10 percent of the specific questions to be asked. When appropriate, this interviewing plan has the double advantage of letting the respondent talk freely without interruptions by the interviewer and of providing the interviewer with an inventory of specific facts needed to cover all important relevant information.

Choosing Between Open-Ended and Closed-Answer Questions

A question with an open-ended answer is one that does not supply a set of answer options, for example, "What did you like most about College X?" Contrast this to a question with a closed answer: "Which of the following things did you like most about College X: the social life, the academic program, the sports program, the location, the physical plant, or the political orientation?" Obviously, if the question with the closed answer were used, it would be easier to code the answers and give a quantitative summary of the results from a large number of interviews. There are, however, conditions which make this increased efficiency meaningless, because supplying the answer choices biases the information.

Before using questions with closed answers, we must be sure that several important conditions have been fulfilled. First, the interviewer must understand the topic enough to know *most* of the possible answer categories in advance of the interview. Second, the answer categories must be relevant to both the central purpose of the interview and to the nature of the reality being investigated. Third, the categories must be clearly meaningful to the respondent. If these conditions do not exist, we may be systematically biasing the responses.

Often, an attempt is made to avoid omitting important answer categories by simply adding an "other" category. This practice may be helpful, but if three answer categories are provided in a situation where there are actually a dozen possibilities, simply adding "other" is of little value. A valid way to avoid the problem of omission is to start with exploratory open-ended interviewing. Thereby, the interviewer can discover the range of possible answers and then design the questions with closed answers using all of these answers plus the "other" category. Now any respondent who says "other" may be probed to discover exactly what he or she means.

This process of using the open-ended question in search of valid closed-answer questions may in some cases prove that no closed-answer questions can be legitimately used. Unfortunately, many interviews are designed to use closed-answer questions without the advantage of exploratory open-ended interviewing.

Three techniques are available for applying the principle of closed-answer questions: (1) the interviewer may word the question to include the answer choices; (2) the interviewer may ask the question and hand the respondent a card with the answer categories and say, "Please give me the letter opposite the answer that applies to you personally"; or (3) the interviewer may ask an open-ended question without showing the answer categories to the respondent but use the set of possible answers as a checklist for recording the answer.

When the appropriate conditions are fulfilled, the closed-answer question has several advantages over the open-ended one. It saves time for both the interviewer and the respondent; it reminds the respondent of the possibilities to be considered thereby reducing forgetting; in some cases it may supply the chronological order to help the respondent answer more easily; it may reduce ego threat by supplying an acceptable vocabulary or by allowing the respondent to say a letter rather than an embarrassing word or phrase; and it facilitates a quick statistical summary of the results of several interviews. When the conditions necessary for valid use of closed-answer questions cannot be met, then the open-ended form of question must be used.

One common interviewing error occurs when the form of a question unintentionally implies a highly restricted choice of a "yes" or "no" answer. For example, an interviewer who wants to evaluate an educational movie might ask, "Did you like the movie in your first-aid class?" The question implies that the interviewer wants a simple "yes" or "no" answer. Fortunately, many respondents would not take this easy way out; instead they would give their opinions on the movie. Unfortunately, others would choose either a "yes" or a "no" answer when in reality there were things they both liked and disliked.

This hidden yes-no form of the question can bias the response in three ways. First, it loads the question toward liking rather than disliking the movie because it did not ask whether the respondent "liked or disliked" the movie. Second, it implies that the respondent either likes or dislikes the movie instead of having both positive and negative reactions. Third, it excludes the possibility that the respondent has no strong reaction one way or the other.

Instead, the interviewer should ask, "What did you think of the movie in your first-aid class?" This question would invite a fuller discussion of the pros and cons of the movie from the respondent's point of view.

Usually, it is easy to correct these hidden yes-no questions by changing the form of the question slightly from "Did you do X in that situation?" to "What did you do in that situation?"

Choosing Between Direct and Indirect Questions

As we have seen, in some cases a broad question may be an indirect approach because it avoids more specific questions that call the respondent's attention to ego-threatening implications in the information. Other forms of questions are valuable for the same reason.

The *hypothetical* question has the advantage of allowing the respondent to answer without ego threat. For example, instead of asking a direct question like "Are there any houses of prostitution in this neighborhood?," an indirect form could be used: "What if some people wanted to start a house of prostitution in this area, do you think they could get away with it?" Often such an indirect question prompts the respondent immediately to volunteer information that is *not* hypothetical such as, "I know they could get away with it and they *do* because there is one in the middle of the block on the other side of the street." If the person sticks to the hypothetical answer, whether it is "yes" or "no," the interviewer can follow up with a probe: "What makes you think that?" or "If there was one in this area do you think you would know about it?" Often the respondent is challenged to show that he or she knows what is going on and proceeds to tell about a real case.

Another indirect type of question asks not about the respondent's own behavior, own family, own neighborhood, or own organization but about *other people's* behavior, families, neighborhoods, or organizations. For example, "Do you think that there are fences who buy stolen goods located in some of the neighborhoods near your own?" or "What do you think most people would do if they learned that an appliance repair shop in their block was really a fence?" Whether the respondent goes beyond the hypothetical response to reality depends to a great extent on how the interviewer reacts to the hypothetical information. For example, if the respondent says, "Most people wouldn't do a thing about it," the interviewer could say, "I guess they might be afraid of what would happen if they did, right?" If respondents feel that the interviewer is understanding rather than righteously judgmental, they might take the opportunity to admit their own failure to do anything about the situation.

Using Intentionally Leading (Loaded) Questions

In wording a question we must avoid *unintentional* loading. As pointed out earlier, we can load a question by using emotional words, implying only one side of a dichotomous situation, suggesting a specific answer from among many possible answers, and including a hidden argument in the context or the question itself.

In some circumstances it is better to use an intentionally loaded question rather than a neutral one. Research has shown that if all four of the following conditions prevail in a given interview, the loaded form of the question will obtain the truth more often than the neutral form.[9]

Relevant Information Must Be Clear in the Respondent's Mind. If the needed information is *not* clear in the respondent's mind because memory has faded or because images and feelings are confused or ambiguous, then the respondent is open to the power of suggestion in the loaded question and can be influenced away from the truth with no intention of deceiving the interviewer. Therefore, the first condition for using a loaded question is that the respondent has the relevant information clearly in mind.

The Respondent Must Tend to Withhold Information. Even though a respondent may have the information clearly in mind, he or she may still withhold it to avoid an admission of socially unacceptable behavior. In this case the respondent may simply say that he cannot remember or he may fabricate a socially acceptable answer. For example, an interviewer for a state health department asks a twenty-one-year-old male, "Have you ever been to a prostitute?" there would be a strong tendency on the part of the respondent to answer "no" even though the experience was fresh in his memory.

The Question Must Be Loaded in the Socially Unacceptable Direction. The interviewer makes it easier for the respondent to answer by loading the question in the direction of the socially unacceptable answer. This was found to be true in interviewing for the Kinsey Report[10] in which loaded questions on sexual behavior were used. Instead of asking "Did you ever...(engage in a certain form of sexual behavior)?" the interviewers used a loaded form of the question such as "When did you first...(engage in this behavior)?"

This third condition for the successful use of loaded questions is not always easy to apply, because the socially unacceptable direction is not always clear. For example, when the author was closely associated with gangs as a recreation director, he found that some fourteen-year-old boys were reluctant to admit they had never been to a prostitute after they heard the older gang members bragging about their experiences. In this case what was socially acceptable within the gang and what was socially acceptable to a parent or school teacher were opposites. Under such circumstances the correct direction for loading the question would depend on whether the respondent perceived the interviewer as an insider or an outsider. Once an interviewer is well acquainted with the type of respondent, the general social setting, and the respondent's view of the interviewer, it is not difficult to know the correct direction in which to load questions.

The Loaded Question Must Be Followed with Probes.   The loaded questions should usually be followed by additional probes to obtain *concrete detail* about the respondent's admission. This safeguard is useful because a respondent can easily claim in general terms to have had a certain experience, but when probed for detail cannot quickly fictionalize convincingly. For example, the fourteen-year-old-boy claiming to have been to a prostitute may be tripped up by probes such as these: "Where did you meet her?" "What did she say?" "What did you say?" "How much did it cost?" "When did you pay?"

Loaded questions can be helpful if they are used judiciously under the right conditions, but they should never be used unintentionally.

SUMMARY

This chapter assumes that the interviewer already has questions that are logically relevant to the purpose of the interview and is now concerned with wording the questions to facilitate valid responses. Most question formulation is done as part of planning—before face-to-face encounter with the respondent. Still, the same principles of wording questions apply in formulating probes and impromptu questions during the give-and-take of the interview.

The principles of selecting question forms to facilitate valid responses are summarized here:

1. Try to minimize ego threat and forgetting.
2. Try to maximize recognition and empathy.
3. Provide verbal contexts where needed.
4. Select appropriate vocabulary.
5. Know when to use narrow and broad questions.
6. Know when to use open-ended and closed-answer questions.
7. Know when to use direct and indirect questions.
8. Know when to use intentionally loaded questions and unloaded questions.

NOTES

1. Raymond L. Gorden, *Interviewing: Strategy, Techniques and Tactics* (Chicago: Dorsey Press, 1987), chapters 5 and 6.

2. Norman A. Polansky, *Ego Psychology and Communication: A Theory for the Interview* (New York: Atherton Press, 1973).

3. Alfred Schultz, *Collected Papers,* vol. 1, ed. Maurice Natanson (The Hague, Netherlands: Martinus Nijhoff, 1962).

4. B. V. Moore, "The Interview in Industrial Research," *Social Forces* 7 (1929): 445–52.

5. Ralph E. Dakin and Donald Tennant, "Consistency of Response by Event-Recall Intervals and Characteristics of Respondents," *Sociological Quarterly* 9 (1968): 73–84.

6. Stephan A. Richardson, "The Use of Leading Questions in Non-Scheduled Interviews," *Human Organization* 19, no. 2 (1960): 86–89. See also Barbara Dohrenwend and Stephan A. Richardson, "A Use for Leading Questions in Research Interviewing," *Human Organization* 23 (1964): 76–77.

7. Fred E. Inbau and John E. Reid, *Criminal Interrogations and Confessions,* 3rd ed. (Baltimore: Williams and Wilkins, 1985).

8. Raymond L. Gorden, *Interviewing: Strategy, Techniques, and Tactics* (Chicago: Dorsey Press, 1987), 323–24.

9. Lois R. Dean, "Interaction, Reported and Observed," *Human Organization* 17 (Fall 1958): 36–44; Barbara Dohrenwend and Stephan A. Richardson, "A Use for Leading Questions in Research Interviewing," *Human Organization* 23 (1964): 76–77.

10. Alfred C. Kinsey et al., "Interviewing," in *Sexual Behavior in the Human Male* (Philadelphia: W. B. Saunders, 1948).

Exercise 3-A
RECOGNIZING QUESTION FORMS
THAT FACILITATE VALID RESPONSES

Carefully read the following interview purposes and dialogue. Then re-read as needed to answer the fifteen questions that follow. Use the answer sheet supplied by your instructor. Be prepared to defend your answers and ask questions in the group discussion.

PURPOSES OF THE INTERVIEW

This interview is one of the early interviews in an exploratory study of the changing roles of women in the United States. Since the role of women cannot be changed without also changing the role of men, and since men have been politically and economically dominant in the past, it is important not only to know women's attitudes and expectations but also to know men's beliefs, expectations, and feelings on the issue. The interview is being conducted by a member of a campus women's group to discover how men on campus view the issue.

Since the study is in its initial exploratory stage, many questions are broad, open-ended, and sometimes impromptu. It is hoped that subsequent interviews can be more structured and yield more precise and quantifiable information.

INTERVIEW DIALOGUE

I-1: Hello, I'm Nina Channing!
R-1: I'm Sam Gould!
I-2: Thanks for coming Sam. I appreciate your help. Have a seat! As you know, we are interested in the changing role of women in the United States. Since the role of women cannot be separated from the role of men, I need to get your view as a man on some of the issues. Any questions?
R-2: No. It sounds interesting to me.
I-3: If you don't mind I will have a video camera running. We may pick two or three of the sample of 100 students we are interviewing to be

broadcast on a special program on the campus television station in April or May.

R-3:   I see.

I-4:   To begin with I'd like to ask you whether you feel that the principle of equal pay for equal work regardless of gender is fair or unfair?

R-4:   Sure, why not? I guess that's what was wrong with slavery—the pay was not equal.

I-5:   What do you think about the people in the Women's Center on campus?

R-5:   In my opinion they are separatists. They want to just talk among themselves and don't want to talk to men. Sometimes they give the impression that to be really for women's liberation you have to be lesbian. They also get hung up on silly issues like how to spell women. Some insist that it should be changed to w-o-m-y-n to take the "men" out of "women." It seems to me that they should be concerned with getting an equal education, having equal access to a full range of jobs, and getting equal pay for equal work.

I-6:   I see. You feel that they should get away from silly issues like how to spell *women* and on to something more serious, right?

R-6:   Right, that's how I feel.

I-7:   I'm interested in what gives you the impression that they feel that to be for equality of women one must be a lesbian?

R-7:   Well, they seem to be men-haters and give the impression that they view all men as rapists.

I-8:   I see. How does this make you feel?

R-8:   It makes me angry. It's like having them assume that I personally am a murderer because most murderers are men. Also, by putting the emphasis on the rape issue they can support a feeling that they are really morally superior to men since women don't rape men. They are morally superior because they don't do the physiological impossible.

I-9:   What if your best male friend got married and his wife went to work immediately and earned $5,000 a year more than he did, how do you think he would feel?

R-9:   That's hard to say for sure, but I think he would be a little happier if he could make just a little more than she did.

I-10:   Would he feel happy about her working if she didn't make more than he did?

R-10:   He would be happy because at the beginning of a marriage the family can always use the extra money.

I-11:   At the beginning? How long is that?

R-11:   Until they have kids.

I-12:   And you agree that they won't need the money after they have kids?

R-12:   Not that they won't need the money, but that they won't need it as much since he would be more established in his job—no longer at the entry level. But also, she would not have time to be a good mother and work at the same time, particularly when the children were small.

I-13: Now I would like to go into a different angle. I want you to think about your home when you were growing up, particularly during the time you were in elementary school between the fifth and eighth grades. Where did your father work?

R-13: At Lockheed Aircraft I believe.

I-14: Did your mother work at the time?

R-14: Yes.

I-15: Did she work full time?

R-15: I suppose so. She was usually home when I got home from school. I came on the bus from North Hollywood High School. It took an hour and a half to get to Sun Valley.

I-16: What sort of role relationships were there between your parents at that time?

R-16: They got along fine. No fights or arguments. And they were proud of me because I got mostly A's in school and helped a lot with the work around the house. We lived out in the country where we raised chickens and rabbits and had a vegetable garden from about April to October. You can do that in California. I couldn't go out for sports because I always had to catch the bus right after class to get home. There was no public transportation. I did lots of chores when I got home.

I-17: I see. Which of the many courses here at college have you had which deal with the problems of sex and gender in modern society?

R-17: Well, I've had Anthropology 201 and Journalism 220.

I-18: Thank you. You have helped me a lot in getting ideas for making up the questionnaire we'll be using later to get a more quantitative picture of men's views on the role of women in society. Thanks for your time. I know it is a busy time of the quarter.

QUESTIONS ABOUT THE DIALOGUE

Use the answer sheet supplied by your instructor and answer these questions.

1. Which of the questions or statements by the interviewer is most likely to be ego threatening to the respondent?
2. Which two questions are most likely to involve difficulty in recalling the answers?
3. In which question does the interviewer try to give recognition to the respondent?
4. Which response gives the interviewer a good opportunity (which she misses) to give recognition to the respondent?

5. In which two questions or probes does the interviewer show empathy with the respondent?
6. In which question does the interviewer go ahead without showing empathy for the previous response?
7. Where is the first instance in which the interviewer uses a verbal context to a specific question?
8. What is the main function of this verbal context?
    a. To reduce ego threat
    b. To facilitate recall
    c. To define terms used
    d. To provide a time perspective
    e. To provide a spatial perspective
    f. To supply facts needed for judgment
9. Which two questions are loaded in a way they should not be?
10. Which question is too narrow in scope for that point in the interview?
11. Which question is too broad for the circumstances?
12. Which question would clearly benefit by providing a multiple-choice answer card?
13. Which question is a hypothetical question?
14. Which response shows that the respondent has lost track of the original question?
15. What are some additional ways the interview could be improved that are not touched on in questions 1 through 14?

The most skillful interviewing may be doomed to failure when there are strong negative influences in the physical setting or social definition of the interview situation.

4

Establishing a Communicative Atmosphere

To ESTABLISH A COMMUNICATIVE ATMOSPHERE, the stage must be set before the actors (interviewer and respondent) begin their purposeful conversation. The stage is set in two ways. First, a suitable physical setting and props are selected to make the respondent more willing and able to talk. Second, an appropriate social-psychological atmosphere is established by the introductory remarks and questions of the interviewer. Do not expect, however, a sharp cut-off point at which stage setting has ended and purposeful conversation has begun. Part of the stage setting is done via conversation and so may blend into the part of the interview that focuses on objectives.

If the stage is not set to establish a communicative atmosphere, even the most skilled interviewer will be operating at a disadvantage, and in some settings the interview may be doomed to failure. Let us first look at how certain features of the physical setting may be designed or selected to maximize the interviewer's chances of success.

PHYSICAL SETTING

The degree of control that can be exercised over the physical setting of an interview varies greatly between a *field interview* setting (for example, a news interview, a study of homelessness, or a public opinion survey) and an *institutional interview* setting (for example, an employment interview, police interrogation, or most social work interviews). In the field setting the interviewer goes out to find the respondent and in some cases has a choice of respondents. In some cases the interviewer may be selected because he or she can increase access to respondents or make respondents more willing to give relevant information. For a survey in which the respondents are housewives, it would be better to have female interviewers because they would have a better chance of being admitted into an urban home during the day when the housewife is alone. Even though in the field survey theoretically the interviewers could be selected to match the respondents, in actual practice little matching is done, because often the survey organization has trained one set of interviewers to interview anyone (as in a random sample) on any topic.

Some institutional interviewing is less flexible than field interviewing because there is less control over the time and place of the interview. For example, in a field survey of people involved in international trade, the interviewer may choose to interview the respondent at home, at the office, at the club, or in some publicly accessible place such as an airport or restaurant. In contrast, a personnel manager probably meets all applicants in the office.

The art of selecting the most appropriate respondent, interviewer, time, and place for field interviews is described in another book.[1] Here we will focus on the types of physical arrangements and props that may be used in the institutional interview—where the respondent comes into the interviewer's territory. To a limited extent, some of these uses of physical setting are relevant to the field interview.

Desk Arrangement

In any situation in which it is important to put the respondent at ease rather than to impress him or her with the interviewer's power, status, or importance, the interviewer should *not* sit behind a desk. The desk is not only a physical barrier, but it acts as a social symbol that might inhibit the respondent by triggering an ego threat or an etiquette barrier. Even though the interviewer may need a desk for paper work, when a client enters, the interviewer should usually abandon the desk.

Chair Placement

For interviewing purposes, two chairs should be in place away from the desk. Unless the interviewer wants to intimidate the respondent or control the respondent (as might be the case in certain interrogation situations), certain precautions should be observed in placing the chairs. The chairs should be of the same type, for example, not one straight-backed wooden chair and one overstuffed chair. They should be a proper distance for a private conversation, that is, arranged so that the eye-to-eye distance between the two seated persons is about three or four feet. For some types of helping interviews in which clients are likely to need strong emotional support, the interviewer should be able to reach out and touch the respondent. Lastly, the two chairs should be directly facing each other.

Lighting

Lighting is an important aspect of physical setting. For example, neither person should be facing a glaring light such as a bright desk lamp or a sunny window. Each person should be able to see clearly subtle changes in the other's facial expression. Older people, particularly, may have difficulty in seeing another person's face against bright backlighting.

Quiet

The interview location should be quiet enough so that the respondent does not have to speak loudly to be heard; even soft, soliloquizing remarks should be clearly audible. Sometimes the sounds of office equipment, conversations, air conditioners, or traffic interfere with clear reception of normal conversation, particularly if the respondent mumbles or speaks in an accent different from the interviewer's.

Privacy

The place of interview should afford both visual and auditory privacy. The respondent must have no fear that any confidences will be overheard or that emotional responses will be observed. The interviewer must remember to close the door. The privacy requirement may be difficult to put into practice. Think of office architecture characterized by cubicles with half walls or glass walls. In such cases special areas for private conversations are necessary so that the conditions for quality interviewing can be met.

Amenities

Certain amenities may be helpful: paper tissues (for colds, weeping, or perspiration); an ashtray with lighter or matches (in some cases there must be a segregated smoking area); drinks (coffee, herb tea, cold drinks, water); and nearby toilet facilities. Other items that can be helpful to the client who is coping with the bureaucratic process are a parking ticket validation stamp, a floor plan of the building, and a written list of names, addresses, and phone numbers of individuals and agencies to which the client might be referred.

Visual Props

Certain visual props may be used as reminders of the interviewer's basic interest in helping the respondent. What is appropriate depends on the nature of the agency and the purpose of the interviews taking place in that agency. For example, in a health agency props might consist of slogans, posters, pictures, or magazines dealing with maximizing health. In a multiservice center aimed at getting welfare mothers out of poverty, there might be a schematic diagram or cartoon titled Steps to Economic Self-Sufficiency. The interviewer in a childcare agency or a pediatric clinic might display photos showing the interviewer's young children. In situations where the interviewer talks to clients about a limited range of problems month after month, considerable thought should be given to the possible effects of visual props of various kinds. Some of the props might even remind the interviewer of the objectives or the procedures of the agency.

Note Taking

Physical preparations should be made to facilitate note taking and to make it as unobtrusive as possible. Since the interviewer should not be at a desk, a spiral-bound notebook or a clipboard (particularly if forms are used) should be placed in advance within reach of the interviewer's chair. The interviewer should be careful not to let the note-taking process distract either person in the interview. If the interviewer needs to discover many details and no questionnaire form is being used, there is danger that copious note taking will distract from attentive listening and thinking. In such cases it might be advisable to use a tape recorder and prepare summary notes from the tape later.

Tape Recording

If a tape recording of the interview is required, then its physical setup is important. No attempt should be made to hide the tape recorder or microphone, yet they should both be as unobtrusive as possible. Neither the microphone nor the machine should be directly in the line of sight as interviewer and respondent look at each other. The tape should be long enough so that the interviewer does not have to turn it over or insert a new tape in the middle of the interview. Consider placing the microphone on a small table to one side; even though it is visible, its distracting effect will be reduced if other objects, such as a vase or a book, are also on the table. Later in this chapter we will discuss what the interviewer should say about the tape recorder.

Dress and Grooming

Establishing a communicative atmosphere involves not only the "stage set and props" but the "costumes" of the actors. In the interview situation the interviewer must be aware that dress and grooming affect the respondent's judg-ment of the interviewer. Often the respondent is seeking clues to whether the interviewer is the kind of person who "would understand my problems" or "would be shocked by the realities of life" or "can be trusted with my secret." A youth agency worker who talks with street gangs obviously should not dress like an MBA being interviewed for his or her first job. The corporation for which the MBA might work expects certain standards of dress and grooming that would create distrust in the teenage street gang. Even police interrogators at a police station find they get better results when they are not in uniform. This may be surprising because suspects know they are in the police station and that anything they say can be used against them in court. Field interview-ers find that they will more often be denied entrance to a home if they are dressed like a detective, an FBI agent, or a bill collector.

As pointed out by Rogers,[2] some of the characteristics that can be commu-nicated by clothing are cultural background, regional origin, sex identifica-tion, generation identification, personality, occupation, ethnic affiliation, and social strata. All of these characteristics of an individual tend to create ingroup-outgroup boundaries and determine what information will or will not be shared.

If the other person is like me, I am more willing to listen to and talk to that person. Any performer is more appreciated if the audience feels that the performer "is one of our own." For example, a ballet company that gave per-formances in the public schools of a city found that the teenage audience was much more attentive throughout the concert if the dancers wore blue jeans in the first number. The idea that the same person could wear Levi's and a tutu was a revelation that allowed the audience to identify more easily with the dancers.

No set of regulations can tell an interviewer how to dress or what hairstyle will yield the best results. In general, we need to know how the respondent views different kinds of dress as being more or less "like me." We also need to know whether the interviewer wants to establish an insider or an outsider rela-tionship with the respondent.

One pitfall that interviewers must avoid is the appearance of masquerad-ing. If a white person using the vocabulary of a college graduate tries to dress like the black ghetto resident he or she is interviewing, the spectacle would ap-pear ridiculous to the ghetto resident. Similarly, Peace Corps trainees in Bo-gotá, Colombia, who dressed like poor Colombian farmers were considered either puzzling or humorous by the Colombians. In either case the effect is the opposite of that intended. To the respondents, the interviewers appeared to be pretending and to believe that they could fool the respondents easily. Such situ-ations do not lead to trust.

Often the best way to dress may be a compromise between that typical of the higher-status people in the organization sponsoring the interview and that of the respondent. It may take considerable experience to determine a practical and optimum form of dress and grooming for a particular interviewing func-tion, but we must begin with recognition of its importance.

In general, the physical setting and props of the interviewing scene have both a physical and a symbolic (psychological) effect on the communicative atmosphere. At the physical level, the arrangements can make it either easier or more difficult to hear and to be heard and to see and be seen; they also can make the respondent more or less physically comfortable. At the psychological level, the surroundings can suggest to the respondent that the interviewer is trustworthy or not, sympathetic or not, understanding or not, competent or not, nonthreatening or threatening. Success in designing a communicative atmosphere depends to a great extent on the interviewer's understanding of how different physical aspects of the setting are interpreted by the respondent.

VERBAL SETTING

The verbal setting includes everything the interviewer says to the respondent to *define the situation* before the formal interviewing begins. It includes any introductory remarks, explanation, self-presentation, or rapport building the interviewer engages in to reduce the inhibitors and to increase the facilitators of communication before getting down to the specific business of the interview. The interviewer must be aware that anything he or she says can affect the respondent's views of the interviewer and the respondent's willingness to cooperate.

All of the following specific suggestions about what may need to be explained and defined to make the respondent more communicative do not need to be used at the beginning of every interview. Which ones are needed in a specific interview depends on several variables: the purpose of the interview, the extent to which the respondent is familiar with the interview situation, and whether the respondent took the initiative in arranging the appointment.

The interviewer should begin by asking, "Do I know enough about the respondent and the situation to know which aspects of the verbal setting need to be supplied in a particular case?" If the answer is "no," the interviewer must learn more before deciding to omit any portion of the verbal setting. On the one hand, the interviewer should avoid unnecessary explanations. On the other hand, the interviewer must carefully deal with any doubts or anxieties the respondent has about the interview situation.

Basically there are nine questions the interviewer needs to consider in planning the interview. The first seven questions arise in the respondent's mind and the last two arise in the interviewer's mind.

Who Is This Interviewer?

In addition to giving their names to respondents, interviewers should explain their roles in the organizational setting. Terms that reduce potential ego threat and etiquette barriers are most beneficial. For example, instead of saying, "I'm Mrs. Caldwell, the case manager in this department," the interviewer could say, "I'm Jeanne Caldwell; my job is to see what kinds of help you need and to show you where to get it." Obviously, the second introduction is less threatening and less officious; it also shows more sympathetic interest in the respondent, who is more likely to feel that the interviewer is on her side.

We all have experienced bureaucracies that are obsessed with dealing with people quickly and efficiently. Sometimes their interviewers feel they cannot afford the time to introduce themselves and that the respondents don't care about who is questioning them anyway. In some instances such bureaucratic procedures do not have any serious negative effects; for example, think of people coming into a state license bureau to renew their auto license plates. Such procedures can, however, seriously reduce the effectiveness of most human services (social, legal, medical, and educational) where trust is needed to encourage the sharing of personal information and problems.

What Can You Do for Me?

In situations where the respondent takes the initiative in making the appointment, it may be necessary to begin by asking the respondent what he or she wants. This information is necessary to determine whether the respondent is contacting the right person in the right organization at the right time. Once it is clear that the respondent is coming to the right person, the interviewer should explain in general terms not only what he or she can do for the respondent, but also what he or she cannot do and why. This second aspect may sound negative, but it prevents the respondent from becoming resentful for not receiving some type of help that is beyond the power of the interviewer or the agency represented. A foundation of agreement on expectations is important and can be reinforced through written materials given to the respondent before or after the interview.

Why Do You Want to Interview Me?

If the respondent took the initiative and made an appointment with the interviewer, then the interviewer's task is to discover why the respondent has come in. In the initial contact the interviewer should be sensitive to possible emotional reasons for coming in versus the more formal, superficial, and rational-sounding reasons.

On the other hand, if the interviewer took the initiative (for example, a case manager called in a client to discover why he or she dropped out of vocational school, or a public opinion interviewer contacted a randomly selected member of the population), then the interviewer must explain non-threateningly to the respondents why they are being interviewed at this time. In the first example the case manager should make clear that the primary concern is helping the respondent succeed in the vocational training program. In the second example the interviewer should explain why a random sampling process is important, why it is needed to be sure "that people like you" are included, and how people were picked by chance.

What Are the Objectives of the Interview Session?

Although this question may sound similar to What can you do for me?, a distinction is often needed between the general-purpose intent or long-range goals and the more specific objectives of *one* interview. This distinction is not needed in a public opinion interview where the respondent and interviewer have never seen each other before and do not expect to meet again. However, in many types of helping interviews by lawyers, social workers, counselors, or medical personnel, there may be an ongoing series of interviews. Here it is important to set specific goals at the beginning and to review what has been accomplished at the end. Without setting goals and reviewing, the respondent may expect too much of the interview and feel that little was accomplished.

Why Are Certain Types of Personal Information Needed?

Experienced interviewers sometimes find that a respondent cannot see the connection between a specific question and the stated objectives of the interview. As a result, the respondent may suspect that the interviewer has some hidden motives or may feel that the interviewer is being unnecessarily curious about personal matters. If the interviewer does repeated interviews with many clients on the same topic, he or she can anticipate the questions at which the respondent is likely to balk. To avoid this negative reaction the interviewer can simply tell the respondent in advance why specific information is being sought. For example, an interviewer could explain that social security numbers and other identifying information are required to obtain certain services for the respondent. Even when a general statement is made before the interview begins, it is advisable to repeat the explanation whenever one of the sensitive questions arises. For example, the client in a social service program may need to be reassured that the agency has a policy of never giving a phone number or address to a bill collector or to anyone who is not performing social services.

Why Are You Taking Notes and/or Tape-Recording?

Without making too great a point of it, the interviewer can explain that he or she needs to make a few notes so that "I won't forget some of the things I need to know to be of help and will remember any promises we may make to each other about what we are going to do." The exact explanation must be worded to fit the nature of the particular interview situation and the level of the respondent's understanding. Usually, after the first interview in a series, explanation is no longer needed. In any case, the interviewer should neither make a big display of taking notes nor appear to be trying to conceal it. To do either might arouse suspicion in the respondent.

The same principle applies to the use of the tape recorder. There should be no attempt to conceal it, but it should not be used in a way that is distracting to the respondent. Physical arrangements to minimize inhibiting effects of the tape recorder were described earlier, but what kind of verbal explanation is helpful? In my experience using a tape recorder in many interview situations in both the United States and Colombia, I have found that the most effective explanation of the presence of the tape recorder is one that (1) copes with the respondent's fears of violation of confidentiality and (2) shows how it allows the interviewer to pay closer attention to what the respondent is saying. At the same time, the explanation of the advantages must maintain a delicate balance between *not asking* the respondent's permission yet giving the respondent an opportunity to object to its use. For example:

> I want to use a tape recorder so that I won't forget the important things you have to say, and since I don't know shorthand, I can still let you go at your own speed. Also, we won't need a third person in the room to take notes. I want to devote my full attention to what you mean and be ready to ask for clarification if it is needed. No one else will hear the tape but myself. What I do is listen to the tape and dictate off the most important stuff onto another tape and then use the first tape over again for another interview.

Of course, all of these points should be made only if they are true and the promises can be kept. For example, if the interviewer is not going to select and then dictate the relevant information, but a typist is going to transcribe the whole tape, then something like the following can be used:

> The tape will be transcribed by a typist who is instructed to delete your name any time it is mentioned. The original tape is erased and I am the only one who sees the transcription after that.

As important as *what* the interviewer says is *how* he or she says it. If the interviewer sounds doubtful, apologetic, or anxious, the respondent may feel unsafe and ask that the tape recorder not be used. If the interviewer does not sound apologetic and worried that the respondent will object, but seems to be simply explaining the routine, the chance of objection is small.

As interviewers have more experience in tape-recording interviews, they usually become less concerned about any problems, and their confidence is credibly communicated by nonverbal signals.

Will What I Say Be Kept Confidential?

Assuring a respondent that the information given in the interview is confidential may mean that only the interviewer can link the information with the respondent. In some cases this degree of confidentiality is not in the best interests of the respondent; others beside the interviewer may need the information to coordinate their efforts for helping the respondent. For example, a case manager in a social service agency must give information such as the respondent's social security number, telephone number, address, income, size of family, marital status, education level, and condition of health to other agencies in order for the respondent to receive any one of many social services. In this situation the degree of confidentiality promised could be expressed like this:

> I will not give any of the information you are giving me to anyone else except to people in agencies that I know can help you in some way. If they don't need the information to help you, they don't get it. So you don't have to worry about bill collectors or ex-spouses. Okay!

In any case, the interviewer cannot ethically promise more confidentiality than will actually be enforced.

In some types of interviews it is helpful or necessary to promise the respondent complete *anonymity*, which goes beyond confidentiality to the extent that not even the interviewer knows the identity of the respondent. For example, anonymity may be needed in a study of the workings of a crime syndicate where the respondents would be in fear of their lives if their identity leaked out. Techniques for preserving absolute anonymity are described elsewhere[3]; since they are rarely used in either field or institutional settings, we will not review them here.

The extent to which the respondent is put at ease by assurances of confidentiality depends on several factors: the interviewer's tone of voice when giving the reassurance, previous experiences of the respondent, and whether the physical arrangements in the interview setting make it clear that others will not overhear. In some cases we cannot expect the respondent to accept immediately assurances of confidentiality. Trust will come in a series of encounters in which the interviewer shows the ability to use the information to the respondent's advantage.

Should the Interviewer Engage in Any Self-Disclosure?

In interviews where the respondent is expected to disclose information that under most circumstances would be considered private, personal, or intimate, some degree of self-disclosure on the part of the interviewer may increase the respondent's ease and trust. It is, however, very difficult for the interviewer to know when and how much self-disclosure to use. It has been pointed out that even between married couples too much self-disclosure may be harmful to the marriage.[4] Also keep in mind that the respondent might not be under the same ethical or professional constraints regarding confidentiality as is the interviewer. Despite the potential dangers of self-disclosure, studies suggest that the right amount at the right time can contribute to trust and reciprocity.[5]

The problem for the interviewer is to realize how much self-disclosure is prudent and helpful under the circumstances. Ross[6] summarizes some of the variables that must be taken into consideration by the interviewer in making a decision. First, the interviewer must be able to clearly distinguish between *necessary* and *discretionary* disclosures. As we have already pointed out, it is necessary for the interviewer to give his or her own name and function in connection with the interview, but it would be discretionary to mention, for example, that one has children or a spouse or that one was an alcoholic. Once the interviewer recognizes certain information as discretionary, he or she can give it due consideration before revealing it. Interviewers should never engage in self-disclosure as a means to their own catharsis. A strong need for catharsis could damage the interviewer's judgment about the appropriateness of self-disclosure for helping the respondent.

Second, the interviewer must consider whether the interview is a one-time event or part of an ongoing relationship. Generally the amount of openness and self-disclosure that is prudent can increase as a relationship deepens with time. Small and relatively safe confidences early in a relationship can lay the groundwork for more intimate self-disclosure later by both the interviewer and the respondent.

Third, the interviewer must consider the risks involved in self-disclosure. Does the disclosure end here or will it be told to the world? Does it matter? Will the disclosure be interpreted by the respondent as undue pressure to reciprocate with self-disclosure? Will the interviewer be sorry later? What will be the respondent's attitude toward the information disclosed?

Finally, the interviewer must consider whether any self-disclosure is needed to increase the respondent's trust in the interviewer. Long-term relationships can lead to trust on the basis of what the interviewer has been able to *do* for the respondent as well as on the basis of reciprocal self-disclosure.

The foregoing discussion does not provide firm rules about when to allow self-disclosure and how much, but it does provide some relevant guidelines for the interviewer. Ultimately, the ability to use any guidelines will depend on the interviewer's experience, empathic sensitivity, and degree of familiarity with the respondent and the social setting of the interview.

Can the Interviewer Reduce Time Pressures?

What the interviewer says before the formal interviewing begins can either increase or reduce the respondent's feeling of time pressure. If the respondent is anxious about whether there is going to be enough time to get into a problem, he or she may simply avoid mentioning the problem entirely or give a superficial, over simplified, or incomplete account. Sometimes the respondent will not take the time to reflect and accurately recall critical details of a past situation.

The respondent's feeling of time pressure is often a result of the interviewer's nonverbal behavior such as shuffling papers, looking at the clock, speaking rapidly, and so on. For example, a patient in a doctor's office may withhold information because the doctor's manner suggests that he or she is too busy to deal with more than one symptom in one office visit.

If an interview calls for in-depth exploration of problems, symptoms, facts, values, and attitudes of the respondent, then the pace must by slowed down and time constraints must be removed. Often this suggestion is dismissed as impractical or too idealistic by agencies with a backlog of people in the waiting room or lined up outside the door. Yet social agencies may fail to help clients, physicians may fail to diagnose correctly or to order the proper laboratory tests, lawyers may be surprised by testimony of their own clients on the witness stand—all because of failure to take time to listen and probe their respondents sufficiently.

At the verbal level the interviewer should assure the respondent that there is plenty of time or that a certain amount of time is available for this interview and if that is not enough, another appointment can be made. Sometimes the amount of time needed for clients can be reduced by preparing written explanatory materials or simple questionnaires to be used before and/or after the interview, thus creating more time for in-depth interviewing at critical points.

Often institutional and societal pressure to speed up the interview process has its roots in a profound miscalculation of the costs and benefits of rapid, unsuccessful interviews versus slower, successful interviews.[7]

In view of the realities, what the interviewer can honestly say to the respondent may have only a limited effect on the respondent's feeling of time pressure. Nevertheless, the interviewer's own verbal and nonverbal behavior should not add to the feeling of pressure.

SUMMARY

The chances of success in an interview can be enhanced considerably by establishing a communicative atmosphere *before* the first question is asked. The communicative atmosphere consists of both physical and verbal dimensions.

The following *physical dimensions* should be planned whenever they are applicable and when the interviewer has the opportunity:

- Desk arrangement
- Chair placement
- Lighting
- Quiet
- Privacy
- Amenities
- Visual props
- Note taking
- Tape recording
- Dress and grooming

Keep this checklist in mind whenever planning the interview setting. It may not be within your power to control all ten dimensions, but any positive action on any one of them help the interview.

In establishing the verbal setting of the interview, we are trying to produce a social-psychological definition of the situation that will establish trust and maximize the respondent's feeling of security to enhance the free flow of relevant information. There are nine questions the interviewer needs to answer in planning the interview. The first seven are questions that arise in the respondent's mind; the last two arise in the interviewer's mind.

1. Who is this interviewer?
2. What can you do for me?
3. Why do you want to interview me?
4. What are the objectives of the interview session?
5. Why are certain types of personal information needed?
6. Why are you taking notes and/or tape-recording?
7. Will what I say be kept confidential?
8. Should the interviewer engage in any self-disclosure?
9. Can the interviewer reduce time pressures?

In certain circumstances answers to the respondent's questions do not have to be given explicitly because of previous knowledge and experience of the respondent. If there is any possibility of doubt in the respondent's mind, however, it is better to repeat an explanation that is not needed than to omit an explanation that is needed.

Regardless of institutional and cultural restraints, if these suggestions for creating a communicative atmosphere are used whenever possible, the quality and efficiency of the interview will be improved.

NOTES

1. Raymond L. Gorden, "Strategy of Interviewing" in *Interviewing: Strategy, Techniques and Tactics,* 4th ed. (Chicago: Dorsey Press, 1987).
2. William Rogers, *Communication in Action* (New York: Holt, Rinehart & Winston, 1984), 92–93.
3. Raymond L. Gorden, *Interviewing: Strategy, Techniques and Tactics,* 4th ed. (Chicago: Dorsey Press, 1987), 258.
4. Georg Simmel, "The Secret and the Secret Society," in *The Sociology of Georg Simmel,* ed. K. Wolff (New York: Free Press, 1964), 329.
5. Zick Rubin, "Disclosing Oneself to a Stranger: Reciprocity and Its Limits," *Journal of Experimental Social Psychology* 11 (1975): 233–60.
6. Raymond S. Ross, *Essentials of Speech Communication* (Englewood Cliffs, N.J.: Prentice-Hall, 1984), 113–15.
7. For example, if one social agency takes more time and expense to do successful diagnostic interviewing, it may solve a problem that financially benefits some other institution. There is, however, no financial or other reward for the first agency's contribution to overall effectiveness. To make matters worse, the first agency may be criticized for becoming less efficient because it does not handle as many cases per week as it did previously.

EXERCISE 4-A
ARRANGING THE PHYSICAL SETTING
OF THE INTERVIEW

PURPOSE OF THE INTERVIEW

Assume that you are a case manager in the Brighton Multiservice Center. Your main function is to help clients find the combination of services they need to get out of poverty and become employed so they can have a decent standard of living. Typically, the client is a woman who dropped out of high school and who has pre-school children whose father deserted them. For this person to get out of poverty she must first obtain a high school diploma and then obtain specialized vocational training so that she can find an appropriate job. To be able to finish her education, she will need support services such as day-care, financial aid, health care, transportation, perhaps a housing subsidy, and other occasional special services.

You have an appointment with a client who has been receiving this package of services but has been absent from vocational school for a week. You have worked with her for over a year but have not seen her for three weeks. You have asked her to come in for an interview. Your purpose is to diagnose the reason for her failure to attend classes and to offer whatever help and encouragement you can to get her back into school.

MAKING THE PHYSICAL ARRANGEMENTS

Your instructor will furnish a *floor plan* of your office showing the location of your desk, file cabinet, door, windows, plants, and coffee table which has a hot plate and pot of coffee on it. *None* of these features can be moved in making the physical arrangements.

You are to tape-record the interview with a small, battery-powered cassette recorder with a microphone on a six-foot cord.

1. Show where you would locate two chairs for yourself and your client.
   a. Draw them in the same size as the one in the lower left corner of the floor plan. Draw in *pencil* so you can revise easily.
   b. Indicate how many inches apart the front edges of the chairs are.

c. Put the letter *I* in the seat of the chair used by the interviewer.
2. You have a small table you can use if you wish. It is twice the width of a chair seat and about nine inches longer.
3. Show where you would put the following items using the letters in parentheses as keys: microphone (M), ashtray (A), Kleenex (K), recorder (R).
4. Show where you would put a picture, poster, or sign on the wall and succinctly describe its content in the space provided at the top of the floor plan.

COMPARE, DISCUSS, AND REVISE

1. Compare your plan with another person's in the class and note similarities and differences.
2. Discuss the points of difference. (Why did each person do it his or her way? Is one way better? Why?)
3. Revise your plan if you think you can improve it based on your discussion.

Exercise 4-B
SUPPLYING THE VERBAL SETTING OF THE INTERVIEW

THE PROBLEM

The American Restaurant Association (ARA) in its study of business mortality in the restaurant industry made a surprising discovery. It found that many small restaurants that had been in business for years failed *after* they had a sudden growth period. The association hired Research Associates (a group of social scientists) to discover the reasons for these failures. The ARA hopes that the failures and the resultant unemployment and loss of service to the public could be avoided in the future through the training of restaurant personnel. Research Associates sent a letter to every person in the sample explaining the purpose of the study, why the respondent's help was needed, and how his or her response could help the industry. The letter also said that an interviewer (name was given) would be making contact in the next few weeks. The managers of all the restaurants in the sample agreed to cooperate.

Research Associates obtained from the ARA a list of small, independent restaurants that had been in business for at least ten years and a list of restaurants that had recently experienced a sudden spurt in growth. They selected a random sample of each type and interviewed a sample of employees in each. Thus, interviews were with managers, cooks, waiters and waitresses, busboys, and hostesses. All interviews were tape-recorded so that they could be carefully compared and analyzed by the Research Associates staff.

One interviewer was assigned to the sample of restaurants in Detroit. The interviewer's task was to make appointments with the selected respondents and interview them on their off-duty hours, usually at their home. Assume that you are this interviewer and you are going to call one of the waitresses, Rhoda Monarsky, to make an appointment for an interview.

THE PROCEDURE

There are three steps in this exercise. First, you will write a report (not more than one typewritten page) showing what you would say to the respondent to obtain her cooperation. Second, you will meet with another class member to discuss the similarities and differences in your reports. Third, you will participate in a class discussion of the various proposed solutions.

1. Written report
   a. Put in quotes everything you would say on the telephone to the waitress. You dial the number, she answers, and you say . . .
   b. Put in quotes what you would say when you arrive at her apartment to do the interview. You ring the doorbell, she opens the door, and you say . . .
2. Discussion in pairs
   Meet with another member of the class to compare and discuss your written reports. Follow these steps:
   a. Exchange written reports and analyze your partner's report to discover which essential points were covered. Use the *analysis sheet* supplied by your instructor. Fill in columns A and B according to the instructions on the sheet.
   b. Compare your and your partner's analysis sheets and fill in column C using a 0 where neither you nor your partner included the point, a 1 where only one of you included the point, and a 2 where both of you included the point.
   c. Discuss the items that neither of you included to see if you now both think it would have been a good idea to include them.
   d. Discuss the items that only one of you included. The person including it should give his or her reason.
   e. You and your partner take turns suggesting improvements on each other's verbal setting at each of the points you earmarked in column B. Try to show *why* you think a point needs improving and specifically *how* it could be improved. If you put no 1's (improvement is needed) in column B, you will have no suggestions at this point.
   f. If there are any insights or understandings you gained in this process and you have not already discussed them, describe them to your partner and see if he or she had the same experience.
3. Class discussion
   Your instructor will guide a discussion aimed at discovering the range of solutions, evaluating their relative effectiveness, and discussing questions that have arisen in the process. Bring your written report and completed analysis sheet to the discussion.

A translation is no translation, he said, unless it will give you the music of the poem along with the words of it.
—Synge, The Aran Islands

5

Delivering the Question

CHAPTERS 2 AND 3 POINTED OUT that to be useful a question must be relevant to the purpose of the interview and worded to motivate the respondent by making him or her willing and able to give a complete, valid answer. Chapter 4 showed that even the most carefully formulated question may not meet with complete success unless it is used in a physical and verbal setting that establishes a communicative atmosphere *before* the question is asked.

These first chapters dealt with the *planning* phase of interviewing. The current chapter is the first to deal with the actual delivery of the question. A *verbally* well-formed question asked in a communicative atmosphere may still fail if the *nonverbal accompaniment* to the question is not appropriate. The success of a Broadway musical depends not only on the words, scenery, and costumes but also on the appeal of the music. Verbal and nonverbal aspects of the message must reinforce one another for the maximum effect.

IMPORTANCE OF NONVERBAL BEHAVIOR

In general, the verbal formulation of a question deals more with conveying the meaning of the question and nonverbal accompaniment deals more with motivating the respondent to answer. This is not, however, an absolute difference between the verbal and the nonverbal. As we have already shown, the wording of a question deals with *both* the meaning of the question and the motivation of the respondent. Similarly, nonverbal accompaniment deals with both the meaning of the question and the respondent's motivation to answer.

Studies[1] of communication estimate that as much as 65 percent of the meaning of a spoken message can be determined by the nonverbal accompaniment. Nonverbal factors include tone of voice, facial expression, gestures, and posture. These factors affect both meaning and motivation. They affect motivation by communicating the interviewer's attitude toward the question, the respondent, and the answer. The interviewer's nonverbal cues also convey an impression of the interviewer to the respondent. They determine to a great extent whether the respondent feels that the interviewer is likable, sympathetic, and trustworthy. In addition, the way the question is delivered signals to the respondent whether the interviewer really expects an answer and is accustomed to receiving an answer to such a question.

Research on nonverbal communication reveals some important characteristics and principles relevant to the interviewing task. First, most nonverbal behavior is automatic and *unconscious* and, therefore, more difficult for either the interviewer or the respondent to consciously control than is verbal behavior. For example, Passons[2] points out that clients in counseling sessions are more aware of their words than of their own nonverbal behavior.

Second, if one person attempts to deceive another with words, there is usually a conflict betrayed by *leakage* of nonverbal cues. By leakage we mean those nonverbal messages that are sent unintentionally and unconsciously. A respondent may give a verbally deceptive message only to have his repression of the truth show in nonverbal leakage. Another respondent might succeed in suppressing one nonverbal cue (like facial expression) only to have the truth revealed by leakage in the form of other nonverbal cues—perhaps in movements of the hands or feet.

If nonverbal leakage is detected, the listener will usually give greater credibility to it than to the verbal message. For example, we can all recall a person who when asked "How are you?" says "I'm fine" in such a way as to mean "I'm tired and disgusted." To be most convincing, the verbal message must be in harmony with the nonverbal message, and all of the nonverbal cues must be consistent. Gazda et al.[3] have shown in counseling interviews that if there is a contradiction between verbal and nonverbal cues, the nonverbal ones are usually believed by the client.

Third, different types of nonverbal cues are usually interconnected and congruent in manifesting the same attitude or emotion. For this reason, it is possible for different people witnessing the same interview to come to the same conclusion about the respondent's or interviewer's attitudes, even though one observer might concentrate on the tone of voice while another pays more attention to visual cues.

Finally, it is not safe to try to assign meaning to a very specific nonverbal cue out of its verbal, nonverbal, situational, and cultural context. For example, an Asian woman who is brought before a judge to testify might look down at the floor instead of at the judge. Her action might be wrongly interpreted by the judge to mean that she is lying. It may simply mean that in the part of Asia where she was brought up, women do not look men of high status in the eye because to do so would show disrespect.

INTERVIEWER'S NONVERBAL BEHAVIOR

More research has been done on the observation and interpretation of the *respondent's* nonverbal behavior than on the interviewer's. But remember that if you can make judgments from seeing and hearing the respondent's nonverbal behavior, the respondent can also make judgments from your nonverbal behavior. Nonverbal communication is a two-way street!

In a book focused on practical skills needed in many interviewing settings, we cannot examine all of the implications of the research on nonverbal behavior, nor can we discuss all of the possible nonverbal stimuli emanating from the interviewer and their possible effects on the respondent. Instead, we will focus on a few of the most basic nonverbal behaviors which can be learned and controlled by the interviewer and which have been found helpful in motivating the respondent to answer more candidly and completely.

Conversational Distance

In dealing with the physical aspects of the communicative atmosphere, we mentioned that the chairs for the interviewer and respondent should usually be placed so that the eye-to-eye distance is about three to four feet. This is within the range referred to by Hall[4] as "personal space." However, this distance is a cultural pattern that varies from one country to another and to a lesser extent, within a country by region, ethnicity, social class, and sex. The major principle that must be applied to a particular interview situation is this: People feel freer to discuss different subjects at different distances. Intimate conversations must take place at a closer distance than mere personal or private conversations, which take place at a closer range than public conversations. Different distances call for different volume and tone of voice and bring into play different senses in the communication process. For example, the senses of smell or touch and the observation of such details as dilation of the pupils can come into play only at a very close range. In contrast, hearing loud voices and noting a person's posture and actions can take place at long distances.

The appropriate distance depends on the topic being discussed. For example, a female counseling an abused housewife should be close enough to hear whispers, to touch the respondent's hand, and to use soft comforting tones of voice. On the other hand, someone interviewing a governor about election issues would be prudent to sit farther away and not be surprised if the governor speaks in an official, public tone of voice.

As shown by Lecomte,[5] in interviewing for personal and private information, the distance of three to four feet allows a softer tone of voice that is less likely to be overheard by others. It also allows both parties to note finer nuances of vocal and facial expression. This distance enables the interviewer to lean forward and touch the other person if emotional support is needed and acceptable under the circumstances.

The distance of three to four feet is not a rigid rule, because most of the research deals with middle-class, white Americans and results may vary with different combinations of interviewers and respondents. This distance should be treated as a tentative beginning point for the interviewer who should remain alert for signals that the respondent feels too close or too far away for comfort.

If the interviewer is too close, the respondent may unconsciously lean back or turn sideways, as shown by Graves and Robinson,[6] as a signal of the desire to escape, to disengage, or to reduce the intimacy of the situation. Other signals of the desire to disengage include looking away, folding arms, crossing legs, or in some other way erecting a physical or psychological barrier. So to be able to regulate his or her own nonverbal behavior appropriately, the interviewer must be sensitive to the respondent's nonverbal behavior.

Body Position

The interviewer's body position should indicate interest in the respondent as a person and show attention to what is being said. Instead of slouching in a La-Z-Boy chair at right angles to the respondent's line of sight, for example, the interviewer should *face* the respondent squarely to show maximum attention and *lean forward* toward the respondent, at least some of the time. Some practitioners suggest that the interviewer should lean forward far enough to rest the forearms on the thighs.[7] Any leaning back has the same effect as moving the chair farther away. The extreme case of withdrawal is turning one's back on another. This is what we do when we are forced into greater proximity than we want as, for example, on the subway when we counteract the effect of forced closeness by turning our back on the other person. Knapp[8] illustrates many of the ways in which people create bodily defense barriers against the violation of spatial privacy.

The interviewer must be alert for the need to deviate from the sit-close-lean-forward rule and keep in mind that most of the research supporting this rule was developed in the helping interview. It will not apply, for example, in the case of a journalist interviewing the mayor.

Touch

Some experimental studies clearly demonstrate that people have a more positive feeling toward someone who touched them during a conversation than toward someone who did not touch under identical circumstances. One such study was done by Borensweig[9] in the clinical social work setting. We must be wary, however, of generalizing too widely from a few such studies. An indiscriminate use of touching in an interview could lead to negative reactions from the respondent. Studies done with female psychotherapists helping female clients may have little relevance when, for example, the problem is rape and the counselor is male. There are also wide cultural and subcultural differences in what is considered the appropriate time, place, and manner to touch a person of the same or opposite sex. For example, Barland[10] compared American and Japanese behavior patterns and found great differences in the socially acceptable amount and type of touching between sexes and within the sexes in public and private.

This area of scientific research, called *haptics* (the study of touch as a form of human communication), is not developed to the point that fixed rules can be given about how touch can be used to enhance communication under the wide range of circumstances in which interviewing is done. All that can be said in reference to acquiring touching skills in interviewing is that touch is a positive influence when done in the right way under the right circumstances. Touch seems most effective when interviewer and respondent are of the same sex and the respondent needs and will accept emotional support in this form.

Eye Contact

Another way to convince the respondent that you are giving your undivided attention is to make regular eye contact. One reason that the interviewer sits close to and facing the respondent squarely is to facilitate eye contact. Lack of eye contact suggests a lack of interest or sympathetic understanding. Too much eye contact, on the other hand, may suggest greater intimacy than is appropriate for an interview.

Practitioners in counseling have suggested that more mutual gazing or eye contact tends to occur when the distance between counselor and client is greater, when comfortable topics are being discussed, when interpersonal involvement between counselor and client is greater, when listening rather than talking, and when the parties involved are females.[11]

If a single eye contact lasts more than two or three seconds, particularly between members of opposite sex, it might suggest that the initiator is seeking intimacy, depending on the accompanying general facial expression and/or tone of voice. If the facial expression is not friendly but the eye contact is prolonged, the action may suggest the attempt to overpower and "stare down" the other person. The aim of the interviewer should be to use enough eye contact to indicate sustained interest and sympathetic understanding without suggesting an intimate or repressive relationship.

Facial Expression

In facial expressions there are two common pitfalls to be avoided: the blank "neutral" expression and extraneous facial movements. An interviewer may use the neutral expression to indicate a nonjudgmental attitude or to hide real reactions to the respondent or to something said. The same effect can be achieved, however, by showing interest in the respondent as a person and in what he or she is saying. To show interest does not necessarily mean agreement. Also, the interviewer should indicate an appreciation of the effort being put forth by the respondent who is trying to respond candidly.

The second pitfall to avoid is extraneous facial movements. If the interviewer is nervous, he or she might show it by grimacing, by biting or wetting the lips, by squinting the eyes, or by simply overreacting, for example, with a smile that is too broad or artificial. This pitfall is rarely a problem for an experienced interviewer who feels comfortable in a situation.

On the positive side, the ideal facial expression for an interviewer is one that is basically calm but alert and responsive. A general expression of attention and interest is the baseline from which the interviewer may vary to convey meaning to the question or to show empathy with the response. In showing empathy, the interviewer should not overact by using extreme or stereotypical facial expressions. The respondent can notice, sometimes at an unconscious level, whether even the most subtle facial expressions of the interviewer are appropriate or inappropriate.

Another useful principle to remember is that the interviewer's facial expressions should be synchronous and congruent with the respondent's emotional state. The interviewer's expression should not be fixed—it should be flexibly responsive to the emotional expressions of the respondent. Note that the interviewer's expressions should be congruent with but not identical in all cases with those of the respondent. For example, if the respondent is clearly in a depressed or angry mood, the interviewer does not respond with equal depression or anger but with an expression of sympathetic understanding.

Also, to be congruent in expression means that the interviewer should not try to counteract negative feelings in the respondent by expressing the opposite. For example, if the respondent is depressed and sad, the interviewer should not try to exude an attitude of optimism and joy. Such a reaction can be interpreted as rejection by the respondent. The more fruitful response is to recognize the respondent's suffering; do not act as though it is not real, but show that you have heard and sympathize with the respondent's plight.

On rare occasions the principle of congruence can be thrown to the winds. For example, if you feel that the respondent is fabricating or exaggerating and can be discouraged from this deception by challenging or contradicting the response, you might openly show disbelief or doubt. At the end of an interview with a depressed or angry person, the interviewer might try to counteract the emotion with some expression of cautious optimism. Care must be taken, however, not to respond this way to a particular bit of information from the respondent who might then feel that the interviewer does not care, understand, or sympathize.

In general, it is easier for interviewers to improve their performance by becoming aware of their feelings and attitudes than by being aware of specific ways these are being communicated by facial expressions. Often it is more fruitful to work on one's attitudes than to try to use the "correct" facial expression. Any attempt to change the outward manifestations without changing the inward attitude is likely to result in a form of ambiguous expression leading to mistrust. More is said on this topic by the author in another book.[12]

Tone of Voice

The interviewer's vocal quality (loudness, pitch, intonation patterns, and timbre) must be adjusted in two ways. First, it must be adjusted to the mood of the respondent. For example, if the respondent is sad and subdued and speaks softly, the interviewer should not respond in a loud, enthusiastic tone. This would indicate a lack of empathy with the respondent. In any case the tone of voice should be spontaneously conversational and should avoid any suggestion of a formal, routine, bureaucratized reading of a script.

The second way in which vocal quality should be adjusted may sound contradictory to the first aim of adjusting to the respondent's mood. Sometimes the interviewer's vocal quality should be used to *change* or *direct* the respondent's behavior. It may be used to regulate turn taking in the dialogue, or it may be used to change the respondent's mood. For example, if the respondent is agitated, excited, and speaking rapidly in an interview where a thoughtful, reminiscent mood is needed to accurately recall relevant material, the interviewer should not adjust his or her tone of voice to imitate but should try to have a soothing effect on the respondent. In other situations the respondent may need to be roused from a lethargic mood and stimulated to think, to verbalize, or to act. In these cases the interviewer should not adjust to the respondent's tone of voice and mood. Even so, there may be a problem if the interviewer is suddenly too forceful in pushing in the opposite direction when more gentle persuasion is needed.

Interviewers should not sound condescending or bored unless they are trying to move the respondent away from an irrelevant topic. Generally, a flexible conversational tone is appropriate to express an accepting, nonthreatening, nonjudgmental attitude. The interviewer's tone of voice should indicate that candid answers are expected and should not sound doubtful or apologetic about any of the questions asked.

Pacing

Pacing the conversation in an interview may refer to either the rate of speech or the frequency of turn taking in the dialogue. Pacing is crucial to good interviewing for several reasons. It determines the extent to which either superficial or deep information can be given. The pace may appropriately be fast to ask name, age, birth date, or marital status; but to ask the respondent to recall details of past events or to search emotional ambivalences, the pace must be much slower. Establishing a more thoughtful, reminiscent mood requires a slower pace, which the interviewer needs in order to stimulate recall, to discourage imprecise reporting of facts, and to encourage self-examination.

A slower pace banishes the feeling of time constraints upon the interview; it gives the respondent the feeling that the interviewer is interested and sympathetic enough to spend some time and that the interviewer recognizes the value in the responses. The slower pace also avoids the ego threat produced when an interviewer asks profound, complicated questions and seems to expect instantaneous answers. The syndrome of "give me your life history in thirty seconds" makes some respondents retreat within themselves whereas others become angry and hostile. In any case, the flow of needed information is seriously inhibited if the pace is too rapid.

How can the interviewer affect the pacing of the interview? There are several ways, but first the interviewer must accept the fact that he or she either consciously or unconsciously will have a strong effect on the pace. As interviewers, we must sensitize ourselves to how we do this. Then we can have the effect needed at a particular point in the interview.

Perhaps the interviewer's most obvious influence on the pace is the *speed* of the interviewer's own speech. Speech rates vary by cultural background (regional, rural-urban, ethnic), individual temperament, and mood. Some interviewers must learn to slow down their normal speech rate and others need to speed it up a bit.

A second powerful tool in regulating pacing is the use of *silence*. Too often interviewers abhor silence as nature abhors a vacuum. The tendency to leap in the moment the respondent finishes a sentence is irresistible for some interviewers. In other cases the interviewer may not even wait until the respondent finishes a sentence, and both talk at once for a few words until the respondent is squelched.

A much more subtle and prevalent form of interruption occurs when the interviewer leaps in at the first pause without waiting to see if the respondent intends to say more on the subject. My research has shown that respondents talking about their experiences in a disaster tended to leave less than a second's pause between one sentence and another. However, if the interviewer waited two seconds before speaking, there was a 77 percent chance that the respondent would continue to elaborate on the response. (The chance that the respondent would continue without being asked another question steadily dropped to 9 percent for a nine-second silence.) The general tendency of inexperienced interviewers is to jump in before they are sure the respondent has finished. Two seconds is not a long time to wait to avoid interrupting the respondent's momentum.

When the interviewer uses silent probes of two or more seconds in length, he or she must observe carefully to determine whether the respondent is thinking and intending to respond further or is looking expectantly at the interviewer. The insensitive use of needlessly long and often fruitless silence can be threatening to the respondent. On the other hand, the failure to allow any silence puts pressure on the respondent to speed up the interview by speaking faster, making responses shorter, or both. In either case the chance of getting valid and complete information is reduced.

A third tool for controlling the pace of the interview is bodily *gestures*. If the interviewer looks at a clock or watch, glances at the door, appears bored, anxious, or uninterested, the respondent might feel it is time to move on. Research by Duncan[13] shows that the concept of turn-taking signals is useful here. For example, the listener in a dialogue who wants to talk can signify this by such cues as inhaling audibly, raising an index finger, straightening or tightening posture, or nodding rapidly. If the interviewer demonstrates such actions, the respondent will usually stop speaking. The interviewer must likewise become sensitive to cues from the respondent who desires to speak.

Finally, there is a special kind of pacing on the interviewer's part that is best described as *hesitating* and *groping*. Instead of delivering a question smoothly and evenly, the interviewer starts a question, interrupts it, starts again, rewords it, and may even comment on the difficulty of formulating the question. For example:

> So the first time you smuggled drugs was when you had gone on vacation to Italy and you got the idea of putting hashish in books about the Uffizi Gallery. Why ...uh, or what were you thinking...what I really want to know is you had to go through some decision making before doing that...so what were some of the pros and cons that occurred to you at *that* time?...uh, *not* what you *now* feel you *should* have been thinking of...can you remember some of your thoughts at that time?

After beginning with a reference to something that the respondent has already said, the interviewer began to formulate a question. Instead of asking the spontaneous question, "Why did you do it?" which might have sounded judgmental, the interviewer struggled to reformulate the question. Then, realizing the danger of the respondent confusing his thoughts at the time of the event with his reflections while spending time in jail, the interviewer added "at that time" and pointed out "*not* what you *now* feel you should have been thinking of."

Perhaps this hesitation and groping is simply bad interviewing which allows the respondent to lose respect for the interviewer and permits the whole interview to get out of control. This criticism is often leveled by people who are used to a dominant role, for example, a police officer interviewing a suspect or a manager interviewing an employee. In these cases the criticism has some validity. In other types of interviews, however, more of a collaborative relationship or a helping relationship exists between interviewer and respondent. In such interviews the effect of hesitation may be positive for several reasons. First, it creates a thoughtful mood and sets an example of thinking out loud and correcting one's first impressions. Second, it reduces ego threat by showing the respondent that the interviewer is also groping and exploring with some difficulty and that such groping is permitted. Third, it militates against the image of a dominant, bureaucratic, and efficient interviewer who expects instant answers in grammatically correct sentences.

Hesitating and groping is more natural when the purpose of the interview is exploratory and new ground is being broken. Also, even though the interviewer may have planned all of the main questions so that they flow smoothly, hesitating and groping may be natural if the first response to a basic question needs to be probed more deeply by another question designed on the spot. The author has done interviews in which it proved helpful to avoid delivering even the basic questions in too smooth a manner. The respondents felt better when even basic questions seemed to be formulated to fit their personal experience.

As interviewers we need to be aware that groping and hesitating is not always bad. We should accept it in both ourselves and in our respondents, particularly when it is a symptom of conscientious, thoughtful effort to make accuracy of content more important than elegance or efficiency of form.

Distracting Behavior

Often interviewers develop mannerisms that are distracting to the respondent and difficult to eliminate because the behavior pattern is unconscious. For example, interviewers may tap their fingers, tap pencils, bounce their knees, rub their noses, scratch their heads, shuffle papers, doodle, fidget in their chairs, or chew gum. Any of these mannerisms can prove quite distracting for the respondent.

To eliminate patterns of distracting behavior, the interviewer must not only realize that they are undesirable, but also become aware of them in his or her own behavior.

SUMMARY

Even the best formulated question used in an ideal physical and social setting can fail. The question needs to be delivered with appropriate nonverbal accompaniment because much of the *meaning* of the question and the respondent's *motivation* to answer it depend on nonverbal cues. If there is a conflict between the verbal and nonverbal portions of a message, the listener is more likely to believe the nonverbal; such a discrepancy is usually viewed (often unconsciously) as evidence of an attempt to deceive with words.

Nonverbal aspects of the interviewer's delivery can affect the respondent's image of the interviewer as a person. Whether the interviewer is perceived as trustworthy, interested, and sympathetic or sneaky, bored, and judgmental depends to a great extent on the nonverbal factors that accompany questions.

Nonverbal behavior also affects the general mood and pace of the interview. Does the respondent feel pressured to give quick, superficial answers? Or does there seem to be time for free association, thoughtful recall, verbalization of feelings, and correction of superficial responses? The respondent's perception depends to a great extent on the nonverbal aspects of the interviewer's delivery of questions and follow-up probes.

Among the interviewer's nonverbal tools for delivering questions with maximum meaning and motivation are the following skills which can be learned and controlled:

1. Assume the optimum conversational distance.
2. Maintain a body position that conveys interest in the respondent by facing the respondent squarely and leaning forward some of the time.
3. Touch the respondent if it is appropriate and acceptable to do so.
4. Maintain eye contact with the respondent without staring.
5. Show appropriately responsive facial expression.
6. Employ a suitable conversational tone of voice.
7. Pace conversation carefully by controlling your own rate of speech, length of silent probes, and turn taking; have no fear of honest hesitating and groping.
8. Eliminate distracting behavior mannerisms that might make the respondent feel you are not interested or sympathetic.

Becoming skillful in the use of these eight nonverbal tools requires an awareness of one's own nonverbal behavior, sensitivity to the respondent's needs, and the ability to control one's own nonverbal behavior.

NOTES

1. Randal Harrison, "Nonverbal Communication: Exploration into Time, Space, Action and Object," in *Dimensions in Communication,* ed. James H. Campbell and Hall W. Hepler (Belmont, Calif.: Wadsworth Publishing, 1982), 101. See also Timothy G. Hegstrom, "Message Impact: What Percent Is Nonverbal?" *Western Journal of Speech Communication* 43, no. 2 (Spring 1979): 134–42.

2. W. R. Passons, *Gestalt Approaches to Counseling* (New York: Holt, Rinehart & Winston, 1975), 102.

3. G. M. Gazda et al., "Awareness of Nonverbal Behaviors in Helping," in *Human Relations Development,* 3rd ed. (Boston: Allyn & Bacon, 1984).

4. Edward T. Hall, "Space Speaks," in *The Silent Language* (Garden City, N.Y.: Anchor-Doubleday, 1974).

5. C. Lecomte et al., "Counseling Interactions as a Function of Spatial-Environmental Conditions," *Journal of Counseling Psychology* 28 (1981): 536–39.

6. J. R. Graves and J. D. Robinson, "Proxemic Behavior as a Function of Inconsistent Verbal and Nonverbal Messages," *Journal of Counseling Psychology* 23 (1976): 333–38.

7. Robert R. Carkhuff and Richard M. Pierce et al., *The Art of Helping* (Amherst, Mass.: Human Resources Development Press, 1977), chapter 2.

8. M. L. Knapp, *Nonverbal Communication in Human Interaction,* 2nd ed. (New York: Holt, Rinehart & Winston, 1978).

9. H. Borensweig, "Touching in Clinical Social Work," *Social Casework* 64 (April 1983): 238–42.

10. Dean C. Barnlund, "The Public Self and the Private Self in Japan and the United States," in *Intercultural Encounters with Japan,* ed. John C. Condon and Mitsuko Saito (Tokyo: The Simul Press, 1975).

11. William H. Cormier and L. Sherilyn Cormier, *Interviewing Strategies for Helpers,* 2nd ed. (Monterey, Calif.: Brooks/Cole Publishing, 1985), 73.

12. Raymond L. Gorden, "Nonverbal Techniques and Attitudes," *Interviewing: Strategy, Techniques and Tactics* (Chicago: Dorsey Press, 1987), 370–84.

13. S. P. Duncan, Jr. "Some Signals and Roles for Taking Speaking Turns in Conversations," *Journal of Personality and Social Psychology 23* (1972): 283–92.

Exercise 5-A
OBSERVING A
QUESTION DELIVERY DEMONSTRATION

Delivering a question properly consists of using all of the nonverbal skills along with the verbal to convey the meaning of the question and to motivate the respondent to answer the question as fully and accurately as possible. To a great extent the nonverbal message motivates the respondent if it shows the respondent that the interviewer is paying attention, is interested, and is sympathetic, but is not gullible.

Before you are asked to practice and demonstrate your own question delivery skills, this exercise will give you an opportunity to observe two demonstrations of question delivery and to compare the two in a systematic way. Your instructor will supply you with a copy of the *question delivery observation form.* You will record your observations of the first demonstration in column A and record your observations of the second demonstration in column B.

Focus your attention on eight questions regarding the interviewer's attending behavior:

1. Does the interviewer maintain an appropriate distance from the respondent?
2. Does the interviewer face the respondent squarely?
3. Does the interviewer lean forward slightly at times?
4. Does the interviewer's face show interest in the respondent?
5. Does the interviewer make appropriate eye contact with the respondent?
6. Does the interviewer engage in any form of distracting behavior?
7. Does the interviewer's tone of voice sound natural and show interest?
8. Is the interviewer's pacing appropriate (not too fast or too slow)?

After you have recorded both sets of observations, your whole class will discuss their experiences.

EXERCISE 5-B
PRACTICING QUESTION DELIVERY

In the previous exercise you had an opportunity to *observe* demonstrations of good and bad question delivery. This exercise allows you to *participate* directly in the interview process both as interviewer and respondent.

OVERVIEW OF THE PROCEDURE

1. Your instructor will supply copies of the same question delivery observation form used in the previous exercise. Use the form to remind you of the behavior patterns you should manifest in your role as interviewer and to remind you of what to look for in your role as observer.
2. Form teams of three and decide among you who is to be interviewer, respondent, and observer in the first role-play. At the end of the following set of instructions for each of these roles, you are told which role you are to assume in the next role-play; each person thus has a turn at each of the roles.
3. Select the topic you want to use in your turn as interviewer. If you prefer to use a topic other than one suggested here, you are free to do so. Be careful to select a topic that is easy for the respondent to talk about. Each member of the team should choose a *different* topic. Here are some possible topics:
   a. Differences between high school and college
   b. Ideas of a dream vacation
   c. Ecology problems in the United States
   d. Plans after graduating from college
   e. Hobbies, recreation, or leisure
4. Prepare for your role as interviewer by designing an opening question and some possible follow-up questions to keep the respondent talking for three minutes.
5. Study the role descriptions given in the next section, particularly the one you are to assume in the first role-play.
6. Do the first role-play.
7. Discuss the first role-play according to the procedure presented in this exercise.
8. Repeat the process to give each person a chance at each role.
9. After completing three role-plays return to the class for a discussion.

DESCRIPTION OF ROLES

1. Interviewer's role
   a. Review the kinds of attending behavior you are to manifest by scanning the question delivery observation form.
   b. Arrange chairs for yourself and your respondent and invite your respondent to be seated as you immediately begin your attending behavior.
   c. Ask your opening question and continue your attending behavior while the respondent answers.
   d. If there is time, ask some follow-up questions to get your respondent to elaborate or clarify something he or she said. The observer will stop you in three minutes.

Take the role of respondent in the next role-play.

2. Respondent's role
   a. Don't sit down until the interviewer invites you to do so.
   b. Answer questions candidly and spontaneously.
   c. Do *not* try to give the interviewer a hard time; remember that in a few minutes it will be your turn to be interviewer!

Take the role of observer in the next role-play.

3. Observer's role
   a. Locate your chair (with writing arm, if possible) at a point no closer than six feet from the respondent or interviewer and at an angle where you can see both people's faces.
   b. Start timing the interview from the moment the interviewer sits down and asks the opening question. Be prepared to stop the interview in exactly three minutes, even though you must interrupt.
   c. Carefully observe the interviewer and fill out your question delivery observation form.
   d. Call "time" at the end of three minutes and finish checking your observation form.
   e. Start the discussion (again note the time) and direct it along the lines suggested in number 4 under "discussion format."
   f. Stop the discussion when it is no longer productive or at the end of 10 minutes, whichever comes sooner.

Take the role of interviewer in the next role-play.

4. Discussion format
   a. Ask the *interviewer* to give his or her impressions: "How do you feel you did?" (Any mistakes? Easy or difficult?) "What would you try to do differently next time?"
   b. Ask the *respondent* to give his or her impressions: "How did the interviewer do from your point of view?" "How did it feel to be the respondent?" (What was easy? What was difficult?)

  c. Give your *own* impressions (as shown on your observation form) of the interviewer's attending behavior.

  d. Are there any ideas or impressions of differences in the three points of view?

After each member of the team has lead the group in discussion, the team should return to the class for a discussion of the different teams' experiences.

It is the disease of not listening,
the malady of not marking,
that I am troubled withal.
—Shakespeare, King Henry IV

6

Listening
to the
Respondent

I F WE HAVE FORMULATED a relevant and motivating question, arranged the physical and verbal setting to establish a communicative atmosphere, and delivered the question with the most appropriate nonverbal accompaniment, then we are well on our way to success in an interview.

All of these actions may have little value, however, if we fail to *listen* to the respondent's answer. Even when a respondent answers willingly and spontaneously, there is no guarantee that what is being said is relevant, complete, and valid. Failing to listen effectively is like neglecting to harvest a crop after carefully ploughing, planting, fertilizing, and irrigating. Yet it is precisely at the harvesting point that many interviews are weak.

Few people are excellent listeners. This statement should not be surprising in view of the fact that, unlike other basic communication skills such as reading, writing, or speaking, listening is rarely if ever taught in schools and colleges. Perhaps we should expect this situation in our individualistic and competitive culture where persuasion and demonstrable performance are emphasized. It is easy to impress people by performing *outgoing* communication activities such as acting, singing, speaking, and writing, but how can we impress an audience with our skill in listening? Often this is merely a rhetorical question, but researchers are discovering that the results of skillful listening *can* be demonstrated.

IMPORTANCE OF LISTENING

Students who know how to listen do better in college than those who don't. Managers who can listen to employees are more effective than those who cannot. Of course in the process of interviewing, if the interviewer cannot listen effectively there is little hope of success. But aren't we all born listeners? No! We have to be taught. Nichols,[1] an excellent researcher on the listening process, says that most of the individuals he has studied usually listen at no more than 25 percent efficiency. We have no more native ability to listen than to write or speak effectively. Yet success in medical diagnosis, management, politics, social research, and all of the helping professions depends on the ability not only to ask relevant questions but also to listen effectively to the answers.

The first step in becoming an effective listener is to know the difference between merely *hearing* and *listening*. Hearing is the automatic physiological process of sound waves being received by the ear; it is a matter of sensation only. To say hearing is automatic means that it happens under given physical and physiological conditions regardless of the intent, desire, or motivation of the hearer. Hearing is a passive process that does not require intellectual effort on the part of the receiver. This is quite different from listening.

Listening is not automatic; it occurs only with intent, effort, and concentration on the part of the receiver. It is a high-order mental process that includes interpretation, comprehension, evaluation, appreciation, and response.

To interpret is to give meaning to what is said. The meaning of any response depends on the assumptions in the listener's mind about the topic. If the listener's assumptions are congruent with the speaker's, then the meaning intended by the speaker will be the same as that interpreted by the listener. Listening is an intellectually active process of *trying to comprehend* meaning in larger verbal, nonverbal, and situational contexts and of *trying to evaluate* the message in terms of the objectives of the listener.

In interviewing, active listeners constantly ask themselves questions such as these:

- Is it clear what that means?
- Is she saying this or that?
- Is that really relevant to the question?
- Is the answer complete?
- What does that tone of voice mean?
- How did he feel about that at the time?
- Is that really the truth?

- Is the answer complete?
- Should I interrupt now to probe or should I wait till later?

The ability to evaluate responses depends to a great extent upon how clearly the interviewer understands the objectives of the interview as a whole and of the specific question being answered. The active listener is never at a loss to probe when the respondent stops. In fact, there is a danger that the very active listener may be too eager and interrupt the respondent too frequently. The interviewer must listen empathetically to appreciate adequately and respond appropriately.

Some might object to including appreciation and response as part of the listening process, but research on interviewing indicates that a good listener is a person who empathetically appreciates not only the significance of what the respondent is saying but also the effort the respondent is making to be candid and complete. In a sense, internalized appreciation in itself is a response; nevertheless, a further external response is needed to *show* the person being interviewed that the interviewer is listening empathetically.

Appreciation, empathy, or warmth in reply to a particular response can be outwardly expressed by a variety of nonverbal cues as pointed out by Johnson.[2] Tone of voice, facial expression, and eye contact are the main cues received by the respondent. Just as the interviewer tries to "read" the respondent's nonverbal behavior, the respondent reads the interviewer's. Maurer and Tindall[3] show that if the interviewer assumes a posture that is congruent with that of the respondent, that action has an effect on the respondent's perception of the interviewer's empathy.

As indicated by Ivey and Simek-Downing,[4] empathy, warmth, encouragement, and recognition can also be expressed to the respondent by the interviewer's verbal comments. A comment might emphasize the content of a particular response or show appreciation of the effort the respondent is making. Spontaneous remarks such as the following demonstrate that the interviewer is understanding and appreciating the respondent: "Really!" "That must be scary!" "I know it's hard for you to tell me this." "You are doing very well!"

Another way the interviewer expresses empathy, or the lack of it, is in the nature of the probes that follow a response. Even though the interviewer may try to appear interested and empathic, a basic lack of appreciation of the respondent's experiences can be communicated unintentionally by the nature of probes. Here, for example, are two excerpts from interviews on the same project where one interviewer was empathic and the other was not. The interviews were with two women who survived a tornado that obliterated their small, rural village in Arkansas. In the first excerpt the interviewer shows very little empathy:

I: Tell me what happened to you in the storm.
R: Well, I heard this sound . . . like ten locomotives roaring down the track, but it was coming right through the middle of Bald Knob. I looked out the win-

dow and saw this black funnel cloud and a funny yellowish light. The back door flew open and I went to close it. I was holding it shut when suddenly there was a blast and I was flying through the air and landed in the mud in the pecan orchard. I was all wet and had only one shoe on.

I: What time was that?

The respondent is recounting the most frightening encounter she has ever experienced and all the interviewer wants to know in response is "What time was that?" This apparent callousness occurred because the interviewer heard almost identical stories from ten to twenty previous respondents. Yet, some interviewers were able to retain their empathy as shown in the next excerpt:

I: Tell me what happened to you in the storm.

R: It was terrible. I had heard of tornados but had never been in one and don't want to be again! The kids were at school and my husband was working at the strawberry plant when it started blowin' and rainin' and then hailstones as big as golf balls started beatin' down. I looked outside and saw this black cloud just a churnin' up everything in its path. I was thinkin' about headin' for the root cellar in back when the house blew apart and I was sittin' on the living room rug sailin' through the air and I came down with a thump in the strawberry patch.

I: That must have been terrible! Then what happened?

Generally respondents are quick to sense a lack of interest and boredom in the interviewer and will react by retreating to abbreviated answers. However, in this case of disaster victims, it was difficult to discourage respondents because of their strong need to tell someone about their frightening experience. Even so, analysis of the interviews indicated a general decline in the length of the interviews and in the amount of relevant information from the end of the first week of interviewing to the end of the fourth. The decline was due mainly to the interviewer's loss of interest and boredom. If one human being can become bored with another's recounting a life-threatening experience, how much easier it must be for a worker in a service agency to become bored with stories of family conflict.

Active, empathic listening is obviously helpful in any profession involved with human relations. It is also the key to success in many nonprofessional roles such as husband, wife, son, daughter, student, or lover. Yet there are many obstacles to the practice of good listening which we should recognize and deal with in order to improve our listening.

OBSTACLES TO LISTENING

Even if the interviewer has the objectives of the interviewer set deeply in his or her consciousness and is highly motivated to achieve them, there are obstacles that might interfere with active listening. These obstacles can be separated into three general types: physical, semantic, and emotional. Strictly speaking, the physical obstacles involve *hearing* rather than listening, but it is useful to include them in our examination at this point.

Physical Obstacles

We have already mentioned how some of the physical obstacles to hearing can be removed by carefully arranging the physical setting; for example, choose a quiet place or adjust the seating as necessary. Other physical obstacles include visually distracting activities by the respondent, mumbling or whispering by the respondent, and fatigue or hearing impairment in the interviewer. Rarely do these purely physical factors act as a major obstacle to listening.

Semantic Obstacles

The respondent does not have to be speaking a foreign language to present a semantic obstacle to the interviewer. Common English words have different meanings in different social contexts. Contexts differ from one region of the United States to another, from one social class to another, from one ethnic group to another, and from one occupational group to another. The interviewer who is not familiar with the respondent's vocabulary and special meanings cannot listen effectively and will not know whether a question has really been answered.

Sometimes it is readily apparent to the interviewer that a certain word has a special meaning because it is obviously a technical term not found in the dictionary. Consider this example:

> *I:* Since you were working at home, why didn't you continue the job on your own personal computer when the company's broke down?
> *R:* My PC is an Apple II G-S and uses WordPerfect converted for a ProDOS system which is not compatible with IBM WordPerfect. For example, the path names for Save and the menus are very different. Also, I can't use the large floppies on my 3.5 disk drive.

If the interviewer does not understand the technical terms used in talking about computer hardware and software, he or she will not understand the response. In this example, the interviewer would at least be aware that technical terms were being used and could ask questions about them.

Sometimes interviewers do not have the advantage of being aware that a word has a special meaning. They may be familiar with one meaning but not realize that the same word has several different meanings in other circumstances. For example, in the army "CO" means commanding officer, in a Mennonite community it means conscientious objector, in some local teenage gangs it means cop out, and in a telephone company it may mean chief operator.

Sometimes common words that are neither abbreviations nor acronyms have very special meanings in certain subcultures. For example, in the following excerpt an interviewer born in Chicago is interviewing a disaster victim in White County, Arkansas. The italicized words were frequently misunderstood by the interviewing team from Chicago.

I: Tell me what happened to you in the tornado.

R: When I saw this big black funnel comin' I wasn't *excited* at all. While I was trying to hold the door shut the *window light* went out. Then it got so dark I couldn't see across the room. I must have got a *lick* on the head because I took a big headache. As soon as I come to myself I was *proud* my sisters *worked off*. I *lit out* for Judsonia on foot because my car was all buggered up by the blow. I came across a *cookie drummer* from Bald Knob then I knew Bald Knob was hit, too. . . . I found my mother with a broken hand and I borrowed a truck from a neighbor to get her to the hospital, but the roads were all blocked with trees and telephone poles so I finally *carried* her out across the fields to Searcy. I *studied* all night long for the first four or five nights after the storm and didn't get much sleep.

To interpret the correct meaning, the listener had to make the following "translations":

- People who are *not excited* may still be frozen with fright, but they are not hysterically active and out of control.
- The *window light* is the glass pane in the window which was knocked out by the wind.
- The *lick* was a blow (on the head).
- *Proud* has nothing to do with pride; it simply means happy or glad.
- *Worked off* means that the sisters worked away from home, or originally, "off the farm."
- *Cookie drummer* is a traveling sales or delivery person who delivers cookies to stores in the area.
- *Carried* simply means took (in this case in the truck) not picked up and carried by hand.
- *Studied* has nothing to do with things academic; it means worried.

Now re-read the excerpt and it will have a more accurate meaning for you.

We do not have to travel to a different region of the country to find a universe of discourse that is unfamiliar to us. Just move from one college campus to another, or from the plumber's shop to the carpenter's shop. You will find both obviously technical words and common words with special meanings. Before an interviewer can comprehend, interpret, evaluate, or respond to a statement, he or she must be familiar with the universe of discourse of the respondent—including technical terms and special meanings for common words.

Emotional Obstacles

Even if there are no physical obstacles to hearing and no semantic obstacles to understanding, several emotional factors can, if present in the interview, act as obstacles to listening.

Lack of Interest in the Interview Topic.   Interviewers who are not genuinely interested in the topic communicate their boredom to the respondent. For example, an interviewer may display little active effort to interpret, evaluate, and verify the validity of responses. An interviewer's lack of empathic facial and vocal expression can show a lack of interest or complete boredom. Under such conditions the interviewer cannot perform the job well and the respondent is not motivated to answer candidly and fully.

The remedy is either to select interviewers to fit topics or to educate the interviewers on topics so that they appreciate the subjects' significance.

Lack of Interest in the Respondent.   Even though an interviewer may be interested in the topic of the interview, he or she may lose interest in a particular respondent. Perhaps the interviewer is prejudiced against a certain category of person such as a "yuppie," "hard-hat," "redneck," "ignoramus," "fundamentalist," "Klan member," "criminal," "egghead," "senior citizen," "bluestocking," or "AIDS victim."

A historian studying the contribution of construction workers to American urban architecture will have difficulty listening effectively if she has a strong prejudice against "hard-hats." A public health worker studying the epidemiology of AIDS will not be effective if he fears AIDS victims.

Prejudice against the respondent can usually be hidden to some extent by the interviewer, but its effect on listening may be seen in the interviewer's failure to probe for clarification or elaboration at crucial points in the conversation. Prejudice may be betrayed by the interviewer's condescending tone of voice. It may be shown by the interviewer's inability to empathize with the other's feelings and to demonstrate this empathy by facial and vocal expression. There may be a general loss of spontaneity in the conversation. The prejudiced interviewer may also fail to give any verbal expressions of appreciation of the respondent's efforts to supply relevant information.

These problems can be avoided by selecting interviewers who do not have a prejudice against a particular type of respondent. Interviewers also can be educated so that their prejudice is reduced and/or the challenge to achieve the objectives of the interview becomes dominant over the lack of interest in a particular type of respondent.

Biased Expectations.   One of the principal causes of failure to hear correctly what the respondent says involves the interviewer's expectations of what the respondent is going to say or should say. Interviewers have a strong tendency to interpret any ambiguous or unclear response by bending its meaning to fit what they expected. This tendency has been documented in many studies, beginning with pioneering efforts like that of Smith and Hyman.[5] When interviewers tend to hear what they expect to hear, they fail to probe adequately. Instead of probing to clarify meaning, the interviewer merely assumes that the respondent means what was expected.

An interviewer who has a strong attitude on a controversial issue may bias the recording of the responses even in cases where "verbatim notes" are taken. This was admirably demonstrated in a classic experiment by Fisher[6] which showed that interviewers tended to hear more frequently those responses that agreed with their own political views. This tendency occurs in many professional settings; here is one example.

The following exchange between a physician and his patient demonstrates the failure to listen due to strong preconceptions on the part of the doctor. A man had brought his wife to see the doctor two days earlier, and the doctor had diagnosed her condition as hepatitis. Now the man has come to see the doctor about his own condition. He was interviewed by the doctor as follows:

Doctor: What seems to be your trouble?

Patient: I have this sharp pain right here. [Indicating below the rib cage just right of center.] It was so strong in the middle of the night that I had to get up and pace the floor. It subsided after about an hour, but it still hurts and is very tender if I press it. Maybe it was related to the big dinner I ate.

Doctor: I know you are worried about your wife's hepatitis, but I doubt if you could have it. The kind she has is not very contagious. But we might as well give you a gamma globulin injection which will prevent you from catching it from her.

The doctor gave him the injection and said, "You will probably feel better now. If you aren't better in two days call me."

The wife had collapsed during the plane ride back from Mexico and could hardly walk into the doctor's office. The doctor had noted how concerned the husband had been over his wife's condition when they had come two days before. Now, the doctor seemed to assume that the husband's condition was psychosomatic—he imagined that he had caught hepatitis from his wife.

The fact that the information given by the husband contradicted this theory was not noted by the doctor. For example, the husband and the doctor knew that the wife had no pain with her condition and that she had completely lost her appetite. Yet the fact that the husband reported having sharp pains and having eaten a large dinner had no effect on the doctor's diagnosis. He seemed to assume that even if the gamma globulin was not needed to prevent hepatitis, it would have a placebo effect on the husband's assumed hypochondriac reaction. The doctor's failure to listen resulted in a a faulty diagnosis and failure to provide appropriate treatment.

Life is full of examples of people who hear what they expect to hear or want to hear and ignore information that does not fit into their preconceived scheme of things. The human mind tends to set up a matrix of expectations and to remember things that fit the scheme and ignore what does not. The interviewer's task is to examine his or her preconceptions related to an interview topic and to lay them aside, at least temporarily, until all the evidence is in. It takes practice to acknowledge that we have this tendency and then to hold it in abeyance.

Reactions to Emotionally Charged Words.   Another type of emotional reaction to a response is apparent in the effect of a particular emotionally charged word. Sometimes a respondent who feels at ease in the interview interjects obscenities that disconcert the unprepared interviewer. As a result, the interviewer may fail to hear the rest of the respondent's sentence. Racist, sexist, religious, or ethnic slurs can throw the unprepared interviewer off course. To become an effective listener, we should be shockproofed against emotionally charged words. If we are able to interview only people who never use obscenities, who are not bigoted, or whose prejudices agree with our own, we are highly restricted. Our task as interviewers is to discover the experiences, feelings, and values of the respondent, not to agree or disagree with them!

Desire for Self-Expression.   In ordinary sociable conversation, the participants want to have at least equal time and often they compete for the spotlight. Thus, one definition of a bore is "a person who is talking when he or she should be listening to me!" Another notable feature of much sociable conversation is that it is an exercise in self-expression. While one person is speaking, the other person, instead of listening, is thinking about what to say as soon as there is a pause. Good listening is so rare a skill that in some social circles anyone who is a good listener may be called an excellent conversationalist.

But interviewing is *not* ordinary sociable conversation. Interviewers must control their desires to give judgments and opinions or to show off knowledge. We have all seen interviews on television in which the interviewer was so busy showing off knowledge and suggesting answers that we wish he or she would be quiet and give the respondent a chance to talk. Instead of listening and probing crucial points the respondent has made, the undisciplined interviewer is trying to steer the respondent to a cue for the interviewer to speak some more. If we are to listen accurately and be alert to assess the relevance, validity, and completeness of a response, we cannot be concerned with finding opportunities to express our own views.

Performance Anxiety.   Another obstacle to effective listening is the interviewer's anxiety about his or her own performance. This is a problem particularly for neophyte interviewers or even for seasoned interviewers who are attacking a new topic of investigation. One of the most common causes of interviewer anxiety is the feeling that the interview may be getting out of control: "I'm sure what the respondent is saying is only partly relevant, but I don't know if I should interrupt to get back on track, and if I do, what exactly should I say or ask?" The interviewer is preoccupied with what should be done next and so fails to listen carefully. If the respondent has already caught the interviewer off guard (for example, with no question to ask), the embarrassment might build up a general fear in the interviewer.

There are several ways the interviewer can avoid this type of performance anxiety. First, there should be no time pressure put on the interview so that the pace can be relaxed. Second, as a last resort, the interviewer can always stall for time by saying something like, "That's very interesting! Let me take a second to see what we still need to cover (looking at the interview guide). Yes, I'd like you to tell me more about..." Third, to avoid having to use this last resort, the interviewer can take *probe notes*, which are sketchy reminders of what the respondent has said with indicators (such as underlining or arrows) to show what needs to be explored a little more deeply. Probe notes should always con sist of specific words or phrases used by the respondent so that the interviewer can say, "Tell me more about_____"—filling in the blank with the specific words or phrases used by the respondent. Fourth, in Chapter 9 on probing, we will present a variety of *neutral probes* which can be used to keep the respondent talking without biasing the content of the response.

Another source of performance anxiety is the interviewer's lack of familiarity with the topic and the precise objectives of the interview. The more clearly the interviewer has mapped out the major objectives, their subobjectives, and the possible routes for moving from one objective to another, the more flexible the interviewer can be. The interviewer can allow respondents to follow their own patterns of free association in answering without fear that the interview will get out of control.

Interviewers sometimes fear that important information will be forgotten if the respondent is talking faster than the interviewer can take notes. The need for taking notes depends a lot on the topic, how many interviews of this type the interviewer has done before, and the proportion of the response that is relevant to the objectives of the interview. As will be discussed later in Chapter 10 on recording information, the use of a tape recorder can often act as a safety net to prevent anxiety about losing relevant information.

Now that we have pointed out the three types of obstacles to good listening (physical, semantic, and emotional), let's consider the three basic *objectives* of listening. By keeping these objectives firmly in mind, we can surmount some of these common obstacles.

OBJECTIVES OF LISTENING

Interviews have different purposes and different specific items of information that are relevant to those purposes. But the general objectives of listening are the same for all interviews. First is to *understand* the meaning of what is said. Second is to *evaluate* the information received in terms of the objectives of the interview. Third is to *judge* the emotional state of the respondent to detect any need for encouragement and support. Let's take a closer look at each objective.

Understanding the Meaning

In order to understand the meaning of what the respondent is saying, we must focus on hearing the words in their larger *context*. This context of meaning includes the verbal context of what has been said before, the audible nonverbal accompaniment of the verbal messages, and the more general social context of the interview situation. (Visual cues as an additional context will be described in the next chapter on observing the respondent.) In listening for meaning interviewers must not prejudge what respondents will say and must not project their own expectations or assumptions into the interpretation process. The process of understanding the respondent's meaning undistorted by one's own feelings, assumptions, and expectations is the first basic objective of listening. Information must be understood before it can be evaluated.

Evaluating the Information

The second objective of listening in any interview is to evaluate the information in terms of the objectives of the interview. The three aspects of evaluation can be expressed by three questions the interviewer must keep in mind while listening to the response:

1. Is this information *relevant* to the specific objectives of the question?
2. Is this information *valid* (true or accurate)?
3. Is this information *complete*?

Let's look at relevance first.

We have already seen the importance of formulating questions that are relevant to the objectives of the interview. The problem of evaluating the relevance of *answers* to a question is similar. Before judging the relevance of an answer, we must know precisely what the question means and how the resulting information is to be used. In Chapter 8 on evaluating responses you will learn more details about this evaluation skill. Here, be aware only that evaluating the relevance of a response takes constant, concentrated, analytic listening.

It is not uncommon for respondents to speak voluminously on what superficially appears to be an answer to the question while skillfully evading the crux of the matter. This is a skill used by successful politicians and anyone else who has need to erect verbal defenses. If respondents would simply say "no comment" when they do not wish to answer a question instead of using an evasive smoke screen of irrelevancies, life would be much simpler for interviewers.

Irrelevance, of course, is not always intentional evasion. It can also be due to the respondent's lack of clear understanding of the question, desire to please the interviewer by saying something that sounds interesting, or simply desire to talk about a favorite subject.

A second aspect of evaluation is judging the validity of the response, which is quite different from relevance. If the answer is relevant, it logically falls within the area outlined by the question. However, information can fall within the area and still be useless because it is untrue. To be valid, the response must be true and accurate. The interviewer cannot accept fiction whether it is fabricated out of self-defense, politeness, or poor memory. Luckily, people who are interviewed do most of their evading by giving irrelevant facts rather than by fabricating, which they realize is difficult and dangerous.

The third aspect of evaluation is judging the completeness of a response. An answer can be relevant to the question, free of any defects in validity, and still not be complete. An interviewer may be so pleased by a clearly relevant and frank response that he or she forgets to check the answer for completeness. In situations where there will be no second opportunity to talk to the respondents, incompleteness can be a serious problem. It can be avoided only by careful listening and immediate probing for completeness. To recognize whether the response is complete, the interviewer must not only listen carefully for the meaning, but also must know precisely the objectives of the particular question in the context of the overall purpose of the interview.

Evaluative listening is necessary before we can learn to probe a response effectively. Responses are rarely totally relevant or irrelevant, valid or invalid, complete or incomplete. They often fall somewhere between the extremes, and only an alert interviewer will know what probes are needed to improve or test their relevance, validity, and completeness.

Judging the Emotional State of the Respondent

The third general objective of listening is to judge the emotional state of the respondent. The interviewer must listen for clues while asking himself or herself the following questions:

- Am I going too fast for the respondent?
- Is it too soon to answer that question?
- Does the respondent need encouragement, praise, or support?
- Does the respondent feel insecure in long silent periods?

To do this type of evaluation, the interviewer must listen carefully to both the verbal and the nonverbal messages.

At this point, we have discussed the importance of listening, outlined some of the main obstacles to listening, and spelled out the three basic objectives of listening in any interview. With this background, we are ready to analyze the most practical question of *how* to listen.

HOW TO LISTEN

Much of this section will sound familiar because it can be deduced from what has been said earlier. Here we will distill and convert previous explanations into seven action statements: know your objectives, know your respondent, pay attention from the beginning, control your urge for self-expression, listen actively, listen empathetically, and be patient.

Know Your Objectives

Although it may seem obvious that the interviewer must know the objectives of the interview to listen effectively, often an interviewer has only a vague and general notion of the objectives. To be intimately acquainted with the objectives, the interviewer must understand how each question contributes to the overall objectives of the interview. Furthermore, the interviewer must have a clear picture of the interrelationships among the questions. For example, it is critical for the interviewer to understand how certain questions act as pivots, so he or she can determine which line of questioning is appropriate for a particular respondent.

To understand the objectives of a specific question, the interviewer must realize what difference one answer or another makes to the overall objectives of the interview. The interviewer must know what crucial distinctions have to be made among answers so he or she is prepared to probe a response for a clarification that improves relevance, validity, or completeness.

Know Your Respondent

Of course as interviewers we may not be able to know every respondent personally. To listen effectively, however, we need to be familiar enough with respondents' accent, vocabulary, life-style, and social background to hear what they say, understand the meaning, and not feel that they are so strange or exotic that we cannot readily empathize.

How complete our knowledge of respondents must be depends to a great extent on the topic or purpose of the interview. For example, minimal knowledge of the respondent is needed in a public opinion poll to discover which presidential candidate the respondent intends to vote for. This requires only that we understand the respondent's language.

In other cases the interviewer needs no special knowledge of the respondent's unique personal history, but must be familiar with the characteristics of a category of people that includes the respondent. The category might be one of social class, ethnicity, geographical region, age, sex, vocation, age, marital status, health, vocation and so on. To be a good listener the interviewer must be aware of any special vocabulary needed, any taboos or values that would affect the conversation, and any physical characteristics that might affect speech or hearing; the interviewer must also be free of prejudice against the particular category of people.

In some cases it is very important for the interviewer to have an intimate knowledge of the unique life history of the particular respondent. A journalist writing the life story of a public figure, a sociologist studying a criminal's career, or a historian interviewing an army general to reconstruct a battle need intimate knowledge of the respondent's unique background both to ask meaningful questions and to listen intelligently and empathetically.

Pay Attention from the Beginning

If the physical setting is prepared for the interviewer to see and hear the respondent clearly and if the interview situation has been verbally defined for the respondent, the interviewer should then be ready to pay attention to the first response. Often, however, interviewers rush into the interview and ask the first question before they are ready to listen. After asking the first question, they may spend a few moments looking for a pencil, turning on the tape recorder, looking for the case file folder, thinking about the last person interviewed, or just trying to refocus their attention on this particular respondent. This confusing atmosphere gives the interview a bad start for two reasons: relevant information in the first response might be lost and the inattentiveness can dampen the respondent's motivation.

It pays to prepare calmly, settle down, and focus attention on the respondent *before* launching the interview. This initial attentiveness must be sustained throughout the interview.

Control Your Urge for Self-Expression

As a good listener, the interviewer is not engaged in the free give-and-take of a sociable conversation. Statements, as well as questions, by the interviewer must be carefully controlled and selected. Some interviewers are plagued by the urge to give their own views. Others mistakenly believe that sharing their experiences indiscriminately will build rapport; in reality, all that is needed is their undivided attention and empathic facial and vocal expressions.

The urge for self-expression often leads an interviewer to interrupt the respondent. We have already seen that we can interrupt psychologically without cutting in at mid-sentence. All we do is fail to allow the few seconds of silence we normally allow when determining whether the respondent intends to continue without being prompted. This does not mean that interviewers should *never* interrupt, but they should not interrupt habitually merely to fulfill their urge for self-expression. If the respondent has been talking about something that is completely irrelevant to the purposes of the interview, it is appropriate to interrupt, but do it gently and diplomatically. For example, "That is a very interesting story but what I need to know is. . ."

The interviewer must resist the urge to change the subject unless the respondent is off the topic or has already given a valid and complete answer to the question. A problem often occurs because something the respondent has said reminds the interviewer of another question, so the interviewer asks the new question without being sure the answer to the previous one is complete. The interviewer who interrupts with new questions often realizes later that pieces of the previous answer are missing and has to go back to patch up the holes. The respondent is thus jerked forward and backward, and free association, recall, and spontaneity are jeopardized. An interviewer's interruptions and premature changes of topic can reduce a respondent to taciturn answers such as "yes," "no," "I don't know," and "That's right."

Listen Actively

To listen actively, the interviewer must listen to both the verbal and the nonverbal (paralinguistic) channels of communication. The active listener is mentally summarizing what is being said in relation to the objectives of the interview and is noting what needs to be probed further to make it more relevant, valid, or complete. The active listener is less likely to be caught without a good probe, statement, or question when the respondent stops talking.

Listen Empathetically

Listening empathetically requires the interviewer to be both a sensitive *receiver* of feeling signals and a *sender* of responses that show appreciation and sympathy. As a receiver, the interviewer listens for verbal cues that either directly express or indirectly imply feelings and for nonverbal cues that do the same. As a sender, the interviewer communicates that the respondent's feelings have been heard and appreciated. This is done by the interviewer's posture, eye contact, facial expression, and by noninterrupting vocalizations such as "hmm," "uh-huh," "really," "wow," "scary," and so forth.

Two-way communication is important because the interviewer's listening in itself does not encourage the respondent to give more relevant and candid information. In addition, the interviewer must *show* that he or she is listening sympathetically. People have little motivation to pour their hearts out to a granite-faced interviewer.

Although empathic responses by the interviewer are desirable, do not overuse them. The term *overuse* does not refer to the frequency of use but to the strength and vividness of the response, which should be somewhat subdued or understated. This is important! If the interviewer *seems* to feel the respondent's experiences more vividly than does the respondent, the respondent will probably think the interviewer is acting and is insincere. Respondents are usually aware of the most subtle expressions of empathy that are normal for a sympathetic listener.

Be Patient

To be able to pay attention, to listen actively, and to listen empathetically for the duration of the interview, interviewers must avoid impatience with themselves as well as with respondents. The interviewer's patience creates a thoughtful, permissive, and relaxed atmosphere.

In being patient with oneself it is important to realize that you do not have to be speedy and efficient in extracting relevant information. An interviewer will make errors, but they can usually be corrected. If a response indicates a question has been misworded, simply reword it and try again. Do not expect every probe to hit the mark; be ready to try another probe to obtain the same clarification or elaboration.

Being patient means avoiding overcontrol of the respondent and refusing to panic if the interview seems to be getting out of control. It also means avoiding value judgments about the respondent's reported behavior, beliefs, values, or ignorance. A nonjudgmental attitude toward the respondent and toward the information received should be supplemented with positive responses in appreciation of the respondent's efforts to report candidly and completely. Patience is the basic ingredient needed to sustain active, empathic listening.

SUMMARY

Effective listening is a basic communication skill that is vital to success in many fields. Yet unlike other communication skills such as reading, writing, and speaking, listening is rarely taught at any level of academia.

The first step in learning to listen is to appreciate the great difference between the passive, physiological process of hearing and the active, mental process of listening. The second step is to recognize and eliminate as many of the obstacles to listening as possible.

The obstacles to listening can be put into three major categories: physical obstacles to hearing, semantic obstacles to understanding, and emotional obstacles to understanding, concentrating, and empathizing. The emotional obstacles include a lack of interest in the interview topic, a lack of interest in the type of respondent, biased expectations, reactions to emotionally charged words, desire for self-expression, and performance anxiety.

Once these obstacles to listening are removed, the interviewer can concentrate on the objectives of listening. Regardless of the specific topic of the interview, there are three major objectives toward which the interviewer should strive. The first is to understand the meaning of what is being said. Second is to evaluate the response in terms of the objectives of the interview. This objective includes judging whether a response is relevant, valid, and complete for the purposes of the interview. The third objective of listening is to judge the emotional state of the respondent by listening for clues to fatigue, boredom, anxiety, or needs for encouragement and support.

The above conceptions of the nature of listening, the obstacles to listening, and the objectives of listening all have a bearing on the following list of action statements on *how* to listen.

Seven action statements summarize how to listen:

1. Know your objectives: Understand the objectives of the interview precisely so you can determine whether a particular response is relevant or irrelevant or complete or incomplete.
2. Know your respondent: Be familiar with the respondent's accent, vocabulary, and social context so you are able to understand what he or she means and to show interest and appreciation.
3. Pay attention from the beginning: Have all preparations made in advance and focus your attention on the respondent from the beginning of the interview.
4. Control your urge for self-expression: Do not deviate often from these three golden rules: stop talking, don't interrupt, and don't change the subject.

5. Listen actively: Strive to understand the meaning of what is being said; evaluate the information in terms of its relevance, validity, and completeness; and evaluate the respondent's motivation.
6. Listen empathetically: Be a sensitive receiver of feeling cues and a responsive sender of cues that indicate you have heard and sympathize.
7. Be patient: Expect to make errors and be prepared to correct them. Expect misunderstandings and irrelevancies from the respondent and be prepared to make repeated efforts, if necessary, to correct them. Avoid overcontrolling and judging the respondent.

NOTES

1. Ralph G. Nichols, "Do We Know How to Listen?" *The Speech Teacher 10* (1961): 118–24.
2. D. W. Johnson, *Reaching Out: Interpersonal Effectiveness and Self Actualization*, 2nd ed. (Englewood Cliffs, N.J.: Prentice-Hall, 1981).
3. R. E. Maurer and J. H. Tindall, "Effect of Postural Congruence on the Client's Perception of Counselor Empathy," *Journal of Counseling Psychology* 30 (1983).
4. A. E. Ivey and L. Simek-Downing, *Counseling and Psychotherapy: Skills, Theory and Practice* (Englewood Cliffs, N.J.: Prentice-Hall, 1980).
5. H. L. Smith and Herbert Hyman, "The Biasing Effects of Interviewer Expectations on Survey Results," *Public Opinion Quarterly* 14 (Fall 1950): 491–506.
6. Herbert Fisher, "Interviewer Bias in the Recording Operation," *International Journal of Opinion and Attitude Research* 4 (Spring 1950): 393.

Exercise 6-A
LISTENING FOR MEANING

OBJECTIVES

Before you can evaluate a response, you must be able to hear accurately the meaning of that response. You must concentrate on what the respondent is saying rather than on your next question. This exercise is designed to give you practice in listening for meaning.

GENERAL PROCEDURE

Work in groups of three—interviewer, respondent, and facilitator—and use a tape recorder. The interviewer asks a question, the respondent gives an answer, and the facilitator interrupts after 10 seconds. The interviewer then repeats (also on tape) his or her version of what the respondent just said. Next the facilitator leads a discussion of the accuracy of the interviewer's repetition. Repeat the process three times with people keeping the same roles and the same interview topic. Then rotate roles and repeat the process three more times with the second person acting as interviewer. Each person has three opportunities as interviewer to listen and repeat what the respondent says, three opportunities as respondent to correct any errors in the interviewer's repetition, and three opportunities as facilitator to lead the discussion and note the types of discrepancies that occur.

SPECIFIC STEPS

1. Teams of three are formed and each team decides who will act as facilitator, interviewer, and respondent in the first set of three role-plays.
2. Respondent selects a topic he or she would like to talk about from the following list below or any other topic.
   a. Improvements needed in the quality of campus life
   b. Things people do that bother you most
   c. Your favorite type of movie
   d. Important qualities in a friend
   e. Good or bad points about the American government

    f. Attitudes toward cocaine use

3. Interviewer formulates an opening question on the topic selected by the respondent, turns on the tape recorder, asks the question, and listens.
4. Respondent begins to answer the question freely and spontaneously.
5. Facilitator times the response by counting subvocally "one thousand, two thousand," and so on up to ten thousand and raises hand to stop the respondent.
6. Respondent sees the hand signal, finishes the sentence, stops, and listens carefully to the interviewer's repetition of the response.
7. Interviewer repeats the *meaning* of what the respondent just said using the same words and inflections as much as possible, then turns off the recorder.
8. Facilitator directs a discussion in three steps:
    a. Asks the respondent if the interviewer's repetition was accurate and if not, in what way was it inaccurate: different words? different meaning? different inflection of voice?
    b. Asks the interviewer if he or she agrees with the respondent's points. If not, where is the disagreement?
    c. Replays the response and the interviewer's repetition to verify points of agreement or disagreement.

REPETITIONS

Without changing roles in the triad, repeat steps 3 through 8 two more times modifying step 3 to formulate a *continuing* question rather than the opening question on the *same* topic. This continuing question or probe should be worded based on what the respondent has already said on the topic.

ROTATION OF ROLES

After the three repetitions with triad members in their initially assigned roles, all three members rotate to new roles and do three repetitions in those roles. Then they rotate again so that each person has had three repetitions in each of the three roles. When the roles are rotated, the new respondent may pick a new topic or a previously used one, whichever is more comfortable. The following chart illustrates the pattern of rotation that will give everyone a different role with each rotation:

	ROTATION		
Person	1	2	3
A	Interviewer	Facilitator	Respondent
B	Respondent	Interviewer	Facilitator
C	Facilitator	Respondent	Interviewer

So if you are first assigned to the role of facilitator, you follow the rotation pattern of person C.

IMPORTANT HINTS

1. Triads should be far enough apart not to distract one another.
2. The facilitator should sit further from the interviewer and respondent than they are from each other and should be in a position that the stop signal can be seen easily by the respondent.
3. The microphone should be situated so that both the interviewer and respondent can be heard clearly. Test it before you begin. An external microphone that can be passed back and forth is preferable.
4. The interviewer should pick an opening question (or continuing question) in an open-ended form that does not provide multiple-choice answers or suggest a "yes" or "no" answer. The question should give the respondent a chance to speak spontaneously.
5. The respondent should pick a topic of interest, talk candidly and spontaneously, and finish the response as soon as possible after the 10 second signal from the facilitator.

Exercise 6-B
LISTENING FOR NONVERBAL CUES

OBJECTIVES

Your active participation in this exercise will sensitize you to audible nonverbal cues and will demonstrate that (1) emotions are communicated nonverbally; (2) auditory cues, without visual cues, are enough to communicate emotion; (3) the same words have different meaning depending on how they are said; and (4) we are often not conscious of the specific cues that communicate an emotion, yet are correct in our judgment of the emotion.

GENERAL PROCEDURE

Your instructor will call on some members of the group to act as *demonstrators* of emotional communication while the remainder of the group will act as *listeners* who will classify the emotion expressed and try to detect and describe specific cues. After several demonstrations there will be a discussion based on a summary of the results of the whole group's listening.

ROLE OF DEMONSTRATOR

You may be among those selected by your instructor to demonstrate the nonverbal expression of emotions. You will have several ways of demonstrating feeling:

1. You may be asked to recite the alphabet in a way that demonstrates a particular one of four basic emotions (anger, fear, happiness, or sadness).
2. You may be asked to say a short sentence three times to demonstrate one basic emotion.
3. You may be asked to do four short demonstrations. The instructor will give you a card telling which emotion to demonstrate in each and when to use the alphabet or the sentence as the vehicle for the emotion.
4. You may be asked to use the alphabet in two of four demonstrations and a sentence in the other two. The particular sentence you are to use will be given by the instructor. Use the same sentence both times.

When demonstrating an emotion, do *not* think about *how* you are going to show a particular feeling. Instead, concentrate on producing the feeling in yourself. As you continue reciting the alphabet or repeating the sentence, your mood will become stronger and the feeling will show more clearly. During your recitation, *stand with your back to the audience* so that they will not see your facial expression and fold your arms in front of you so that they cannot see your hands!

ROLE OF LISTENER

After each demonstration of one emotion (which will last about ten seconds), note the emotion you think is being demonstrated, the two main nonverbal cues that expressed the emotion, and two words describing the cues. Your instructor will give you the *audible nonverbal cues recording form*.

SUMMARIZING

After 10 to 20 demonstrations, your instructor will ask your help in summarizing the results of the whole group's listening to answer these questions:

1. How much agreement is there on which emotion is being expressed?
2. How much agreement is there on which cues were predominant?
3. How much agreement is there on the descriptive words used?

DISCUSSION

When the summary is finished, the instructor will lead a discussion related to the basic objectives of this exercise.

More believed and trusted
than sonorous word,
Is the tell-tale gesture
seen but not heard.

7

Observing the Respondent's Nonverbal Behavior

I N THE PREVIOUS CHAPTER we dealt with how the interviewer *listens* for the respondent's *audible* nonverbal (paralinguistic) cues. In this chapter we will focus exclusively on how the interviewer *observes visible* nonverbal cues.

WHY OBSERVE THE RESPONDENT?

Just as it is true that audible nonverbal cues such as tone of voice, pacing, and volume affect the meaning of spoken words, it is also true that visible nonverbal cues such as eye movement, facial expression, and posture affect the meaning of the verbal message by reinforcing, supplementing, or contradicting. This additional visual channel of communication helps the interviewer achieve the three major objectives of any interview: (1) to *understand* the meaning of the message, (2) to *evaluate* the relevance and validity of the information received, and (3) to evaluate the *motivational* state of the respondent.

Visual cues are important for understanding the meaning of a response. For example, Rogers[1] has shown that if a listener is allowed to hear the tone of voice of the speaker but not to see head and hand gestures, there is a 20 to 30 percent loss in comprehension.

Visual cues are also important in evaluating the general emotional state (including the motivational state) of the respondent. People communicate their current feelings by unconscious physiological reactions. This close connection between emotional states and physiological events is shown in common expressions such as lost your head, chin up, hair-raising, or butterflies in my stomach. Emotional states and their physical expression are major themes in Schutz's[2] book about human awareness.

People who are more sensitive to nonverbal cues make better interviewers. Studies, for example one by Rosenthal et al.,[3] show that individuals vary considerably in this sensitivity and that, in general, young people are less sensitive to nonverbal cues than are older people. So the evidence suggests that the ability to read nonverbal cues comes with life experience and can be learned.

How easy it is to note and interpret a particular visual cue depends on whether the cue is *subtle* like the dilation of the pupil in the eye or *gross* and obvious like posture. Some cultures, such as those in the Middle East, sensitize people more to pupil dilation than do others. Research in the United States has shown that a man's pupils double in size when he is shown a picture of a nude woman and that good card-players and magicians know that a person's pupils widen involuntarily when he or she is dealt a good card.[4]

Another factor affecting the noticeability of a visual cue is the extent to which the body language is *intentional* versus *involuntary*. Intentional cues, such as shaking the fist, are usually more noticeable and more easily interpreted. The involuntary ones, such as the dilation of the pupil or increased breathing rate, are not as noticeable, but under certain circumstances they are more useful and dependable. Because they are unconscious and involuntary, the respondent cannot use them to deceive the interviewer.

In general, intentional gestures have two basic functions: emphasis and description. We can emphasize anger by pounding the table or shaking the fist, thus reinforcing the meaning, particularly the emotional content, of the message. Observe a descriptive gesture by asking someone to define the word *spiral*. The urge to use a descriptive gesture instead of a verbal definition is often overpowering. The intentional gesture helps convey the *meaning* of the verbal message.

In addition to helping us interpret the *meaning* of the message, particularly the emotional content, the unintentional (unconscious) gesture may also give clues to the *validity* of the response. If there is incongruity between the verbal message and the unconscious gestures accompanying that message, the discrepancy may be a clue to a respondent's inner conflict or attempt to deceive the interviewer with the verbal message.

VISUAL CUES AND INTERVIEW OBJECTIVES

Observing the respondent's visual cues has the same objectives as listening to the audible nonverbal cues. Both the visible and audible nonverbal cues are helpful in (1) interpreting the meaning of the response, (2) evaluating the validity of the response, and (3) judging the emotional state of the respondent.

Interpreting the meaning of a particular response has two dimensions. First, visual cues can help interpret the *cognitive* (denotative) meaning of the response. For example, a respondent may say "yes" while shaking his or her head to mean no. To say the least, this response cannot be interpreted as a clear "yes" and it definitely needs to be probed; it might be discovered to really mean "no."

Second, visual cues can help interpret the *affective* meaning (feeling) or strength of the conviction in the response. For example, the interviewer might ask, "How do you feel about the increase in the number of rapes on campus?" The male respondent might say, "It's a bad thing" while shrugging his shoulders. This response would certainly bear further probing to see just how bad he feels it is. Perhaps the conflicting verbal and visual nonverbal cues indicate that the respondent feels that rape is not good but far too much is made of it, or that he doubts whether there is any such thing as rape. In any case, the visual nonverbal cues could help substantially if the objective of the interview is to determine how strongly the respondent feels against rape and whether he would be interested in joining a group to protect the women on campus.

The second objective in observing nonverbal behavior is to evaluate the validity of the response. In this context validity refers to the truth and accuracy of the response. As shown earlier, respondents may not give valid information because they are unable or because they are unwilling to give the whole truth. The willing-but-unable respondent may be difficult to detect because he or she may speak volubly without realizing that the information is not correct, and the respondent's obvious desire to please the interviewer often tends to make the interviewer a less critical observer.

Often the inability to answer is due to the lack of recall of concrete details from past experience. This can occur particularly if there is time pressure in the interview. Possible invalidity of a glib response may be indicated, for example, by the absence of visual cues such as a facial expression of thoughtful concentration.

In cases where the respondent is able but unwilling to give an accurate response, even though there is no difficulty in remembering, body language may be more clearly in conflict with the verbal message. Many people can tell "white lies" without any great bodily reaction, but the witness on trial, or the child threatened with a spanking, may have great difficulty in repressing the body language that contradicts the verbal message or the silence. This is the principle, of course, which lies behind the polygraph or lie detector.

A third objective in observing nonverbal behavior is to determine the respondent's emotional state, which includes the general *energy level* of the respondent, the respondent's *mood*, the respondent's *attitude* toward the topic or toward the interviewer, and the respondent's *turn-taking* desires.

A social worker, for example, might need to know if a client will have enough energy to participate in an adult education program. An employer might need to know whether an employee's mood is consonant with a proposal to cooperate with certain other employees. A counselor may need to determine whether a client has a sufficiently trusting attitude to permit guiding the discussion into critical areas.

Many of the clues to negative attitudes are visual. Lack of frequent eye contact, tightly pursed lips, shaking the head unconsciously, shrugging the shoulders, folding the arms across the chest, and so forth, can all be manifestations of such negative attitudes as tension, anxiety, hostility, or indifference.

Visual cues are also useful in determining the respondent's turn-taking desires. To avoid being domineering or unresponsive in the interview, thereby reducing the respondent's spontaneity, the interviewer must be sensitive to the turn-taking signals emitted by the respondent. According to Duncan[5] there are four types of turn-taking signals: those indicating the respondent's desire to let the interviewer continue speaking, those indicating the respondent's desire to continue speaking, those requesting to speak, and those denying the other person's request to speak. All of these desires are manifested by the respondent's visual as well as audible nonverbal cues. The specific nature of the visual cues will be described later in this chapter.

As shown by Exline,[6] when we try to assess another person's emotional state, we generally pay more attention to the person's head and facial cues than to the other body cues. People who want to deceive the listener are thus more careful to control their facial expressions; leakage occurs in the movements of their hands and feet and in posture. For this reason the interviewer needs to be aware of the respondent's whole body rather than the face only.

Incongruence between the expressions of one part of the body and another (or between body language and the verbal message) is referred to as *leakage*—the unintentional communication of nonverbal messages. Passons[7] indicates that because of leakage, the respondent's nonverbal behavior is often a more valid indicator of the respondent's position than is the verbal content of the message.

A respondent may manifest leakage in a variety of visual cues: pupil dilation, smiles, a jutting jaw, speeded breathing, avoiding eye contact, leaning away from the interviewer, twisting and intertwining hands, tapping feet, crossing and uncrossing legs, rocking back and forth, or squirming in the chair. The important point about the concept of leakage is that it does not refer to any particular nonverbal behavior but to the incongruence between one nonverbal behavior and another, or between nonverbal and verbal behavior. So the same bodily cues which in one situation reinforce the verbal message may in another situation invalidate the verbal message by being incongruent.

The interviewer should observe sensitively for such leakage; and when it occurs, the interviewer must probe more deeply to test for verbal contradictions or changes in the story.

Now that we have analyzed the major purposes of observing the respondent's nonverbal behavior, we can focus on the specific visual cues the interviewer needs to notice.

SPECIFIC NONVERBAL CUES TO OBSERVE

In listing specific visual cues we will also discuss interpretations of the meaning. Be warned, however, that these interpretations are not cast in iron; they should be viewed as flexible. A reliable interpretation of any gesture is difficult to make out of context, and at least three different kinds of context influence the meaning of a gesture: the cultural context, the situational context, and the personal context.

Cultures differ in their use of nonverbal expressions. They also differ in the extent to which emotional expression is encouraged or suppressed. For example, the probability that a heterosexual couple conversing over a meal in a restaurant will touch each other depends on the culture in which we are observing. Jourard[8] found that the number of times per hour a couple would touch each other ranged from 180 in San Juan, Puerto Rico to zero in London, England. Cultures also differ about which emotion is supposed to predominate in specific situations. For example, the emotion *expressed* at a funeral may vary from loud and continuous wailing in one culture to serene smiles in another. Of course, the emotion expressed is not necessarily the emotion *felt*. Cultures also differ in the emotional meaning of a specific gesture.

You do not have to go abroad to encounter basic cultural differences in nonverbal communication patterns. Interviewing in many professional settings in the United States involves dealing with members of different cultures. There are rural-urban differences, social class differences, and ethnic differences as well as subcultures based on age and sex.

Within any one culture the meaning of a specific gesture depends on the *situational* context. The degree to which nonverbal expression is used, which expressions are considered appropriate, and even the meaning of specific gestures vary from one situation to another. For example, the cordial handshake and smile means one thing when a politician is greeting a crowd on the street and another when friends meet at a party.

In addition to being influenced by cultural and situational factors, the meaning of gestures is affected by *personal* factors. It is often dangerous to conclude that the respondent's body language has a particular meaning in response to something the interviewer has said. First, the interviewer must know how the individual responds nonverbally to ordinary conversation. For example, some people are always reticent in speech and always have a nervous or apprehensive look on their face no matter what the topic of conversation. Others may be wiggly in their body language most of the time. Before we decide what the person's posture, facial expression, or hand behavior means in response to a question, we must know something about the individual's normal range of response. Then when we notice deviations from a personal norm, we can attach some significance to them.

Despite these caveats about interpreting the meaning of specific body movements, interviewers will find it useful to become sensitized to specific movements of various parts of the body that usually carry meaning in any conversation. In the following discussion we will intentionally ignore emblem-type gestures (for example, winking or thumbing a ride), which are conscious, voluntary, and symbolic; we will concentrate instead on more spontaneous, involuntary, or unconscious gestures which may give clues to things not said.

Eye Behavior

One of the classical expressions of the importance of the eye in human interaction was made by Simmel[9] who said:

> By the same act in which the observer seeks to know the observed, he surrenders himself to be understood...the eye cannot take unless at the same time it gives.

The eyes, poetically, have been called the "windows of the soul" for good reason. We look at a person's eyes for clues to the true meaning of what is being said. A number of different expressions of the eyes have been identified as interacting with the verbal message to convey the total meaning of the message.

Eye Contact.   When the respondent makes direct eye-to-eye contact in response to a question or statement by the interviewer, he or she is usually indicating a willingness to communicate, attentiveness, and a desire to understand what the interviewer is saying. Although studies have shown that in normal conversation there is a tendency for the listener to watch the speaker more closely than vice versa, the respondent—even when talking—will normally make intermittent eye contact. Several variables have been found to affect the amount of eye contact sought in a conversation between two people. In the counseling setting, for example, it was demonstrated[10] that respondents tend to seek *less* eye contact under these circumstances:

1. The client and counselor are physically close.
2. The client is talking about difficult, intimate topics.
3. The client or interviewer is not interested in the other's reactions.
4. The client is talking rather than listening.
5. The client is male.
6. The client is embarrassed, ashamed, or trying to hide something.
7. The client is from a culture that discourages direct eye contact.

With experience in interviewing in a given setting, an interviewer becomes more capable of allowing for some of these variables when interpreting the meaning of the respondent's eye behavior. It is the *variation* in eye behavior within the context of a particular interview that furnishes the most valid clues to the meaning of the message.

Although a certain amount of intermittent eye contact is desirable in the interview situation, too much can cause problems. If short, intermittent gazes are replaced by longer ones, the target person is likely to interpret this action as an indication that the task (the interview) is less important than the personal relationship between the two.[11] This is particularly true if the interviewer and respondent are of similar age and opposite sex.

A reduced degree of eye contact may indicate, on the one hand, avoidance of frank conversational interchange due to embarrassment, shame, or the desire to hide something. On the other hand, it may indicate that the respondent is caught up in reminiscent thoughts, images, and feelings related to the topic of the interview. Such preoccupation might be accompanied by squinting or frowning while looking down, thus giving an even stronger impression that the respondent is puzzling over the question or the response.

If the interviewer asks a question about events of the past, the respondent might pause, look down at the floor or up at the ceiling, and then look back at the interviewer before answering the question. This behavior usually indicates that the respondent is thinking through the meaning of the question, trying to recall events of the past, or trying to put thoughts into words; it should not be interpreted as evasive.

If the interviewer brings up topics that might be threatening, the respondent might freeze his or her gaze on some object or just stare into space in a rigid way indicating fear, anxiety, or preoccupation. In this situation the respondent will often fail to share his or her thoughts.

Usually, if the respondent's eyes are darting quickly from one object to another or are blinking rapidly, or if the respondent's forehead is twitching, excitement or anxiety is the cause (assuming nothing physical is irritating the eyes).

Tears. Tears, which may be profuse or just moisten the eyes, can indicate a wide range of feelings: fear, pain, grief, sadness, self-pity, frustration, anger, tenderness, or joy. In any case tears tend to indicate the *strength* of the feeling; the quality of the feeling must be gained from the verbal context of the tears. In some interview settings tears are so common that the interviewer keeps a supply of tissues on hand. Males tend to repress displays of tears due to feelings of fear, pain, and sadness and are more likely to be moved to tears by feelings of tenderness and joy. This difference in the sexes' expression through tears varies considerably from one culture to another and, perhaps, from one generation to another. The interviewer must be careful not to assign a fixed meaning to tears and be sensitive to the verbal and situational context in which they appear.

Pupil Dilation. The dilation of the pupil in the human eye is a gauge of alarm, excitement, interest, and even satisfaction. There is no evidence that a lack of interest, boredom, or tranquility will cause contraction of the pupils. The eyes' pupils seem to attain a certain size as they adapt to the amount of light available and then expand only momentarily in response to psychological stimulation. Americans are not as accustomed to paying close attention to a person's pupils as are people in the Middle East, but interviewers can learn to observe this telltale, involuntary signal in the respondent.

Facial Expressions and Head Movements

The face is capable of expressing more than one emotion at a time. In some circumstances different parts of the face are expressing conflicting emotions. This is particularly true when the person feels one emotion and social norms expect another. In cultures where a funeral is supposed to be a happy occasion, a relative of the deceased might have a smiling mouth and sad eyes. In another culture where relatives of the deceased are supposed to mourn, a bitter enemy of the deceased might show a sad, drooping mouth contradicted by a merry twinkle in the eyes.

The Mouth.   The mouth of the respondent who is speaking is much more restricted than are that person's eyes. The act of speech demands certain movements and positions of the mouth to articulate the syllables, so most of the expressions of the mouth can be seen most clearly during pauses and while the interviewer is talking. It takes more discipline and experience to watch the respondent carefully while we are speaking than when the respondent is speaking and we are listening. The skill in observing while talking can be very advantageous.

The most frequent expression of the mouth is a smile, but there are different degrees of smiles, different degrees of spontaneity in smiles, and different degrees of congruity with the expression of other parts of the face, particularly the eyes.

In addition to smiling the mouth may show stress, determination, anger, or hostility by pressing the lips together. Which of these emotions are being expressed depends on the verbal and situational context. In cases of extreme anxiety or stress, the lower lip may quiver or be bitten. Another expression is the open mouth which, if it is not a suppressed yawn or a symptom of fatigue, usually indicates surprise or shock.

Other Facial Expressions.   Slackness and unresponsiveness in the face may indicate depression, sadness, or stress. The corners of the mouth tend to droop along with the whole face. The wrinkled forehead with horizontal lines, if momentary, may indicate special interest, attentiveness, questioning, or doubt depending on the context. If prolonged, the same lines might indicate general tension, stress, and anxiety. Flushing of the face may indicate embarrassment, discomfort, or anger.

Head Movements.   In American culture nodding the head up and down may indicate that the respondent is listening, agreeing, or emphasizing and stressing some point. Shaking the head from left to right almost always indicates disagreement or disapproval. Such movements become most useful to the interviewer who is sensitive to slight unconscious head movements either during the time the interviewer is speaking or during silences. They give clues to the respondent's attitudes toward the interviewer's statements and questions and (during silences) toward the respondent's own thoughts. Head movements will often give the interviewer clues about what needs to be probed for clarification and elaboration.

Generally, if the respondent's head is hanging down toward the chest, this action is an indication of sadness, concern, or shame. Depending on the context, however, it could also simply be an indication that the respondent is thinking or concentrating. A rigidly held head may indicate anxiety. A chin jutted out probably shows anger or challenge.

Shoulders

As tension and anxiety develop in an individual, the shoulders tend to rise; when the person is relaxed but attentive the shoulders are in a lower "normal" position; when the individual becomes depressed or discouraged, the shoulders drop still further. It is easier for interviewers to correctly interpret the meaning of shoulder position in a person they know very well because they are familiar with the normal position for that individual.

The position of the shoulders can also be changed by rotating the trunk of the body. The respondent may face the interviewer directly or turn one shoulder or the other toward the interviewer. This turning of the shoulder can mean that the interviewer is getting too close either physically or emotionally. The respondent may bring both shoulders closer or farther from the interviewer by leaning forward or backward in the chair. Leaning forward usually indicates attention, openness, and eagerness to communicate while leaning back may indicate less eagerness to communicate or fatigue.

The most obvious of the shoulder movements is shrugging to indicate uncertainty, ambivalence, or indifference. Which of these it is may make considerable difference for the purposes of the interview; the accompanying verbal context or subsequent probing by the interviewer can usually determine what meaning is being displayed.

Arms and Hands

The hands can be very expressive in voluntary and involuntary ways. We will not deal with the voluntary signs (for example, the A-OK sign or the crazy-in-the-head sign) but with the involuntary, unconscious expressions of the hands that often tell the interviewer more than words alone.

Think of a scale of activity for the hands and arms—a scale ranging from folding the arms across the chest (indicating reserve, avoidance of self-revelation, or even dislike of the interviewer or the topic) to animated, energetic, fluid moving of hands and arms to support, emphasize, or illustrate what is being said. Enthusiasm to communicate and be understood can be shown both verbally and nonverbally. The extent to which hand and arm activity is used to express this enthusiasm varies from culture to culture and from individual to individual, but *changes* in the amount of hand and arm activity within an interview reflect changes in the respondent's attitude toward communicating.

Trembling or fidgety hands can indicate strong anxiety or anger. Often a respondent who is discussing a personal crisis will have trembling hands, but the trembling can be obscured by fidgeting with some object like a pencil, handkerchief, or clothing, or by twisting the hair, wringing the hands, popping the knuckles, or tapping the fingers on the arm of the chair or table. The latter action is more likely to be a mild signal of boredom or impatience rather than intense anxiety.

Anger can be expressed by clenching the fists, pounding the table, and moving the hands and arms quickly with jerky actions. When such gross expressions are repressed, finer ones like trembling hands or holding the arms stiffly at the sides may be substituted. When the interviewer is observing most arm and hand behavior patterns, he or she must depend on the context to sort out indications of fear and anxiety from those of anger and hostility.

Legs and Feet

The legs and feet are used much less frequently in the voluntary expression of emotion and ideas than are the hands and arms. At the involuntary level, too, the lower limbs are less expressive than the arms and hands. Nevertheless, the interviewer will find it useful to be aware of the legs and feet of the respondent, because they are often under less conscious control than are the arms and hands. If the legs and feet appear comfortable and relaxed with very little activity, the respondent probably feels at ease and willing to communicate. The repeated crossing and uncrossing of the legs may signal anxiety or depression. Legs and feet that appear stiff and controlled may indicate anxiety or insecurity.

Whole Body Motions

Rocking forward and backward in the chair can mean anxiety or grief. A generally slouched posture, whether sitting or standing, can indicate fatigue, low morale, or depression. The emotionally poised person tends to be erect without being stiff and comfortable without appearing limp. The body is in balance and the mind is ready to send or receive communication. The way a respondent walks into the room can signal confidence or apprehension. It is not uncommon to see the respondent leave the room after the interview with a slightly different walk.

We have seen that specific visual nonverbal cues have more than one possible meaning and that the reliability of our interpretation of the meaning depends on seeing the specific cue in the larger context. The effective interviewer is alert for meaningful *patterns* rather than isolated specific cues. Let's now look at some of the patterns that are important in the interview situation.

MEANINGFUL PATTERNS

Three important patternings can be observed to interpret the meaning of any specific nonverbal cue, whether it is visual or auditory: (1) the nonverbal cue's relationship to the *verbal* message it accompanies, (2) the nonverbal cue's relationship to another *nonverbal* cue being expressed simultaneously, and (3) *changes* in nonverbal expression during the interview.

Relationship of Nonverbal Cues to the Verbal Message

Incongruence between nonverbal cues and the verbal message might indicate some sort of ambivalence in the respondent, an attempt to conceal emotions, an effort by the respondent to persuade or deceive himself, or an attempt to deceive the interviewer with words. Usually, when there is incongruence between verbal and nonverbal cues of the involuntary type, the nonverbal cue is probably a more valid and reliable indicator of the true meaning behind the message. As Ekman and Friesen[12] point out, nonverbal leakage is the communication of messages that are valid but not sent intentionally. The validity lies in the fact that words can be monitored and selected before being said, but the involuntary nonverbal behavior that accompanies this monitoring process is not nearly so subject to the respondent's control.

Relationship Between Nonverbal Cues

People tend to control their facial expressions more than their body posture, hands and arms, or feet and legs. If respondents want to deceive the interviewer, they may succeed in producing convincing smiles or straight-faced sincerity even though they feel shame and guilt. In these situations the concept of leakage is very important. While the face is being successfully controlled to manifest serenity, the hands might be showing distinct expressions of anxiety. In other cases people are particularly aware of their hands but fail to control their feet. For example, a photographer taping a talk show with a panel of people who took opposite sides on a current controversial issue decided to have one camera focused on the feet of the participants. Ordinarily, when a panel is seated at a table for a television show, nothing that happens beneath the table is seen by the audience, and seasoned panel participants assume this. In this case the camera focused under the table showed shoes being pushed on and off, feet tapping, toes curling, ankles entwining, and other manifestations of tension; meanwhile above the table all was smiles and civility at points of verbal disagreement. In the interview situation such incongruencies indicate a need for further probing or for reassurances from the interviewer. By noting which part of the verbal message is accompanied by the contradiction between non-verbal signals, the interviewer can obtain clues about where to probe.

Changes in Nonverbal Behavior

The interviewer who wants to avoid jumping at unwarranted interpretations of the respondent's nonverbal behavior must remember that there are individual differences in levels of expressiveness and amounts of activity of the face, head, hands, and feet which may be related to various temperaments or cultural backgrounds. What might be a high level of expressiveness in one person might be a low level in another. Some people may rarely frown while others have a permanently knitted brow.

A polygraph operator must find the level of pulse, respiration, galvanic response, and blood pressure of the respondent while the respondent is being asked harmless questions such as, "What day of the week is it?" before drawing any conclusions about the significance of these same indicators when the person is asked, "Did you kill a man in the alley last night?" The significance of the various levels of involuntary bodily functions is in the amount of *change* that occurs when the topic is shifted from harmless to incriminating questions. In a less precise way the interviewer tries to do the same thing. Significant changes are easier to note if the interviewer has had an opportunity to observe the respondent in sociable conversation before the formal interview begins. Lacking this opportunity, the interviewer can become sensitive to changes in the type and level of nonverbal behavior corresponding to changes in the topic of discussion.

In any case, the most significant and most reliably interpreted dimension of nonverbal behavior is the *change* of behavior of a particular respondent in a particular interview situation. A type of nonverbal behavior that continues throughout the interview is very difficult and dangerous to interpret. Whether the respondent's frown means that he or she does not like the interviewer or needs glasses is impossible to judge validly if the frown is a constant throughout the interview.

SUMMARY

Six important points are essential in observing nonverbal behavior:

1. Interviewers should observe respondents' visible nonverbal behavior for the same reasons they listen to nonverbal behavior: (1) to more accurately interpret the meaning of the words, (2) to evaluate the validity of the verbal responses, and (3) to evaluate the motivational state of the respondent.

2. If the visible cues are *congruent* with each other and with the verbal message, then they indicate meaning by showing the relative importance of certain words, the amount of conviction, and whether the word or phrase has a positive or negative emotional charge. The interviewer thus receives clues about where to probe for additional relevant material.

3. If the visible clues are *incongruent* with each other or with the verbal message, then they warn that the verbal message may not be entirely valid. The respondent may be confused, having difficulty in remembering, trying to hide information, or fictionalizing to deceive the interviewer. In any case, this incongruency is an indication that the interviewer should probe and do cross-checks on the validity of the response and/or give more assistance to make the respondent more willing or more able to give valid information.

4. Visible nonverbal cues have a function separate from acting as an interpretive context for the verbal message. They indicate important dimensions of the motivational state of the respondent: the energy level and mood of the respondent, the respondent's attitude toward the interviewer or toward the topic of discussion, and the turn-taking desires of the respondent. These cues help the interviewer decide when to introduce certain topics, when to speed up or slow down the pace, whether the respondent needs encouragement and support, and so on.

5. To note all of the potentially relevant specific cues, the interviewer needs to be aware of the total body of the respondent. Eye behavior and facial expression are extremely important, but the behavior of the shoulders, arms and hands, legs and feet, and body posture where leakage is more likely to occur are also significant.

6. Since the meaning of specific cues may vary with their cultural, situational, and personal contexts, it is safer to interpret the meaning of visual cues by noticing certain patterns. First, visual cues should be seen in relationship to each other; for example, note any apparent incongruencies such as the smiling mouth and the mirthless eyes. Second, they should be seen in relationship to the verbal message; for example, note incongruencies such as the droopy-shouldered respondent saying, "I'm feeling fine." Third, visual cues must be seen in a pattern over time. This is extremely important because the pattern of *change* allows the interviewer to separate the individual or cultural baseline of the respondent's nonverbal behavior from the visual signals associated with a particular question or response.

NOTES

1. William Rogers, *Communication in Action: Building Speech Competencies* (New York: Holt, Rinehart & Winston, 1984), 80.

2. W. Schutz, *Joy: Expanding Human Awareness* (New York: Grove Press, 1967).

3. Robert Rosenthal et al., "Body Talk and Tone of Voice—the Language Without Words," *Psychology Today* (September 1974): 64–68.

4. Eckhard H. Hess, *The Tell-Tale Eye* (New York: Van Nostrand Reinhold, 1975).

5. S. P. Duncan, Jr., "Some Signals and Roles for Taking Speaking Turns in Conversations," *Journal of Personality and Social Psychology* 23 (1972): 283–92.

6. Ralph Exline, "Body Position, Facial Expression and Verbal Behavior During Interviews," *Journal of Abnormal and Social Psychology* 68 (1964): 295–301.

7. W. R. Passons, *Gestalt Approaches to Counseling* (New York: Holt, Rinehart & Winston, 1975), 102.

8. Sidney M. Jourard, "An Exploratory Study of Body-Accessibility," *British Journal of Social and Clinical Psychology* 5 (1966): 221–31.

9. Georg Simmel, "Sociology of the Senses: Visual Interaction," in Robert E. Park and Ernest W. Burgess, *Introduction to the Science of Sociology* (Chicago: University of Chicago Press, 1924), 358.

10. William H. Cormier and L. Sherilyn Cormier, *Interviewing Strategies for Helpers*, 2nd ed. (Monterey, Calif.: Brooks/Cole Publishing, 1985), 73.

11. Michael Argyle, *The Psychology of Interpersonal Behavior* (New York: Harmondsworth-Penguin, 1972), 105–16.

12. P. Ekman, and W. V. Friesen, "Nonverbal Leakage and Clues to Deception," *Psychiatry* 32 (1969): 88–106.

EXERCISE 7-A
OBSERVING NONVERBAL CUES

OBJECTIVES

With your active participation this exercise should demonstrate that (1) emotions are communicated nonverbally; (2) visual cues, without auditory cues, are enough to communicate emotion; (3) the observer is often not conscious of the specific visual cues that communicate an emotion yet is able to correctly identify the emotion; and (4) you can improve your awareness of visual cues.

GENERAL PROCEDURE

Your instructor will call on some members of the class to act as *demonstrators* of visual communication of emotions while the remainder of the class act as *observers* who try to identify the emotion being expressed, name specific visual cues, and describe some of those cues. After several demonstrations, there will be discussion based on a summary of the results of the group's observations.

ROLE OF DEMONSTRATOR

You may be among those selected by the instructor to demonstrate nonverbal expression of emotion through body movement. The instructor will assign four basic emotions to be expressed in a particular sequence. You will be allowed only 20 seconds to express each emotion. You may take a short time between demonstrations to get in the proper mood for the next emotion.

When demonstrating an emotion, first take a moment to get yourself in the right mood; then you may stand, sit, move about, or do anything else except speak. You should act in *silence* and *face* your audience most of the time. In each demonstration focus your attention on generating the feeling and don't worry about any techniques for expressing it.

ROLE OF OBSERVER

After each demonstration of an emotion, which will last for only 20 seconds, you will record the emotion you think is being demonstrated, what parts of the demonstrator's body are giving the relevant cues, and a few words describing what the body is doing.

A *visual nonverbal cues recording form* supplied by your instructor will provide details on the recording procedure.

SUMMARIZING

After 10 to 20 demonstrations have been completed, the instructor will ask for your help in summarizing the results of the whole group's observations.

DISCUSSION

The discussion will focus on this summary and compare it with the summary of the results of the exercise on *audible* nonverbal cues in Chapter 6.

Is the response an adequate answer, a careless irrelevance, or a clever evasion? That is the evaluative question.

8

Evaluating Responses

T HE INTERVIEWER'S TASK does not end with careful listening and observation. The interviewer who has heard exactly what the respondent has said and observed the respondent's nonverbal behavior now is ready to evaluate the information received.

To say that the interviewer evaluates responses does *not* mean that the interviewer makes moral judgments about the respondent's opinions, values, or actions. Instead, it means that the interviewer must have the objectives of the interview clearly in mind and must critically compare the information received with those objectives. The three criteria for this evaluation—relevance, completeness, and validity—are expressed in the following questions which can be asked about the response to any question:

1. Is the information in the response *relevant* to the purpose of the interview? In other words, is the respondent answering the question?
2. Is the answer *complete*? A response may be relevant but still not receive a high evaluation because it is not complete. The interviewer must continually ask if all the important elements and details are present in the answer.
3. Is the answer *valid*? In some instances, the response may be clearly on the topic and be loaded with detail yet be invalid because it is not true.

119

The respondent is not necessarily lying, but of course that is a possibility. The response may also be untrue because the respondent misunderstood the question, was misinformed, or did not remember.

These three criteria must be in the interviewer's mind at all times, so that when a response is judged to be lacking in any one of the three dimensions, the interviewer can take corrective action.

Continual evaluation allows the alert interviewer to correct shortcomings in the information on the spot. It is too late to make corrections when deficiencies are discovered by those trying to code or use the information. The uncritical interviewer can be easily deceived by a respondent who talks freely and rapidly while skillfully evading the point of the question. It can be embarrassing, to say the least, for the interviewer to have voluminous responses which upon closer inspection prove to be irrelevant.

Now let's take a closer look at what is involved in evaluating the relevance of a response.

EVALUATING RELEVANCE

The process of evaluating the relevance of a particular response is closely related to the process of formulating a relevant question as described earlier. To be relevant, a response must logically fall within the area defined by the question. For example, if we ask a farmer about fruit crops, a response about apples is relevant but a response about asparagus is not. In this example it is easy to see the irrelevance of the asparagus response, but when we are dealing with more complex concepts such as terrorism, the presidency, or family conflict, it becomes more difficult to judge the relevance of a particular response.

Let us now examine some of the guidelines to relevance in the context of specific ways in which a response might be irrelevant.

Guidelines to Relevance

Information may be irrelevant in several ways. These negative characteristics form the guidelines for determining relevance. Information may not fit into the definitions of the concepts used in the question; the concept might be applied to the wrong object, person, or event, the wrong time period, or the wrong place. Also, the *why* or *how* aspects of an action may be omitted or the information simply may not be concrete or general enough to fit the objectives of the question.

These guidelines may seem obvious and easy to use, but my experience in teaching interviewers and in analyzing interview data has shown that the novice interviewer may unwittingly accept from 10 to 90 percent *irrelevant* data depending on the difficulty of the interview topic and the type of respondent. The interviewer may be so delighted that the respondent talks in a free and friendly manner that he or she does not notice that much of the response, although interesting or even sensational, is irrelevant! To sharpen our sensitivity to the need to evaluate critically the relevance of each response; let us examine illustrations of each of the guidelines.

Does the Response Fit Key Concepts in the Question? If the interviewer asks about the respondent's children and the response is about parents, obviously the response is irrelevant. The type of irrelevance that is *not* obvious occurs in the response that is somehow related to the question but does not fit within its boundaries and definitions.

For example, assume that you are to do a study to evaluate the effectiveness of a three-year community action program aimed at improving the quality of life for residents of a slum neighborhood. Suppose that you defined *effectiveness* in terms of three basic objectives: (1) to increase the willingness of people in the neighborhood to meet and discuss problems of the neighborhood, (2) to successfully pressure city, state, and federal authorities to meet their responsibilities to help solve the neighborhood's problems, and (3) to mobilize members of the community to take direct action in their block to improve the appearance, health, and security of the neighborhood.

Here is a fragment of a hypothetical interview with the director of the Community Action Council, which is in charge of the project. The three questions correspond to the three objectives just stated.

I-1: In the three years you have been working on Project Upgrade has there been an increase in attendance at neighborhood meetings dealing with the neighborhood's problems?

R-1: I'm so glad you asked that question, because that is one of the major objectives of the project. We recognize the vital importance of grass-roots participation at the neighborhood level if we are to improve the quality of life in the urban slums. If you have time I would liked to invite you to the neighborhood meeting we are having tonight, as a matter of fact. We try to have meetings at least once per month. The last one was three weeks ago. At that meeting there were forty-five people attending compared to only forty three weeks before. I expect at least fifty tonight. The discussion is lively to say the least, and sometimes it is heated!

I-2: Has your organization successfully pressured local, state, or federal authorities to take more responsibility in improving the quality of life in this community?

R-2: Yes. That is what we call the political action phase of Project Upgrade. It is so important in community action to find out who is responsible for collecting the garbage, for removing dead animals from an alley, for fixing potholes, or repairing the sidewalk...or who is responsible for testing for radon gas in these old basements. We are locating and identifying more and more of the individuals and organizations related to various aspects of the quality of life in the local community. At tonight's meeting we are going to launch our third campaign of letter writing to pressure some official. This time it is the local Department of Health.

I-3: To what extent have you mobilized the local residents to take direct action to upgrade their neighborhood?

R-3: We believe strongly in direct action such as getting people to clean up their own yards, paint their own houses, and that sort of thing. Another thing we have stressed is the importance of having lids on all of the garbage cans so that the rats don't feed in them. We have also had one meeting to discuss the need for a neighborhood watch to make the neighborhood more secure and an escort service from the bus stop. All of these things can upgrade the quality of life and can be done by the people who live here.

Here the respondent talks freely, gives a lot of information about the program, and even invites the interviewer to a meeting to see firsthand what is happening. The respondent seems proud and enthusiastic about Project Upgrade. This emotional communication might lead an unwary interviewer to a positive evaluation of the project. But let us evaluate each response in terms of the objectives of the interview and ask: How much of the information is *relevant*?

Response 1: Can we tell from this response whether there has been any trend over the past three years (even in the mind of the respondent) showing either an increase or a decrease in the "willingness of people in the neighborhood to meet and discuss problems of the neighborhood" (the first objective)? Of the three-year period in which there may have been as many as fifty-two meetings we have unverified facts about only two meetings and an optimistic guess about the attendance at the next meeting. There could have been an average attendance of a hundred in the first year. The increase of forty to forty-five in the attendance at two consecutive meetings cannot represent a three-year general trend. If the program was successful, there would be a much greater difference between the attendance in two meetings one year apart than between two meetings three weeks apart. The small difference of five people could have been due to the weather or the scheduling of competing activities in the community. To put it bluntly, there is no information in response 1 that can be used to evaluate the first objective of the project. *It is all irrelevant.*

Response 2: The objective of the second question is to discover whether the program had "successfully pressured" local, state, or federal officials. The response says nothing about *results* in this area. Instead, the response talks about specific *aims* and *efforts*. The aims may be lofty and the efforts might be laudable with or without achieving results. Three years is long enough to have had some concrete results if the program is successful. The respondent has not given the slightest clue to whether past efforts have resulted in any relevant action by the officials. For these reasons, there is *nothing* in this response to achieve the objective of the interview.

Response 3: Again, the respondent talks about a strong belief in the *goals* of direct action and the *potential* for direct action. What is missing is any relevant fact about any specific direct action project either under way or completed. There is *nothing* in this response that would contribute to the third objective of the interview.

This interview fragment, though hypothetical, is typical of my experience; that is, directors of projects tend to see an interview as an opportunity to improve public relations, fear objective evaluation of their work, and feel that the interviewer naively expects quick results in circumstances where realistically only slow and irregular progress is possible. Under these conditions the skilled respondent will be careful to appear cooperative and load the interviewer with information that is related to the topic but that carefully sidesteps the main thrust of *evaluation*.

The basic defense tactic in this example was to avoid talking about the central evaluative concepts like long-run *trends* and specific *results* by showing enthusiasm about *goals* and *activities*. Often the hidden assumption is that, if your heart is in the right place and you get involved in lots of activity, the results will take care of themselves. Nothing could be further from the truth.

Is the Information about the Right Object, Person or Event?   Sometimes in analyzing information it is useful to distinguish between information describing *properties* (qualities, characteristics, traits, features, or attributes) and information designating the *objects* (persons, events, situations) having these properties.

Thus, when a question calls for information on the qualities of a specific object, the response can be irrelevant by being about the right qualities but the wrong object. This form of irrelevance is much more common that you might expect; it is not easily detected and may pass unnoticed by all but the most alert interviewers.

To illustrate, assume that you are interviewing for the U. S. Department of Health and Human Services to obtain a random sample of the adult population's opinions on AIDS. Among the several questions to be asked, you begin with the following.

I: There has been a lot of discussion in the news media about the spread of AIDS in the American population, and we would like to know how you feel about a number of related issues. First, do you feel that children with AIDS should attend public schools?

R: You're right; the news has been full of stories about AIDS and it's scary. I know the story about the school board that voted to exclude the kid who got AIDS from a blood transfusion and the case where they wouldn't let the kid into the school cafeteria. People felt very strongly against having these kids in school because they were afraid they or their children would catch AIDS. Some of the other kids felt so strongly that they probably would have beat the kid up if they were not afraid of getting AIDS themselves. Yes, there seem to be a lot of people who don't want kids with AIDS in school!

The response is irrelevant. Even though it is on the topic of feelings about children with AIDS attending school, the feelings mentioned are *not* those of the respondent, which was the aim of the question. Instead, the response is about the feelings of some unspecified other people reported in the news. This information is strictly irrelevant. The purpose of any random sample survey is to obtain a quantitative estimate of the population as a whole without having to interview everyone. To be sure that the feelings expressed are representative of the population, those feelings must be those of the individuals selected for the sample. People do sometimes project their feelings onto others and, therefore, give an expression of their own feelings disguised as the feelings held by others. Nevertheless, it is not a valid indicator when respondents simply repeat a news story without making it clear whether they agree or disagree with the feelings of the people described in the story.

The tendency for respondents to stray from their own actions, attitudes, or beliefs to those of other people is a common tactic that is used, either consciously or unconsciously, to avoid giving ego-threatening information. A respondent may be testing the situation by waiting to see how the interviewer reacts to a certain point of view expressed by real or fictitious others before venturing to give his or her own views.

Is the Information about the Relevant Time Period?   A response can cover the right concepts as applied to the relevant object (person or thing) but still be irrelevant because it is not related to the relevant time period. In the study of cause and effect in human events, it is crucial to keep the chronology of events clear. If this is not done, there is a high probability that the *effects* of an event will be confused with the *causes* of that event. Straightening out detailed cause-effect chronologies is critical in social-psychological studies of how conflicts begin, how decisions are made, or how communication networks operate, as well as in medical diagnostic interviews to track down sources of allergies or other diseases. The problem is often exacerbated by the respondent's own confusion over the exact chronology of events. Let us look at an example of the problem.

Assume that you are doing buyer-motivation research to discover how the respondents decided to buy the car they are currently driving. You begin by finding out *when* and *where* a respondent bought what kind of car before getting into *why* it was bought. You want to know "why" in the sense of discovering both the internal motivations (values, desires, wishes) and any external pressures (social pressure, economic situation, sales tactics, and so forth) that influenced the decision to buy the particular car.

I-1: What kind of car do you own?
R-1: A 1987 Nissan Sentra.
I-2: Did you buy it yourself?
R-2: Yes.
I-3: New?
R-3: Yes, I bought it new in January 1988.
I-4: Now I would like to get into some of the reasons you bought this car instead of some other car. What were some of the things that made you decide to buy the Sentra?
R-4: I spent a lot of time studying *Consumer Reports* and found that the Sentra and the Toyota Corolla had superior performance and maintenance records. Of course, nothing was available yet on the 1987 models, but I figured if they had been good up to 1986 they would probably continue to be good.
I-5: The performance and maintenance records are certainly important. What else seemed to move you in the direction of the Sentra?
R-5: We love the Sentra for lots of reasons. We can get more luggage in the trunk than we could in the old Chevy which is two and half feet longer overall. Also, there is plenty of room in the backseat for two kids. And the

heater works much faster and better. I drove to work one morning when it was just five degrees above zero. At that temperature the Chevy's heater would not put out any heat at all until I had gone ten miles. The Sentra's heater was putting out after about two miles. Another great thing about the Sentra is that it is easier to park because the turning radius is smaller. It is even easier to put in oil. I'd have to say that the Sentra is just a better all-around car than the Chevy.

Now let us look at the first ninety seconds of this interview to see if there is any information relevant to why the respondent bought the Nissan Sentra. The first three questions are to verify that the respondent did actually buy the Sentra new. Question 4 begins to explore motivations. Response 4 *seems* to be relevant in that the respondent studied *Consumer Reports* before making the purchase. The response is incomplete as it stands, however, because the respondent was impressed by *both* the Sentra and the Corolla; so the response as given seems to support buying a Corolla as well as a Sentra. This deficiency could be corrected by further probing.

The next response (R-5) may be totally irrelevant. It is a list of good points the respondent discovered *after* buying the car and these realizations could not have been causes for buying the car.

It would be easy and natural for the respondent to confuse what he knew *before* with what he learned *after* buying the car. No intent to deceive the interviewer is involved. Often people look for after-the-fact justifications to support their decisions. The good interviewer does not let this chronological confusion slide by; instead, the interviewer probes to verify the chronology.

Is the Information about the Relevant Place?

Often when we need to discover cause-effect in human relations it is useful to first establish the physical location where the event or condition to be explained takes place. If the effect we are trying to explain happens repeatedly in the same place, this suggests that we can narrow our search by focusing on variables in the one place. If the interviewer, however, unwittingly accepts responses about the physical location which are vague, confusing, or incorrect, this may lead to wasting time in exploring situations that are irrelevant.

To illustrate this point let's consider a case where a teacher comes to a psychiatric social worker in the public school system for help with a five-year-old boy in nursery school. Sometimes the boy is destructive and hostile. He destroys toys and materials and injures himself and others in what seems to be an almost random lashing out at anyone or anything within reach. The teacher reports that he is not always this way and at times is under control. She has noticed that just before he goes on a destructive rampage his ears turn bright red. On the basis of the "red ears" clue the social worker suspects that the boy might be having an allergic reaction to something in the environment that affects his central nervous system. An interview with the mother indicated that Bobby never has these destructive spells at home. An initial interview with the teacher gave several important clues: (1) the attacks never happened before 10:00 a.m. recess when the children went outdoors if weather permitted, (2) the attacks didn't happen every day, and (3) the behavior pattern usually subsided before noon when Bobby went home. Based on this information it was decided that the cause must be something in the environment during recess on certain days. So the problem at this point is to discover the difference between the *place* Bobby spent recess on days he had attacks and the place on days when he didn't.

I-1:   When was the last time Bobby had an attack?

R-1:   Yesterday. That was Tuesday. Nothing happened Monday or today.

I-2:   What did Bobby do during recess yesterday?

R-2:   He did the same thing all the kids do every day that the weather permits. They go outside to play for a half hour.

I-3:   What do they do outside and what are the surroundings like?

R-3:   Take for example today. They went out the front door to the golf course which is used only on weekends by the public. The grass is nice and green, well mowed and clean. Sometimes they play tag or other games or just look for four-leaf clovers.

I-4:   Do you know if they use artificial fertilizers or weed killers on the grass?

R-4:   That's an idea. No, I don't know for sure, but since you never see a weed I suspect they use weed killer. We could find out from the gardener for the golf course.

I-5:   In the games the kids play do they ever roll around in the grass?

R-5:   Oh yes, particularly the boys. They love to tussle in the grass.

Unfortunately, this interview led the investigation into a false trail involving interviews with the gardener, a careful exploration of the golf course area where the children played, tests for Bobby's possible allergy to fertilizer, weed killer, grass, and mold. None of this added information led to a solution because the information obtained in this segment of the interview was *irrelevant*. It was about the wrong place. The interviewer did not notice that although question I-2 was heading in the right direction because it was leading up to a description of the place Bobby was before his attack the day before, in R-3 the interview was sidetracked into a description of the surroundings in the place Bobby spent recess *the day of the interview* when he did *not* have an attack.

When the social worker discovered the error, she interviewed the teacher again about the environment where Bobby spent his recess just before an attack. The cause became clear when it was discovered that most recesses were spent in one of two places. The children either went out the front door to the golf course or out the back door to the playground which had a gazebo and a jungle gym made of old railroad ties. This led to the discovery that Bobby was allergic to creosote in the railroad ties.

If this example gives the impression that being an interviewer is sometimes like being a detective, that is correct. Perhaps it is better to say the detective is sometimes an interviewer.

Are the Why and How Aspects Covered in the Response?   In certain interviews we need to know not only who did what, where, and when, but also *why* and/or *how* it was done. Often it may be ego threatening for the respondent to give his or her motivations for an action or inaction. For example, a battered wife may be reluctant to explain why she tolerates repeated beatings by her husband, and the uncritical interviewer may be so impressed by the detailed descriptions of violence that he or she may not notice that the why aspect has been omitted. In some cases it takes skilled probing to discover the why of certain human actions because the respondent is not consciously hiding the information, and the respondent has never been clearly aware of his or her own motivations.

Similarly, if the objectives of an interview call for discovering *how* a certain result was accomplished, the interviewer must maintain a keen awareness of the need for the how dimension to probe for it at appropriate points. It is easy to be so impressed by the respondent's story of intentions and results that the absence of information on *how* these intentions were translated into results may go unnoticed.

For example, this happens in the following exchange in which the interviewer is trying to discover how "crack" is distributed to school children in a ghetto area.

> *I:* How do kids at your school get hold of "crack"?
> *R:* That's no problem here. If you want something bad enough you can always get it. And I mean they want it bad! If they haven't had their fix and it is overdue they will do anything to get it. They even begin to look sick and act sick so anyone who knows "crack" can tell why the person is suffering. I know some kids on "crack" that not only steal to pay for crack but would kill if there was no other way. I know girls that go on the street to raise the money for their fix.

The interviewer should not accept this response as a valid explanation of how crack is obtained. The response instead emphasizes the strength of the person's need for crack. It touches on the how aspect slightly in mentioning how the money to buy crack may be obtained. It does not, however, answer many other how details such as: how does the buyer make contact with the seller; what precautions are taken to avoid being caught; what does the buyer say to the seller; or how do you learn how it is done. Again, the interviewer must have a continual awareness of the need for information on the how dimension to be able to probe at the appropriate points.

Is the Response at the Correct Level of Abstraction?   Depending on the purpose of the interview, a question may require an answer that is specific and *concrete* or it may seek an answer that is more general and *abstract*. Often, when we want respondents to be specific, they are general; and when we want them to be general, they give a specific answer. The unwary interviewer may accept an answer that is not at the appropriate level of abstraction for the purposes of the interview.

To be successful, the interviewer must have a clear understanding of the difference between concrete and abstract information. To say "people sleep about eight hours a day" is a generalization. A more refined generalization might be "the average citizen of Sleepyhollow Township sleeps 7.13 hours per twenty-four-hour period." Such a generalization, to be true, must be based on many concrete instances. One of these concrete instances could be expressed as "I, John Jones, slept soundly for six and a half hours on January 16 in my own bed at home." Note that the concrete event does not stop at specifying the action (sleep), but goes on to specify a particular person who slept a particular amount at a certain time and place. The urge for concreteness is behind the journalist's 5W + H rule, which states that an ideal news story must answer the question "*Why* did *who* do *what, when, where,* and *how?*"

To illustrate the problem of eliciting *concrete* information, let's look at a situation in which the interviewer is looking for specific *examples* of racial discrimination in the local public school system and is interviewing a black student.

I-1:   As you know, there have been charges of racial discrimination at Central High School and the school board has contracted with State University Community Research Department to investigate the situation. I work for the research department and would like to get your views on the issue. How long have you been going to Central High?

R-1:   I have been here for three years. It's the only high school I have attended.

I-2:   Would you say that there is racial discrimination going on at your school or not?

R-2:   It's my feeling that there is.

I-3:   Can you give me an example of it?

R-3:   Yes. For example, the white teachers think that the black students are dumb!

I-4:   I see. Are there any other examples of discrimination you have noticed?

R-4:   Sure. The white teachers don't talk about things the black students are interested in. Also, the coach doesn't let all the black members of the basketball team play in the tough games, and they get tired of sitting on the bench. Oh, and the best example of all is the way some of the white students make remarks about the way the blacks dress.

Although the interviewer is looking for *concrete examples* of discriminatory behavior against blacks, no specific example has yet been mentioned. Instead, the respondent gives broad categories of discrimination or prejudice such as "white teachers think that the black students are dumb." To convert this irrelevant statement into a relevant example, the interviewer would have to probe for an example of a *particular* teacher doing or saying something *specific* at a certain *time* and *place* to a *particular* person which would indicate discrimination. Without such information, the original statement is an unsubstantiated generalization. The same is true of all the statements in R-4. Much more concrete detail is needed to know whether there were any specific acts of discrimination. These statements in R-4 would need extensive, careful probing to obtain specific examples. Then, the detailed examples could be examined and classified logically.

The alert interviewer never accepts vague generalizations in place of concrete facts. When the search is for concrete details about X, then generalizations about X are irrelevant.

Conversely, when the purpose of the interview calls for generalizations, a detailed, concrete case cannot take the place of the generalization. No generalization can be based on one case. When the question asks for a generalization, the respondent may give concrete examples to avoid admitting the generality. The respondent might give selected exceptional cases that are not representative of the generality but are in accord with the respondent's own prejudices. Thus, if a football fan is asked how his team compares with its competition, when his team is near the bottom of its league, he might dwell on the details of the last game that his team won. Similarly, if a staunch advocate of an underdog political candidate is asked about her candidate's chances to carry the election in the local precinct (in other words, how precinct voters in *general* feel about the candidate), most likely she will respond with examples of specific local supporters of the candidate.

To evaluate any response effectively, the interviewer must be acutely aware of which level of abstraction is sought and be sensitive to attempts to respond at the wrong level.

The foregoing illustrations of the five guidelines to judge the relevance of a response may give the impression that a response is always clearly relevant or irrelevant, but this is not the case. In fact, responses come in various degrees of relevance, and it is the interviewer's responsibility to probe the initial response to improve its relevance if necessary.

Degrees of Relevance

In between the clearly irrelevant and the clearly relevant is a large area of *potentially* relevant responses that cannot be classified as relevant or irrelevant until the interviewer obtains additional information by probing the respondent. For example, it may not be clear whether the initial response to a question deals with the basic concepts as defined for the purposes of the interview. It may not be clear whether the information pertains to the correct object or to the relevant time, place, or occasion. It may take considerable probing by the interviewer to help the respondent move up or down the ladder of abstraction to reach the desired level.

Remember that in evaluating the *relevance* of a response, the interviewer should have two basic objectives in mind: first, to avoid accepting irrelevancies as relevant; and second, to avoid allowing the potentially relevant to pass unnoticed and unprobed.

EVALUATING COMPLETENESS

There are two types of completeness. First is the minimal completeness needed to determine whether an initial response to a question is relevant. This has already been discussed. The second type is optimum completeness in which all dimensions of the question are covered with relevant information. Let us now explore this second type of completeness.

The probability that the problem of completeness of coverage will arise depends to a great extent on the breadth and complexity of the question. For example, if the question is "How old are you?" the answer "Twenty-five" gives completeness of coverage. On the other hand, if the question is "What do you think about the illegal alien problem in the United Sates?" then a longer response like "The U. S. Border Patrol has certainly been unsuccessful in keeping them out, but I think that this amnesty idea is good" is certainly not complete. Obviously, it would be foolhardy to expect such a broad question to elicit a complete answer.

As this example suggests, much incompleteness of coverage can be prevented by breaking the broad topical question into many subquestions. This does not necessarily mean that all of the subquestions must be asked, but they do all have to be answered. The subquestions are there to remind the interviewer that answers are needed. Often when questions are arranged in an appropriate order, the respondent may answer two to ten questions of detail for every one that has to be asked. Even if the interview is being tape-recorded to relieve the interviewer from taking notes, the interviewer still must note which subquestions have been answered and which have not as the interview progresses.

Even when a question is fairly simple and narrow in scope, there are several basic reasons why a respondent might fail to give a complete answer. First, the respondent might not understand the full implications of the question. Second, even when the respondent appreciates the full implications, he or she may tend to filter out certain relevant information. Certain portions of the information may be difficult to remember; some information may threaten the respondent's ego; some may cause the respondent to relive a painful experience; or the respondent might feel that a particular bit of information might shock the interviewer.[1]

To illustrate the need to probe for completeness in the answer to a medium-scope question, assume this situation. A manager in the Atlas Data Corporation is interviewing newly recruited computer programmers to see whether they need help in adjusting and whether the management's orientation program for programmers could be improved.

> *I-1:* Thanks for coming in, Rick! As you know we want to see how all the new programmers are doing after their first month here at Atlas. There might be some way I or someone else can help you get settled into your job. How do you feel about the job so far?
>
> *R-1:* Well, things were a bit <u>confusing</u> at first. It was good that we had the two-day orientation before we started. But now things are <u>clearing up</u> and I know my way around a lot better. I'm sure I still have a <u>few things to learn</u> about how things operate. There are a lot of things that are <u>different</u> from my old job at Data Systems. But I <u>feel great</u> about my new job and see that Atlas is going to be an interesting and <u>challenging</u> place to work.

Much of the response is relevant, but it is not complete in many ways. The interviewer's task is to get the respondent to provide more information in order to see more concretely how he can be helped or how the orientation program might be improved. As will be explained in more detail in the next chapter on probing, the skillful interviewer can obtain more relevant detail by acknowledging the relevant points the respondent has made and probing for elaboration. In the preceding example all of the underlined words in the response should be probed. For example, in this case the interviewer could continue with any one of the following probes for completeness.

- That's very interesting! Can you tell a little more about how things "were a bit confusing at first?"
- I'm interested in how "things are clearing up" for you and in what way you "know your way around a lot better."
- You said you had a "few things to learn" about how things operate. What are some of these things?"

Answers to these three questions would contain suggestions for a better orientation program and bring up questions or misconceptions that the manager could deal with immediately in the interview. Of course, the answers to each of these probes might need further probing to obtain a more concrete picture of the problems of the new employee in adjusting to the job.

EVALUATING VALIDITY

A response is invalid if it is untrue. It can be untrue because the respondent is intentionally trying to deceive the interviewer, as is often the case when a police officer is interviewing a suspected criminal. A response can also be untrue for several other reasons. The respondent's reported observations may be highly distorted by strong prejudices. In this case the respondent would feel he or she was telling the truth, but the report might only faintly resemble the reality. In other cases the respondent's memory of a situation or event might have faded and be easily confused, so that much of an honestly attempted report might be untrue. In other situations the respondent may be simply misinformed and report rumors and other forms of misinformation as fact. If the interviewer presses for answers that the respondent is not able to supply at the moment, the respondent might fictionalize some innocuous answer to avoid appearing uncooperative. Finally, a respondent sometimes will withhold the truth not in self-defense, but because he or she assumes that the truth would shock the interviewer.

The interviewer must be skilled in recognizing probable invalidity in a response regardless of its cause. Let's now look at some of the nonverbal and verbal clues to invalidity in a response.

Nonverbal Clues to Invalidity

Chapter 6 on listening to the respondent described and illustrated how *incongruencies* between the verbal message and the audible nonverbal accompaniment give clues to possible invalidity. These paralinguistic cues include the general pitch of the voice, intonation patterns, quality of voice, and pacing. If these audible nonverbal cues are not congruent with the logical meaning of the words, the interviewer may suspect some possible invalidity in the response. When strong incongruencies occur, the nonverbal cues are usually closer to the truth than the verbal message.

The chapter on observing the respondent (Chapter 7) described and illustrated how incongruencies between one visible gesture and another or between gestures and words are indications of possible invalidities in a response. It is not necessary to elaborate at this point on the need to listen for and observe incongruencies among nonverbal expressions or between the nonverbal and the verbal expressions, except to note that they differ from incongruencies between two verbal expressions in an interesting way. Discrepancies involving nonverbal cues are conflicts between two *simultaneous* events, whereas discrepancies between verbal statements are conflicts between two *sequential* events. Let us now look more closely at the verbal incongruencies and how they offer clues to invalidity of the response.

Verbal Clues to Invalidity

In looking for verbal clues to invalidity, the interviewer focuses on *incongruencies*. Since the discrepancies are sequential rather than simultaneous, the interviewer must depend on memory to detect them. In some instances the two incongruent verbal statements may occur in the same sentence, but in others they may occur at widely separated times in the interview. In long, depth interviews it is not unusual to approach the end of the interview and observe the respondent contradict what was said at the beginning. Usually the later statements, those made after the interviewer has been able to build trust and help stimulate the respondent's memory, are more valid.

To avoid multipage examples, the following illustrations of verbal-verbal incongruencies occur in rapid sequence. Of course, then, these examples will be much more obvious than those that occur in real interviews.

Incongruencies between One Generalization and Another.   Often respondents make generalizations that logically contradict one another. This can happen for a number of reasons. The generalizations may be *logically* incongruent but *emotionally* consistent in that they both express or support the same strong feeling. For example, a respondent who is prejudiced against a minority may say that members of that minority are both "lazy" and "pushy" by nature.

Another common reason for inconsistent generalizations is simply that the respondent makes a quick, careless, or premature generalization without giving it much thought. Then later in the interview, after recalling many more specifics, the respondent will make a more thoughtful and valid generalization.

Another type of inconsistency arises when the respondent sees certain ego-threatening implications in his or her generalization and tries to undo it by fabricating an opposite generalization with additional arguments in its support.

Finally, and of equal importance, is the incongruency that is not real but only apparent to the interviewer. In this case, if the interviewer confronts the respondent with the apparent contradiction, the respondent's explanation shows that no real contradiction exists. To illustrate, let's look at an excerpt in which the interviewer is trying to discover the effects of an educational film on members of the experimental audience.

> I-1: As you know, the film *For a Few Pesos More* is an experimental educational film which the producers hoped would be more acceptable to new Navy recruits than the usual type. Let's start by having you just give your overall reaction to the film.
>
> R-1: It certainly wasn't the usual type; it was beautiful. The color, the camera angles, and the background music were terrific. They used one of the tunes from a Clint Eastwood film in the background and it fit the mood very well. Some of the old training films were things like an admiral standing at a podium reading the articles of war. Dry as dust. This one had about eight characters and the setting was in a cantina near the Mexican border and they slipped in information on the pros and cons of different types of life insurance. That's why it is called an educational film. But I agree with a lot of the guys I have talked with. It should never be used in our training center.

The two general statements about the film—"it was beautiful" and "it should never be used"—certainly seem to be contradictory. But further probing about this apparent contradiction made it clear that the respondent meant that the film was technically and artistically very appealing, but that it portrayed Mexicans in negative stereotypes. The respondent felt that the film would perpetuate stereotypes of Mexican Americans. This hypothesis was carefully tested by the study and found to be true, so the film was not used.

Incongruencies between One Fact and Another. Factual incongruencies also arise from a variety of causes. Often in employment interviews, police interrogations, and social science interviews, attempts are made to cross-check crucial facts. For example, a questionnaire might ask for the person's birth date and a subsequent informal interview might ask "How old are you?" to verify the date.

In a police interrogation, for example, the suspect got off work at 10:00 p.m., the robbery took place at 11:30 p.m., and at 1:00 a.m. the police came to the suspect's home, which was about five miles from the suspect's place of work, and found the suspect and a friend in the kitchen eating. Later in the police station the following interrogation took place.

> I-1: When the police came to your house last night, before they knocked on the door, they felt the engine of your car parked out front and it was still very warm.
>
> R-1: Why shouldn't it be? We just got home and were raiding the refrigerator when the police came banging on the door.
>
> I-2: I see.

(One hour later in the interrogation.)

I-97:   Now I'd like to have you account for all your movements after you got off work. You say that you got off work at 10:00 p.m., is that right?

R-97:   That's right.

I-98:   Well the store was robbed at 11:30. You could have picked up your buddy then gone over and cased the store and looked for a good chance for the stick up. What's your story about what you did right after you got off work?

R-98:   My buddy came by work and waited for me to get off and we drove straight to my house from there.

I-99:   But you stopped by the store on the way home!

R-99:   No, I drove straight home!

Two factual statements are contradictory: "We just got home . . . when the police arrived" (at 1:00 a.m.) and "I drove straight home." Straight home would have been a five-mile trip which could not possibly have taken from 10:00 p.m. until about 1:00 a.m.

In interviews where there may be a tendency for the respondent to lie, the interviewer should seek detailed, *concrete facts* that can be checked for consistency. In a case like the one above, the two friends could be interviewed separately for details about the trip between work and home to detect whether they are fabricating a story.[2]

Incongruencies between Facts and Generalizations.   An apparent discrepancy between a fact and a generalization does not necessarily mean that either one or the other is incorrect. A generalization that is correct in 99 percent of the cases might conflict with a concrete example of a single case. It is the interviewer's job to test whether the contradiction is real or apparent. In some cases the respondent may give a large number of factual examples, all of which contradict a generalization. In such cases there is a good chance that the contradiction is real.

Respondents in a long, depth interview commonly give a premature generalization early in the interview. After being probed repeatedly for *factual* support of concrete examples, the respondent begins to realize that the initial generalization was incorrect.

Sometimes the respondents have a prejudice that prevents them from recognizing the discrepancy between the facts and generalizations they are reporting. In some cases the prejudice causes the respondent to give an incorrect generalization; in other cases the respondent selects only the facts which, although exceptional, support the prejudiced generalization. When the respondent makes the reported facts and the generalization fit, it is very difficult to detect fabrication without some independent source of verification. In the following example the discrepancy is apparent. A family relations counselor is interviewing a young husband.

I-1:   Tell me a little bit about how you get along with your wife's family.

R-1:   We get along okay, I guess. I see quite a bit of my mother-in-law. She babysits for us on special occasions. Her husband is dead, so she has quite a bit of spare time. She helped Bea [wife] get her first job. They have lunch together sometimes and seem to get along fine. We've had her mother to dinner a couple of times. When we went to the Bahamas for a week, Bea's mother moved into our house and took care of the kids who were eighteen months and three years old at the time.

I-2: About how often do you see Bea's mother?

R-2: At least once a week we chat a bit when she comes to baby-sit while we have a night out. Then there are other irregular times—at least once a week on the average.

I-3: What effect, if any, has Bea's mother had on your marriage?

R-3: Not much, really. I know that mothers-in-law and sons-in-law are not supposed to get along according to all the jokes. But we never have any spats or conflict of any kind. Although she has never done anything to help our marriage, I can honestly say that she hasn't tried to interfere in any way either.

I-4: So, in general how would you rate your relationship with your mother-in-law?

R-4: Well, I'd say we get along as well as could be expected or maybe better than could be expected.

I-5: I see; and how do you get along with your brother-in-law?

In this example there is a logical conflict between the generalization in R-3, "she has never done anything to help our marriage," and the services the mother-in-law gives to the respondent's family, which are freely mentioned in R-1 and R-2. This discrepancy would have to be probed to discover basic attitudes underlying the relationship.

Incongruencies between Respondents' Statements and Known Facts. In some situations the respondent may be giving invalid information without any *internal* incongruencies. This is why it is important sometimes for the interviewer to have independent *external* sources for testing the veracity of a sample of the respondent's statements to detect any tendency for fabrication and even to show in which direction the fabrication leans.

To illustrate the interviewer testing the respondent's veracity and the direction of his or her prejudices, let's look at an example from my own field experience. I had arrived in Bogotá, Colombia, to do the initial field work in laying the foundation for a cross-cultural study program for American college students.[3] The problem was to design a three-stage program in Bogotá where in the third stage American students would attend a regular Colombian university. The initial problem was to obtain objective comparisons of four major universities in Bogotá to assess their strengths and weaknesses. It became apparent that even Colombians who had never attended any university in Bogotá had strong political biases for and against these universities. To classify respondents as objective or biased, for or against a particular university, I prepared a screening interview in which I asked questions about the four universities. I already had authoritative answers for these questions and noted the accuracy of the respondent's reply. For example:

I-1: Let's talk for a moment about the Javeriana University. How strong is their X department?

R-1: I am very well acquainted with Javeriana. I know the rector personally as well as a lot of the professors and department heads. I'm sure you would find excellent courses taught by superb professors at Javeriana. Students interested in X field would be very happy there.

I-2: Are you an alumnus of Javeriana?

R-2: Oh no. I went to the University of Medellin, but as I say, I have many contacts at the Javeriana and know people at the National University and the University of the Andes, too.

I-3: Very interesting! Tell me your opinion of the University of the Andes for American students interested in field X.

R-3: I would not say that it would be superb like the Javeriana University. They do not have a real department of X at the Andes, just part-time faculty. You could hardly say that the Andes is a real, solidly Colombian university.

This exchange was enough to clearly classify the respondent as having a bias in favor of Javeriana and against the Andes, not because of any *internal* inconsistencies in what the respondent said but because of the discrepancies against *external* sources of information. External sources showed that the Javeriana University never had a department in field X, and the Andes had the most highly developed department in Colombia. Such tactics for smoking out biases work particularly well in situations where the interviewer is assumed to be a totally ignorant outsider.

SUMMARY

To evaluate a response is to determine whether it is relevant, complete, and valid. Continual evaluation must be done while listening to the response so that at the first opportunity the response may be probed to determine or improve its relevance, to complete it, or to test and improve its validity.

To determine the degree of relevance in a response, the interviewer should keep the following six questions in mind:

1. Does the response fit the definitions of the basic concepts used in the question?
2. Is the response about the relevant object, person, situation, or event referred to in the question?
3. Is the information about the relevant time period?
4. Is the information about the relevant place?
5. Are the how and why aspects included when relevant?
6. Is the response at the correct level of abstraction?

The same six questions can be used in a slightly different way to determine the completeness of the response. The interviewer must first be aware of which of the six dimensions of information are required to meet the objectives of the question. Then the interviewer must keep a mental check of the responses to any broad, general question covering several of these dimensions. The interviewer may need to design more specific questions to deal with each of the dimensions separately.

Responses may be relevant to the question and complete but still be invalid because they are not true. Any lack of congruence with reality may be either intentional or unintentional on the respondent's part. The interviewer not only must be alert for simultaneous incongruencies involving nonverbal cues (as described in the previous two chapters), but also must look for sequential verbal cues to invalidity. These cues consist of four types of incongruencies:

1. Incongruencies between one generalization and another
2. Incongruencies between one specific fact and another
3. Incongruencies between facts and generalizations
4. Incongruencies between respondent's statements and information already known by the interviewer

In evaluating responses, the interviewer should sometimes probe responses that seem irrelevant but have potential relevance. If the probing of the potentially relevant yields some clearly relevant responses, then the interviewer may go on to probe for completeness and validity. Remember that the skilled interviewer is at least as mentally active while listening as while speaking.

NOTES

1. For a full treatment of these inhibitors of communication see Raymond L. Gorden, "Inhibitors of Communication," in *Interviewing: Strategy, Techniques and Tactics*, 4th ed. (Chicago: Dorsey Press, 1987).

2. For detailed examples of tactics to detect lying, see Raymond L. Gorden, "The Police Interrogation," in *Interviewing: Strategy, Techniques and Tactics*, 4th ed. (Chicago: Dorsey Press, 1987).

3. This resulted in the founding of CEUCA (Centro de Estudios Universitarios Colombo-Americano) by the Great Lakes Colleges Association.

Exercise 8-A
EVALUATING THE RELEVANCE
OF ANSWERS

OBJECTIVES

This exercise is designed to provide practice in evaluating the relevance of the response to the objectives of the interview. To make such a judgment, you must first be clear about the objectives of the interview and how the question fits into the pursuit of those objectives. Second, you must listen carefully.

A response to a question may be inadequate because it is (1) irrelevant, (2) unclear or incomplete, or (3) invalid (not true). In this exercise you are to concentrate on only the question of *relevance*. A response may be incomplete yet be clearly relevant as it stands, or it could be potentially relevant in that an attempt to clarify or complete it could make it clearly relevant. Other responses may be so clearly irrelevant that it would be a waste of time to try to clarify or complete them.

PROCEDURE

1. After everyone has reviewed the following section on purposes of the interview, two members of the class will be selected for a role-play using the script given in this exercise.
2. The other members of the class will act as observers and record their judgments on the *relevance evaluation form* supplied by your instructor.
3. Your instructor will be sure that the interviewer allows 30 seconds after each response for the observers to classify the relevance of the response and to add remarks as specified in the relevance evaluation form.
4. The instructor will circulate a *relevance summary form* on which each observer will record his or her 10 coded responses.
5. After seeing the amount of agreement and disagreement among observers, the instructor will lead a discussion on the results.

PURPOSE OF THE INTERVIEW

The purpose of the interview you will evaluate is to discover the respondent's most significant reference groups. A reference group is defined as a specific group or category of people to which a person does *not* belong, but which that person uses as a standard of comparison in judging his or her own status and worth, or to determine who he or she is in the social world. We all use reference groups to establish our own social status and identity.

In the following interview, your job is to judge which responses are relevant and which are irrelevant to the purpose of the interview.

INTERVIEW TRANSCRIPT

I-1: I am doing this interview with you as an assignment in my interviewing course, and I need to tape-record it so I can be sure to get everything you say and so the instructor in the course can listen to see if I am using the right method. Is that okay with you?

R-1: Sure, I guess so. I'll be sure not to give you a hard time and make you look good.

I-2: Great. I would appreciate that! What I want to find out is the important reference groups in your life. Since *reference groups* is a special term, let me tell you what it means. It is a group that you don't belong to but which you use as a standard of comparison in judging how well you are doing or who you are. Does that make sense?

R-2: Sure.

I-3: Can you think of any group that you use as a standard of comparison?

R-3: Well . . . that's interesting. I catch myself comparing myself with my brother who went to C_____ University.

I-4: In what way do you compare yourself?

R-4: I guess it's mainly when I'm trying to decide what kind of student I am. You see he was a good student and got mostly A's and some B's and had a good scholarship, but I am at A_____. We don't get grades and sometimes I'm glad because my record might not look as good as my brother's.

I-5: I see! Are there other comparisons you make, but not with your brother, to decide how well you are doing or to identify who you are as an individual?

R-5: Well, I'm a Unitarian and I learned a lot of ideas about the brotherhood of man and working for the good of the whole human race. At times I feel a bit lacking in my performance or in my life aims. I tend to want to attract attention to myself or to shy away from good causes that don't seem too practical.

I-6: Yeah, I guess we all fail to live up to some ideals from time to time. What other group has influenced your life?

R-6: Funny you should ask that question, because two years ago I became very aware that my life had been completely changed for the better by a certain group. You see, I was born with a defective heart valve and every September I went to the local heart clinic where they examined me to see if I would outgrow the problem, but it got worse in my case. But two years ago I went to the Bay Area Coronary Research Institute (BACRI) to have a heart valve implant and since then I have felt great! I can do anything a healthy person can do! That group at BACRI had a tremendous effect on my way of life and feeling of well-being, and how I feel about myself.

I-7: That's very interesting. I'm glad to hear it came out so well! There's another angle you could help me with if you can answer this kind of question. Think of some time when you were very pleased with yourself and thought to yourself, "That's a lot better than such and such a group could have done!" What group might that be?

R-7: Hmm . . . I can't think of a situation like that.

I-8: Fine . . . now when you think of who you are now or who you would like to be, or what you would like to do with your life, can you think of any groups you *don't* want to be like?

R-8: Sure. I don't want to turn out to be a hard-hat, or a Ku Klux Klan type of person!

I-9: Uh-huh, and what other groups do you hope *not* to be like?

R-9: Well, I certainly can say that I don't want to be a fundamentalist born-again Christian!

I-10: Very good. That's the kind of thing I was looking for. Thank you very much for your help with my assignment. If I can do you a favor some time, let me know. Thanks again!

R-10: You're welcome. It was fun for me.

Exercise 8-B
EVALUATING THE VALIDITY OF ANSWERS

OBJECTIVES

This exercise is designed to do three things: to give you practice in detecting invalid answers, to provide an opportunity for you to assess your own skill in this detection, and to spark discussion on the conditions under which such detection is possible or reliable.

Remember that the term *validity* means the extent to which the response is an accurate reflection of reality. Any lack of accuracy may have one of several causes. It may be the result of intentional lying by the respondent or it may be due to the respondent's self-deception. The respondent may be ignorant, misinformed, or confused, or have a poor memory; or the respondent may be trying to please the interviewer.

PROCEDURE

Pairs of students will be asked to do two or three demonstration interviews in front of the class. Each interview will be done by a different pair of students and will involve two topics. The remaining members of the class will act as observers; they will try to detect whether topic A or B contains the most invalid responses by the respondent. The observers' judgments will be summarized and discussed.

INTERVIEWER'S ROLE

1. Your instructor will give you two open-ended questions designated as topics A and B. You will interview the respondent for only three minutes on each. The instructor will time you.
2. Your respondent has been instructed to tell the absolute truth at some points and to fictionalize as much as possible at others, but you do not know the order in which this will occur.

3. Your best tactic for detecting and making the fictional material apparent to the observers is to follow up the initial topical questions with questions designed to get as much specific, concrete detail about the respondent's experiences as possible. You should get specific details on *who* did *what*, to *whom* (or what), *where, when, why*, and *how*. Also, concrete details about the scene or situation in which the action occurs will be helpful.
4. You will have five minutes to plan some of these questions after you see the two topics you have been assigned.
5. After the first three-minute interview topic, you will be given two minutes to record your reactions on a *validity evaluation form* furnished by the instructor.

RESPONDENT'S ROLE

1. The instructor will give you an assignment card giving the two topics you will be interviewed on, the order in which they will be used, and when you are to fictionalize as much as you can. Do *not* let the interviewer or the observers see this card.
2. After seeing the two topics, you will have five minutes to improvise some way to fictionalize as much as possible at the appropriate points.
3. Your truthful responses should be as spontaneous and candid as possible, but if you don't know the answer to a question feel free to say, "I don't know."
4. Your responses when you are fictionalizing should sound as convincing as you can make them.
5. *Important*: During the classroom discussion of your interview, be careful not to give either verbal or nonverbal clues as to when you were fictionalizing until the instructor asks you for your unique point of view on the experience. Be prepared at that time to react to the reasons why different observers labeled your responses as either truth or fiction.

OBSERVER'S ROLE

1. You are to listen and observe carefully to detect any cues or impressions of *invalidity* in the responses. You know that the respondent is going to be as frank as possible at some points and to fictionalize as much as possible at others while trying to hide this from the interviewer and observers. You don't know what is going to be fictionalized, so you will have to be vigilant from the beginning.
2. In trying to detect fictionalizing, note the tone of voice, the rhythmic patterns and pauses, as well as body language. Also listen for verbal contradictions and note any incongruencies between one nonverbal expression and another (whether visual or auditory).
3. At the end of each three-minute interview, you will be given two more minutes to fill out a *validity evaluation form* furnished by the instructor.

DISCUSSION

After all three interviews are finished, the instructor will ask your help in summarizing the results of all the observers and then will launch a discussion of the experience. Depending on the length of your class period and the size of the class, the discussion may have to be done at the next class meeting.

*Broad questions stake out the
claim and reveal the easy gold
lying about the surface, but probes
dig deeper to track the vein and
extract the nugget.*

9

Probing the Response for Information

Once the interviewer has critically evaluated the response and found it inadequate in relevance, completeness, or validity, the interviewer must probe the response! The probe is the interviewer's tool for rectifying inadequacies in the initial response to a question. The essential difference between a probe and a question is that a question is planned in advance whereas a probe must be improvised depending on how the respondent answers the question.

Probes can assume many basic forms. They may be either nonverbal (like the raising of an eyebrow) or verbal. A probe may be either a question or a statement—as long as it has the effect of getting the respondent to clarify or elaborate on a previous response. Even though the probe must be improvised after evaluating a response, certain standard *forms* of probes are frequently used. Improvisation comes in supplying the *content* of the probe to fit the content of the previous response. Learning these standard forms will help the interviewer avoid panic when faced with an inadequate response.

The basic function of the probe, which is to rectify inadequacies in the previous response, can be broken into two parallel functions: (1) to point out to respondents what additional information is needed and (2) to motivate respondents to give that information. The refusal to accept the first superficial response to a question distinguishes what may be called depth interviewing from superficial interviewing. If information can be thought of as gold, then broad questions stake out the claim and reveal the easy gold lying about the surface, but probes dig deeper to track the vein and extract the nuggets.

In learning to probe effectively, you must first avoid some of the errors commonly found in neophytes' interviews. Let's review these common pitfalls before going on to describe the tools and tactics used to avoid them.

COMMON ERRORS IN PROBING

Failure to See the Need to Probe

The interviewer may fail to see the need to probe either because a response is accepted as adequate when it is not, or because a potentially relevant response is mistakenly rejected as completely irrelevant and not worthy of probing.

In the uncritical acceptance of an inadequate response, the interviewer may simply be overwhelmed by the speed of delivery and the great volume of information supplied by a loquacious respondent. It is difficult to evaluate a lot of information critically and quickly. Often the interviewer may be so relieved by the "good rapport" with the respondent, and so grateful for the quantity of information, that he or she becomes uncritical of the quality of the information. Another reason for uncritical acceptance is that the interviewer is simply no match for the skillfully evasive and distracting manner of the respondent.

On the other hand, the interviewer may mistakenly reject a response as completely irrelevant and therefore unworthy of probing because he or she does not see the *potential* connection with relevant information. A respondent who begins the answer to a question with an indirect approach will get to relevant points if encouraged to continue. Also, the verbal response may be irrelevant, but the nonverbal cues may hint at some potential relevance worthy of probing. The interviewer should not fail to probe because he or she fears that the particular probe might not be successful. There is always a chance to probe again if the first attempt does not get results.

Probing Too Much

If the interviewer probes too quickly or too often, the probing tends to interrupt the respondent's free-association pattern; this creates more dependence on specific, detailed questions from the interviewer. To interrupt the respondent psychologically, it is not necessary to begin speaking before the respondent is finished, so that both interviewer and respondent are speaking at once. You can also interrupt by speaking the moment the respondent finishes a sentence or pauses mid-sentence to think. The only way to be sure you are not interrupting the respondent with a probe is to wait until the respondent has indicated, verbally or nonverbally, that he or she is expecting the interviewer to speak. Generally, interviewers should allow about two seconds of silence before venturing a probe. The failure to wait for an indication of turn relinquishing from the respondent is one of the most common mistakes of neophyte interviewers.

Rapid-fire probing may have several negative effects. It may fail to establish a thoughtful pace, and it may make it more difficult for respondents to recall material according to their own natural free-association patterns. It can also suggest that the interviewer is not pleased with the respondent's performance or efficiency in giving answers, which can threaten the respondent's ego. Too many probes tend to make respondents more cautious and dependent on the interviewer for guidance and to shorten their answers to "yes" or "no."

To encourage depth of response, we need to let the respondent move at his or her own pace. A liberal use of silent probes by the interviewer encourages more thoughtful responses and also gives the interviewer more time to formulate effective probes. These warnings against probing too quickly do not mean that the interviewer should *never* intentionally interrupt a respondent, but they are intended to point out that the typical error of the neophyte is to probe too soon and unintentionally to interrupt the respondent's trend of thought.

Using Too Much Topic Control

The term *topic control* refers to the degree to which the interviewer's probe controls the topic of discussion by changing the central focus or by contracting or expanding the boundaries of the topic. The following example illustrates minimum, medium, and maximum degrees of topic control in probing the same response:

> *R-16:*   The first time my husband threatened to hit me I didn't take him seriously. And the next time he threatened I made the mistake of laughing at him. That is when all hell broke loose!

Minimal topic-control probes:
   1. Three seconds of silence while looking expectant.
   2. Really? Wow!

Medium topic-control probes:
   1. What happened then?
   2. What do you mean by "all hell broke loose?"

Maximum topic-control probes:
   1. Are you children still living with you?
   2. When did you file for divorce?

In addition to these three degrees of topic control, there are finer gradations which will be described later in this chapter.

The art of interviewing involves skill in observing when the respondent should be given complete freedom from topic control and when strong topic control is needed. The neophyte usually errs in the direction of using too much topic control in interviews that require more than simple, superficial answers.

Biasing the Response

Biasing the response can be anything the interviewer does or says that tends to make the response less true than it could be. Through biasing, the interviewer contributes to the invalidity of the response. There are two general ways the interviewer's probe can bias the response: First, the probe can communicate that the interviewer desires or *expects* a certain answer. Second, the probe can *suggest* one possible answer more forcefully than another. These expectations and suggestions may be communicated either verbally or nonverbally.

The probe that tends to bias the response is called a *loaded*, or *leading*, probe. In general, this form of probe should be avoided, but there are rare situations in which the loaded question is more likely to obtain truth than is an unloaded or neutral question. The conditions for the fruitful use of intentionally loaded questions were given Chapter 3.

The interviewer's use of leading questions may be intentional or unintentional, conscious or unconscious. Most unskilled interviewers use leading questions unintentionally, often motivated by unconscious biases. There are many ways to load a question and most of them take subtle, not obvious, forms. In many cases not even the respondent is aware that the question is loaded.

Nonverbally Loading the Probe.   The tone of voice in which the question is put can have a biasing effect on the response. For example, a simple encouragement probe like "really" can be said to express pure amazement or skeptical disbelief depending on the tone of voice. A longer probe like "What do you think of that idea?" can be said in a tone that conveys the feeling that the interviewer thinks it is a stupid idea or in a tone that suggests the interviewer is genuinely interested in getting the respondent's personal point of view on the issue.

Verbally Loading the Probe.   Ways of unintentionally loading a question by the way it is worded are described in Chapter 3 on formulating motivating questions (in the section about avoiding unintentionally loading questions). Recall that questions can be loaded by using emotionally loaded words, by suggesting one side of a two-sided issue, by suggesting only one answer of several possible answers, and by including a hidden argument for a particular answer.

It is easier to avoid the unintentional loading of preplanned questions than of improvised probes. In the first case, the interviewer has time for deliberate thought and for discussion with others to obtain their judgments. In the best planned interview schedules and questionnaires, time is allowed to field-test the questions for bias. In using probes, however, the interviewer has no time to deliberate and is free to invent probes on the spot. The opportunity for bias to creep in is much greater when interviewers are probing. A corollary to this statement is that interviews on topics that require more extensive probing must be done by skilled interviewers who have a desire to avoid bias.

To summarize, the four most common errors in probing are the failure to recognize the need to probe, interrupting the respondent's trend of thought, using too much topical control, and loading the probe. In the next sections we will present forms of probes that avoid biasing the response. Becoming skilled in the use of these forms will allow you to avoid the most common errors of probing.

TOOLS FOR PROBING

Probes can be classified according to three dimensions: their degree of topic control, their content focus, and their form. All types of probes are useful in getting beyond the initial superficial response to obtain greater depth in terms of relevance, completeness, and validity.

Degree of Topic Control

The term *topic control* refers to the degree to which the interviewer's probe controls the direction of the conversation. The probe can control by changing the focus of the topic, by contracting the topic, or by expanding it. Let us begin by defining and illustrating the probes with least topic control and progress to those with greatest control.

Active Silence. The silent probe is as close to zero topic control as we can get. By remaining silent at the end of a respondent's sentence, the interviewer in effect invites the respondent to continue talking without exercising any control over the direction of the conversation. The silent probe allows the respondent to proceed in whatever direction is most interesting or meaningful. It avoids changing, expanding, or contracting the topic of discussion, and it certainly avoids biasing the response. For these reasons, it is a highly desirable probing technique, but in circumstances where the respondent needs and wants guidance, it is inappropriate.

The interviewer must learn to distinguish between the "permissive pause" and the "embarrassing silence." To avoid the extremes of too little or too much silence, the interviewer must carefully observe the reactions of the respondent during the silence to determine whether he or she is trying to recall needed information or is emitting turn-yielding signals. In the latter case, the respondent would feel pressured or abandoned by continued silence.

Most beginning interviewers err in the direction of using too little silence. As long as silent probes continue to obtain relevant information, they should be used. The silent probe neatly avoids three of the most common errors: interrupting the respondent, using too much topic control, and loading the question.

In addition to avoiding these common errors, the silent probe has some other virtues. First, it slows down the pace and helps to create a thoughtful atmosphere—as long as the interviewer's nonverbal behavior during the silence expresses sympathetic interest. This gives the respondent both the time and the incentive to associate freely and give more valid responses than could be produced under the pressure of time. A second advantage of the silent probe is that it allows the interviewer time to formulate a verbal probe to be used later. A little silence can often save the interviewer from doing something foolish.

Despite all of the advantages of the silent probe, some neophytes rarely use it; they seem to fear or distrust any silence and feel that their job is to goad the respondent. This is unfortunate, because often two or three seconds of silence may be required to avoid unwittingly interrupting the respondent. With practice, the interviewer learns to trust the silent probe and to reap its advantages.

Encouragement.   The probe of encouragement includes all words, non-verbal noises, and gestures that indicate the interviewer is listening, accepts what has been said, and wishes the respondent to continue speaking without in any way specifying *what* the respondent should talk about. Some examples are: "uh-huh," "really," "I see," "wow," "interesting," "fascinating," a nod of the head, or an expectant facial expression. The encouragement probe has distinct advantages. First, it shows that the interviewer is listening and is interested. Second, it does this without interfering with the respondent's trend of thought. It allows the respondent to follow his or her own paths of free association, which facilitates more accurate recall and increases the validity of the response. Third, it avoids the common error of using loaded probes and obtains responses unbiased by the interviewer's questioning. Fourth, the encouragement probe, like the silent probe, allows time for the interviewer to decide whether more direct probing is needed and to formulate a more specific probe.

The silent probe and the encouragement probe both motivate the respondent to continue without interrupting the free-association flow and without biasing the response, and they both give the interviewer time to formulate more direct probes. These two forms of neutral probes will go a long way in eliciting relevant and valid information. Most interviewers should use them more and interrupt the respondent less.

There always comes a time in the interview when these completely neutral probes allow the respondent to wander too far from the objectives of the interview. Sooner or later the interviewer will have to use probes with stronger topic control to keep the interview on track and prevent it from becoming a string of rambling associations with no relevance to the purposes of the interview.

The interviewer should not, however, always intervene with a direct probe the moment the respondent has given irrelevant information. In the interest of motivating the respondent and allowing more free association, often the interviewer must tolerate a considerable amount of irrelevancy. For example, when interviewing the mother of a child killed in an accident, a police officer should not be so narrowly interested in "the facts" of how the accident happened that he or she would not tolerate the weeping mother's account of what the child was wearing and why.

Interviewing objectives and situations vary tremendously in the amount of irrelevant ramblings that need to be tolerated in order to support the respondent's motivation and to obtain the most valid information. In some cases, allowing the respondent to deviate momentarily elicits more relevant details in less time than does keeping the respondent on track with dozens of specific questions. In other cases, tolerating a lot of irrelevancies does not improve the quality of the data and wastes a lot of time. For example, a census-taker who needs to know the age, sex, race, marital status, and income of a respondent does not need to tolerate rambling success stories.

When we reach the point where silence and encouragement are not enough, we must move on to a higher degree of topic control.

Immediate Elaboration. A probe of immediate elaboration is one that asks the respondent to tell the interviewer more about the topic of the immediately preceding response. This form of probe exercises more topic control than the silent or encouragement probes which do not preclude the respondent's going on to a new topic or back to an old topic. The immediate elaboration probe does not allow such freedom. But it does *not* go so far as to point out anything in particular that the interviewer wants to know about what the respondent has just said. The probe is accomplished with such phrases as "Then?" "Tell me more!" "Would you like to tell me more about that?" "What else could you tell me about that?" "Could you spell that out a little more?" "Would you please elaborate on that?"

Of course, the immediate elaboration probe can be used only when the preceding response was in relevant or near-relevant territory. The immediate elaboration may then confirm or refute the relevance of the response, contribute to the completeness of the response, or verify the validity of the response.

The immediate elaboration probe, like the silence and encouragement probes, still allows some free association without biasing the response in any way. It has the added advantage that it controls the topic by restricting it to the immediately preceding response when it is potentially relevant.

Even though the interviewer hopes the respondent will elaborate or clarify certain specific points in response to an immediate elaboration probe, this does not always happen. When it doesn't, the interviewer can then designate precisely *what* he or she wants to know about a particular point in the preceding response. A little more topic control might be called for in the form of an immediate clarification probe.

Immediate Clarification. The immediate clarification probe not only asks for more information on the topic under discussion, it specifies the kind of information needed. A request for clarification may take two general forms. First, the interviewer might request that the respondent give more detail on some particular portion of the time period covered in the previous response. For example, in a domestic violence case the interviewer might ask, "What happened between the time he hit you and the time you called the police?" Second, the interviewer might probe for more detailed information on some specific aspect of an event or situation. For example, the interviewer might try to elicit concreteness by probing the who, what, when, where, why, and how dimensions: "What were you arguing about?" "What did he hit you with?" "What room were you in when he hit you?"

Retrospective Elaboration.   In the case of retrospective elaboration, the probe has the same intent we described in the immediate elaboration probe, that is, getting the respondent to elaborate on something he or she has already said. The only difference is that the retrospective elaboration probe asks the respondent to elaborate on something said *earlier* in the interview, not in the immediately preceding response. Since this is elaboration rather than clarification, the probe specifies what the interviewer wants to know more about, but it does not specify what the interviewer wants to know about it. Here are two examples: "A while ago you said that your mother didn't want you to go out with girls when you were fifteen years old. Could you tell me more about that?" "Let's go back to the point where you had the argument with Mr. Chomsky; tell me more about that!"

The retrospective elaboration probe may be used when the interviewer has intentionally postponed an immediate elaboration probe in order not to interfere with the momentum of the free-association pattern. Another reason to postpone a probe is to avoid an ego-threatening situation for the respondent; so the interviewer waits hoping the information will come out spontaneously later in a different context where the threatening nature of the point is not so apparent. The interviewer might have to probe later for the point in a new context without referring to the original context.

Another reason for using the retrospective probe is that in the context of the later part of the interview, certain things said earlier now become significant. For example, there may be an apparent contradiction between what the respondent just said and something he or she said earlier. To test the validity of the contradictory statements, the interviewer might ask the respondent to elaborate or clarify the earlier response.

In exploratory interviews where a topic is new to the interviewer, the number of retrospective probes needed may be extremely large because the interviewer cannot recognize the significance and importance of certain points when they are first mentioned. One way to handle this situation is to do a second interview *after* carefully analyzing the first interview and planning the questions and probes for the follow-up interview.

Retrospective Clarification.   The probe of retrospective clarification has the same intent as the one of immediate clarification except that it asks the respondent to supply specific clarifying details about an *earlier* response, not the immediately preceding one. For example, "You said earlier the pusher gave you a free sample of the stuff. Was that crack?" To give another example, "You said that you didn't like the atmosphere in the neighborhood where the night school is located. Do you mean that you are afraid of walking there alone at night?"

Often, when there is reason to doubt the relevance, completeness, or validity of an earlier response, the interviewer may first try a retrospective *elaboration* probe if there are several specific points to be probed. Then the interviewer can use *clarification* probes for the points that remain untouched. If there is only one detail that needs clarifying, it would be a waste of time to use the elaboration probe.

Even if the interview is being tape-recorded, the interviewer should be taking probe notes consisting of words and phrases from the response that need to be elaborated or clarified. Often the probe notes on one response will contain several things to be probed either *immediately* (before going on to another question) or *retrospectively* (after going on to other questions). Whether to probe immediately or retrospectively depends on the interviewer's judgment about the importance of not interrupting the momentum and free-association process at that moment. If immediate probing will not harm the respondent's motivation or thought process, it is better to probe the response immediately. This keeps information organized chronologically according to question and makes information easier to analyze, code, or summarize.

Mutation.   When the interviewer is satisfied that a response to a basic question is relevant, complete, and valid, he or she is free to go to a new *planned* question or to formulate a new question that has been *generated* in the interview.[1]

In the context of degree of topic control, both the planned and the generated question are considered *mutations* because they break with anything that has been discussed previously in the interview. They cut off the momentum and free-association process of the previous topic by introducing a new one.

Sometimes the skillful interviewer can soften the abruptness of the change of topic by using a transition statement that supplies a mental bridge between the old topic and the new topic in the context of the overall purpose of the interview. For example:

> You have given me a detailed picture of the emotional relationships between all members of your family. But in order to understand the sources of some of this stress, we need to understand the financial situation too. Were both you and your husband employed at the time the tension began to build up?

Mutation probes are necessary if an interview is to move ahead. However, the skillful interviewer usually uses them only after he or she has finished probing for a relevant, complete, and valid response to the previous main question. The neophyte interviewer tends to use a large proportion of mutation probes; therefore, the interview is usually shorter, more superficial, less complete, and less valid than one done by a skilled interviewer using fewer mutation probes.

Content: Probing Aspects of the Respondent's Experience

An important dimension we must be aware of in probing for relevance, completeness, or validity—whether at the elaboration level or the clarification level—is the aspect of the respondent's experience on which we want to focus. The term *aspect of experience* is used most broadly to include overt or objective action and two covert or subjective types of activity: cognitive (thinking) and affective (feeling). The following probes are concrete examples of these three levels:

- Overt action: "What did you *do* when the police called and said your son was in the hospital?"
- Cognitive activity: "What did you first *think* might have happened to your son?"
- Affective activity: "How did you *feel* when you answered the phone and found it was the police?"

Whether one, two, or all three aspects of the respondent's experience are relevant depends on the objectives of the particular interview. The important thing in learning to interview is to be sure you have covered the *relevant* levels for the sake of *completeness* and to look for apparent dissonances between one level and another for the sake of checking *validity*. Sometimes apparent dissonances between external events and subjective feelings may, with further probing, prove to be due to differences between the interviewer's and the respondent's definitions of a word. For example:

> *R:* The police called and told me my son was in the hospital. I knew that something had happened to him in the tornado when our house blew away while I was away at work. I didn't get *excited* none. I just jumped in the car and drove to the hospital.
>
> *I:* You say you didn't get excited even though your son was taken to the hospital? Did they say he wasn't hurt much?
>
> *R:* Oh no, they said he was hurt bad and was still unconscious. But as I say, I didn't get *excited* and hysterical and run around wringing my hands and screaming like a lot of people would do. I was *scared* he wouldn't live and wanted to be there when he came to himself. I drove about seventy miles an hour on these White County roads high-tailing it to the hospital.

Many other similar responses collected in 500 interviews with disaster victims in a rural county in Arkansas indicated that the rural male culture made an important distinction between the words *excited* and *scared*. Getting excited meant responding irrationally to a threat and was attributed to females. Anyone who is not a fool is scared in the face of a serious threat, but a person should stay in control and do something rational about the situation. When a man was found to get "excited," it was simply explained that he was "acting like a woman"; if a woman did something rational in the face of a threat, she was "acting like a man."

The interviewer's first reaction to a man saying he "didn't get excited" was to assume that he was lying and did not want to admit fear. But this interpretation was quickly proven incorrect because the men were very ready to admit they were scared in the tornado.

The dimension of overt action applies not only to the actions of the respondent but also to any person, group, or event as long as it deals with some external activity that could be seen, heard, or felt by the respondent. This external dimension can be obtained by using a probe that in no way specifies any actor as the focus; for example, "What *happened* when the tornado hit the ice house and filling station?"

Interviewers discover that the response often does not deal with the same aspect of experience as the probe. If you ask what respondents *did* in a situation where they either did nothing or felt ashamed of what they did, often their response will be in terms of what they *thought* or how they *felt*. Frequently, it is not necessary to ask how people felt if they felt strongly about something. Any question about what they *did* will usually bring responses at the feeling level.

From the standpoint of skills, the interviewer should (1) know which level of information is needed and (2) listen carefully and not be surprised if the question is at one level and the answer at another. In this case, the persistent interviewer probes again. For example:

> You have told me that you felt confused and paralyzed when the tornado struck and you saw the school bus flying through the air bottom-side-up and dropping kids out the windows. That must have been a horrible sight. What were you actually *doing* at this point?"

Several probes later the interviewer discovered that the respondent could not believe what she was actually seeing and assumed that she had gone insane. What she did was lay down on the couch, which was then in the middle of the street, and wait for someone to come and take her to the mental hospital.

Interviewers should not make the common mistake of assuming that objective "facts" are easier for the respondent to talk about than his or her own subjective thoughts, assumptions, or feelings. All three aspects of the respondent's experience are easy to obtain under some circumstances and difficult under others. The interviewer's task is to know what aspects are needed, which have been obtained, and which need to be probed.

Principles of Good Probing

There are three basic principles that interviewers should keep in mind and ultimately build into their probing reflexes. These principles, which help guide the probing process, are (1) to balance freedom and control, (2) to avoid loading the probe, and (3) to use the respondent's own words in referring to a previous response.

Balance Freedom and Control. Too much topic control tends to interrupt the respondent's flow of free associations and reduce the dialogue to a series of questions and answers in which the questions get longer and more specific while the answers get shorter and less spontaneous. Too little topic control, while supplying freedom of association and choice of topic, may produce too many rambling irrelevancies. In this case, the interview deteriorates into unguided expressiveness with a minuscule amount of relevant material buried in a mound of irrelevancies. The result is time wasted by the respondent, the interviewer, and the people who have to transcribe, code, and analyze the data. Often it is necessary for the interviewer to knowingly accept irrelevancies in order to show interest in the respondent and to avoid interrupting the free-association process. The skilled interviewer maintains a balance between too much freedom and too much control. This balance point depends on the nature of the interview topic and the needs of the respondent.

Avoid Loaded Probes.   To avoid loaded probes, it is helpful to use neutral, low topic-control probes such as silence and encouragement whenever possible before using high topic-control probes. Also, in wording the probe the interviewer should avoid emotionally loaded words, answer categories that are restricting, and argumentative probes. All three types of bias and suggested corrections are illustrated in the following example.

Assume that you are the personnel manager from the national office of a large company, and you are called in to analyze the conflict between workers and management in a regional office. You want to know the attitudes and assumptions of the workers because these affect their interaction with management. You are also interested in how workers interpret the actions and motivations of the managers.

Figure 9.1 gives one of the answers given by the respondent followed by six possible loaded probes with six suggested probes that would serve the purpose better. The first two probes are loaded by using emotionally loaded words, the second pair is loaded by supplying restricting answer categories, and the third pair is loaded by including an argument for a certain answer within the probe itself.

In every case, the alternative probes in the column on the right are more neutral or less loaded than those on the left. The skilled interviewer learns to avoid all of the ways of loading the question. In ordinary sociable conversation loaded probes or questions probably outnumber the unloaded ones. Most sociable conversation, however, has the function of giving participants an opportunity to express their own points of view rather than to conscientiously seek another person's point of view.

Use the Respondent's Own Words.   Whenever the interviewer asks for elaboration or clarification of any idea already expressed by the respondent, that idea should be referred to by using the exact words of the respondent. Often a respondent will not recognize the idea if the same words are not used. The words should act as a cue for the respondent to pick up where he or she left off and continue the free-association process. For example:

> *R:* That seemed like it would be a cool thing to do at the time when he said "this little blue pill will help you out of your depression and put you on a high," so I took the capsule.
> *I:* In what way did you think it would be *a cool thing to do*?

For a number of reasons the interviewer's response is much better than paraphrasing by saying, for example, "a good thing to do." Use of the word *cool* not only makes it easy for the respondent to recognize the idea the interviewer

Figure 9.1   Respondent's answer with six loaded probes and alternatives

> *R:*   Every time the boss tells me about some mistake I have made or how I could improve my performance, she takes me into her office to talk. That doesn't set well with me.
>
> | Six Ways of Probing Incorrectly | Six Better Ways of Probing |
> |---|---|
> | *Emotionally loaded words* | *Unloaded words* |
> | 1. Why does it make you *angry?* | 1. How does it make you feel? |
> | 2. How do you think the boss should go about improving the *efficiency* of the plant? | 2. What do you feel the boss is trying to accomplish by this? |
> | *Restrictive response categories* | *Nonrestrictive* |
> | 3. Are the kinds of mistakes she talks about problems of *safety* or *efficiency?* | 3. Give me an example of the kinds of things she mentions. |
> | 4. Does she take you to her office to get more *privacy?* | 4. Why does she take you into her office to talk? |
> | *Argumentative probes* | *Nonargumentative* |
> | 5. That's better than correcting you in front of other employees, isn't it? | 5. How do you feel about going to her office to talk? |
> | 6. Don't you feel that it benefits the employees to make the plant more competitive? | 6. Why do you feel the boss does this sort of thing? |

wants clarified, but also shows that the interviewer has been listening accurately, is interested, and accepts the respondent's own language. In general, using the respondent's own words when asking for elaboration or clarification will be more productive than using synonyms.

To this point we have dealt with three general principles to follow in probing: balance the amount of topic control, avoid the use of loaded probes, and use the respondent's own words. The kinds of probes described thus far are the workhorses of the information-gathering process and might include 75 to 95 percent of the probes in many types of interviews. Now we will look at some additional specific forms of probes that are used in professional settings.

Special Forms of Probes

Some of the most useful special forms of probes are recapitulation, reflection, paraphrase, interpretation, and confrontation. Let us examine the functions of each in facilitating the communication process.

Recapitulating.   To recapitulate means to go back to the beginning of the interview. In terms of topic control, the recapitulation probe is a special form of the retrospective elaboration probe. It has proved most useful in my experience in interviews where the respondent has had a highly emotional experience and the interviewer wants to reconstruct a detailed account of the event. Such is the case in interviews with victims or witnesses of natural disasters, accidents, murders, or domestic violence as well as interviews obtaining life histories.

Whether the "story" to be elicited from the respondent covers a one-hour crisis or a five-year life history, the recapitulation probe skillfully used can be highly productive. It takes advantage of two general tendencies in respondents who are telling their story. First, people want to tell their story of an important event in chronological order. They do not want to be interrupted in the middle or at the end of each sentence with a probe for some factual detail which to them may seem insignificant. Second, respondents tend to go through their story the first time leaving out much detail. The first telling of the story stimulates the recall of more detail; but respondents do not report it all as they go along. If the respondent is given a second chance to tell the story from the beginning, he or she will usually go through the same time period and add a wealth of *new detail*.

The recapitulation probe takes advantage of these two natural tendencies and yields three positive results. First, it saves the interviewer from having to use dozens of specific elaboration and clarification probes; thus it makes the interview more efficient. Second, it avoids interrupting the natural flow of the recall process and so results in more valid information. A concrete detail that is recalled in the natural flow of free association is less likely to be contrived than a detail that must be given, ready or not, to respond to the interviewer's probe. Third, the recapitulation probe reduces the amount of speaking by the interviewer and increases the proportion of listening time. This sympathetic listening is a strong motivating factor for the respondent who is in need of a sympathetic ear.

To use the recapitulation probe skillfully, the interviewer must make it clear, without asking the same specific question again, that he or she wants the respondent to begin at the beginning of the *time period* covered by the interview. It is also important to note that even though the interviewer may intend for the respondent to cover the same time period again, at a different level of detail, the recapitulation probe does *not* directly ask the respondent to cover the *whole* period again. Such a request would probably be disheartening for the respondent who does not realize that the process will actually yield much new information. So instead of asking to "cover the whole time period again," the interviewer merely probes a specific word or phrase quoted from the first response and lets the respondent go on from there.

For example, assume that a fire investigator is interviewing someone who narrowly escaped from a hotel fire in which several people lost their lives. The investigator wants to know the cause and who or what was to blame, so he or she must reconstruct a detailed chronological account from the information received from many participants and witnesses.

> *I-1:*   Just tell me in your own words what happened, beginning with when you first realized that there was a fire. How did you first know there was a fire?
>
> *R-1:*   My wife and I were asleep when this foghorn-like noise started blasting away and I heard people talking in the hall. I called the desk and no one answered; then someone in the hall said that the sound was the fire alarm. Then someone called my room from the desk and said that this was a false alarm and there was nothing to worry about.

The next half hour of the interview reveals that the phone call about the false alarm was incorrect. The fire had started in the kitchen, and smoke was coming up through air ducts and people were being overcome by smoke inhalation. The respondent's story continues to the point the fire department arrived and people were rescued and taken to the hospital or to other hotels for the rest of the night. But much relevant detail on the early phase of the crisis is missing, so the interviewer uses the following recapitulation probe.

> *I-67:*   Back at the beginning you said that you and your wife were asleep when you heard that foghorn-like noise. What was the first thing you did when you woke up?
>
> *R-67:*   My wife was poking me and saying, "What's that?" I said, "Maybe it's an emergency vehicle" and was putting on my shoes when another blast came and it was clear that it was from the hall or somewhere inside the building. Then I thought "fire," so I went to the door to the hall and felt to see if it was hot, but it wasn't so I opened the door and people were in pajamas and bathrobes in the hall.
>
> *I-68:*   What was your wife doing while you were doing this?

Note that R-1 and R-67 do not overlap in content; although they are covering the same time period, new detail is given in R-67. Then in I-68 the interviewer starts leading the respondent through the whole crisis period for the third time, which is probably not advisable.

In my experience the second time through the time period often yields a wealth of additional detail with a minimum of probing. Usually there is not enough missing detail to make a second recapitulation probe fruitful because the few remaining details can be obtained quickly by a more direct approach.

Reflecting and Accepting Feelings.   To reflect and accept the respondent's feelings, a probe can take different forms. It may be a single word, a phrase, a whole question, or a question prefaced by a contextual statement. The following example illustrates different forms of reflecting probes to the same response. The interviewer is trying to discover why a welfare mother has dropped out of night school.

R: I don't have a car to get to night school, so I take the bus. The nearest bus stop is about two blocks from the entrance of the school. At ten o'clock at night that is a lonely walk from the school to the bus stop. It seems that everyone I know at school has a car or comes with someone who has a car, but they don't feel too good about that parking lot either.

I-1:   A lonely walk?

OR

I-2:   Can you tell me more about what you mean by "a lonely walk?"

OR

I-3:   You mentioned that it is a lonely walk from the school to the bus station at ten o'clock at night. Could you tell me a little more about that?

The form in I-3 would be used if the interviewer wanted a *retrospective* probe referring to an *earlier* part of the interview. For an *immediate* elaboration probe, either I-1 or I-2 would suffice.

The interviewer could have probed for many other types of specific relevant detail such as: "Were the streets dark?" "Is anyone else on the street or at the bus stop?" "What kinds of people are around at ten o'clock at night?" Any or all of these might obtain a clearer picture of what the respondent does not like about the area. The feeling-focused question is better, however, because it is less restricting. It does not assume that the lack of street lights or the type of people are the salient factors; it leaves the respondent free to say what is important to her.

Another advantage of the feeling-focused probe is that it motivates the respondent to talk by showing that the interviewer is a sympathetic listener who is interested in what is important to the respondent. The result is information produced efficiently with a minimum of specific factual probes by the interviewer.

Of course there are types of interviews in which the most relevant information does not come attached to the respondent's feelings. This may be because the feelings are irrelevant or because there is nothing emotionally charged about the topic of the interview. Even in situations where feelings are irrelevant, if there are strong feelings, the interviewer will do well to recognize these feelings, accept them as valid, and show some sympathetic understanding. These actions will go a long way in motivating the respondent to tolerate many questions that are not important to him or her.

In most cases *acceptance* of the respondent's feelings is not communicated verbally. The interviewer does not usually say, for example, "I understand how you felt" or "I would be lonely too!" Instead, the interviewer can accept or reject the respondent's feelings by the tone of voice used. This nonverbal expression is most important; if the interviewer verbally accepts the respondent's feelings while feeling quite the opposite, the respondent will correctly sense this insincerity.

There is one form of the feeling-reflecting probe that is rarely productive. It might be called the "echo probe" because the interviewer merely repeats an emotionally laden word or phrase—not as a question but as a *statement*. For example, in the preceding example, the interviewer could say, "The walk to the bus station is lonely!" Because the interviewer has not implied a question in his or her tone of voice, the respondent may not feel that the interviewer wants to know anything more about the subject. In this case, the respondent may say nothing, nod the head, or say "right." Of course if the experience is emotionally charged, the respondent may insist on talking more about it even if the interviewer has not clearly shown an interest.

Showing sympathetic interest in the respondent's feelings almost always motivates the respondent and improves rapport, and with many interview topics it may be the quickest and most efficient way to obtain spontaneous, valid information. Despite all the advantages of the reflective probe, the interviewer must beware of using it in a mechanical way. There are situations where it is not appropriate: when there are no salient feelings associated with the topic, when the same feeling has already been probed once, or when the nature and meaning of the feeling is clear without probing.

Paraphrasing a Response.   A paraphrase is a verbal statement by the interviewer with meaning that is equivalent to a statement made by the respondent. The paraphrase is usually shorter than the original statement. For example:

> *R-2:*   My mother is ill, but for sixteen years she has been taking advantage of her illness to control me. Every time she feels I haven't been giving her enough attention she calls and sort of moans to me over the telephone.
>
> *I-3:*   So your mother for years has been using her illness to get what she wants out of you. Is that what you are saying?

The paraphrase, unlike the reflecting probe, does not pick out a key feeling (stated or implied) as a focus of elaboration or clarification. Instead, it encompasses the total original statement. In contrast, a reflecting probe for this same response might be, "So you *resent* this tactic?"

The paraphrase probe has several important functions. First, it motivates the interviewer, because to be able to paraphrase a response the interviewer must listen carefully. Second, it gives the respondent the opportunity to correct any miscommunication that has occurred. Perhaps the respondent did not say exactly what he or she meant, or maybe the interviewer did not hear accurately. Third, it can motivate the respondent, because it shows that the interviewer is listening and is interested in knowing exactly what the respondent means. The paraphrase often has a rapport-building affect regardless of whether the respondent agrees with the accuracy of the paraphrase. If the respondent does *not* agree, then the additional information given in the clarification or correction is useful.

In order to achieve its effect, the paraphrase must have two main parts which may occur in either order. The paraphrase *statement* encompasses the total area of the original statement, usually in a simplified form. In addition, a *question* invites the respondent to correct the accuracy of the paraphrase, and often it results in not only corrections but additions, clarifications, denials, or other types of information. The question may come before or after the statement and may take many forms such as: "Is this right?" "Do I have the story straight?" "Is that what you are saying?" "Am I hearing you correctly?"

A less frequently used form of the paraphrase is the *summary probe*. Instead of referring just to the immediately preceding response, the summary probe tries to paraphrase a whole section of the interview. In this case, the interviewer must be much more selective and must condense to a greater extent. The interviewer must also be sure to include the most salient points or the general pattern of the responses.

The summary statement should always be accompanied by a question that invites the respondent to correct, elaborate, explain, or deny. If an interview plan has distinctly separate sections, it is sometimes useful to use a summary probe at the end of each section. Often in the process of responding to a set of questions and probes, the respondent recalls forgotten details and gets a new overall perspective and awareness that cannot be expressed until the end of a section or of the whole interview. Some of the most useful material may be expressed in response to a summary probe.

Interpreting a Response.   The interpretation probe has an essential element that clearly distinguishes it from recapitulation, reflecting, and paraphrasing: It *adds* something to the respondent's statement. It may introduce a new *frame of reference* for classifying, analyzing, or judging the respondent's report. It may draw *logical conclusions* from the information given by the respondent. The interpretation probe is *not* an attempt to discover, clarify, or elaborate the respondent's point of view. It is quite the opposite; it is an opportunity for the interviewer to contribute his or her own analysis of the respondent's story. For example:

> *R:* I try to avoid riding on elevators, particularly when they are crowded. It isn't so bad if the alternative is an escalator, but I have walked up ten flights of stairs to avoid an elevator. Another thing I don't like is underground tunnels or even low ceilings in basements. I have dreams about being trapped in caves.
>
> *I:* It seems to me that you are afraid of closed-in places that most people don't mind.

The respondent is free to correct the interviewer's conclusion by showing instances when closed-in places are not viewed as threatening, or to say, "I guess that's true!" and go on to give other examples. In either case, the interviewer has achieved a clearer understanding of the respondent's problem.

The interpretation probe is probably used most in counseling and therapeutic interviewing. It may help the therapist to verify a *diagnosis* or it may help the respondent to obtain some *insight* into the nature of his or her problem. The interpretation probe helps to develop a therapeutic relationship by showing that even though the interviewer does not censure the respondent's behavior, the interviewer does sometimes have a different interpretation or explanation of that behavior. It also increases the interviewer's credibility in the eyes of the respondent by showing that the interviewer not only listens and sympathizes, but also sees more deeply into the problem and sees relationships between the respondent's assumptions, attitudes, and behaviors that the respondent has not noticed or could not verbalize.

The successful use of an interpretation probe depends on the skillful application of three basic rules.[2] First, the interviewer must wait until the client is ready to accept what is in effect a challenge to look frankly at his or her own behavior in a new light. Rarely is this readiness achieved in the first interview. Second, the interpretation should be based on the information furnished by the respondent rather than on biases, prejudices, or assumptions from the interviewer's own experiences or from a too-narrow theoretical framework. The third rule relates to the form of the probe. In the name of caution, honesty, and modesty, the probe should be couched in the form of a tentative hypothesis, beginning with a phrase such as: "It seems to be that you might...," "Perhaps," "I wonder if it could be that..." Also, the interpretation should be in a form that invites the respondent, either verbally or nonverbally, to correct, verify, modify, clarify, or amplify the interviewer's interpretation.

Confronting. A confrontation probe is usually a *statement* that deliberately points out confusions or discrepancies (contradictions and conflicts between the respondent's words, feelings, or actions) followed by a challenge to clarify these.

The confrontation probe can be used in a variety of professional settings ranging from psychotherapy to police interrogation. In the therapeutic interview, it helps clients see their own inconsistencies and explore ways of resolving them in order to change their behavior patterns.

Here is an example of the confrontation probe in the context of the therapeutic interview:

> R: I really don't mind having my mother-in-law live with us. She does some baby-sitting for us and even does a bit of housework now and then. She does bug my wife with being too demanding with the children, and having to have certain kinds of food, and complaining about how food is prepared. Of course these are often things her doctor advises. Also there are times when she assumes that we all want to see the same TV show. She has her own set in her bedroom but she likes to come out in the living room with us, but to see her own show.
>
> I: You say that you don't mind having your mother-in-law live with you, but on the other hand you do have a long list of grievances against her behavior. Do you really not mind her living with you?

The purpose of such a confrontation is to help clients recognize the reality of their feelings, even though these may not be socially applaudable. The acceptance of the real feeling can be a start in reanalyzing the situation and taking actions to correct it.

In the therapeutic interview the success of the confrontation tactic depends on several factors. The interviewer's tone of voice and other nonverbal cues should not indicate that the confrontation is an attack on the client as a person. It should be clear that it is an attempt to help the respondent get a deeper understanding of the situation. Also, the wording of the confrontation probe should clearly indicate the two elements that seem to be conflicting. A confrontation is more likely to be fruitful if it takes place after there has been time for a relationship of trust and rapport to develop between therapist and client.[3]

The use of the confrontation probe in police interrogation is different from its use in any of the helping professions where the respondent's presence is voluntary and the interviewer is trying to help the respondent. Also, in police interrogation if the suspect is consciously lying, it is difficult for him or her to make up a story that is internally consistent in detail and that conforms to objective reality. In such a case, the main function of the confrontation is to convince the suspect that it is useless to try to lie, so he or she might as well tell the truth. The interrogator may show that the suspect has given conflicting versions of events and in this way demonstrate that the attempt to fabricate a story is a failure. The interrogator may also point out an inconsistency between what the suspect says and what is already known from an independent source. Often the interrogator will ask the suspect for detailed information that is already known. If the respondent lies, the lie is pointed out and the truth is revealed. This shakes the respondent's confidence in his or her ability to lie successfully under these circumstances.

Here is an excerpt from the interrogation of a bank robbery suspect who is trying desperately to establish an alibi. After two hours of interrogation the interviewer confronts the suspect.

> *I:* So that's your story! You were driving around with your buddy on the east side of town while the bank was being robbed on the west side. But your story is full of holes. For example, you claim you drove *east* on Riverside to the Grant Tower and took an elevator to the observation deck and got a night view of the city. That is pure fiction because Riverside is one-way going *west* at that point and the observation deck was closed because of elevator problems. Also, we have your buddy in custody and his story about what you did is entirely different. Both of you are very bad at making up stories, so why don't you save a lot of time and tell the truth?

Under circumstances where the respondent is a captive and the interrogator apparently has limitless time to question the respondent, it is extremely difficult for the respondent to fabricate concrete detail without making a mistake.

SUMMARY

A probe is an improvised question or statement that follows the response to a preplanned question. Its purpose is to improve the relevance, completeness, or validity of the response by motivating the respondent to give additional related information.

Several probing errors are commonly made by neophyte interviewers:

1. Failing to probe because of failure to evaluate the response
2. Probing too frequently
3. Using too much topic control
4. Biasing the response by verbally or nonverbally loading the question

Seven types of probes are useful for the interviewer when topic control is necessary:

1. Active silence
2. Encouragement
3. Immediate elaboration
4. Immediate clarification
5. Retrospective elaboration
6. Retrospective clarification
7. Mutation

To probe effectively, interviewers must be aware of the aspect of the respondent's experience on which they wish to focus. Three levels of experience are possible: (1) overt action, (2) cognitive activity, and (3) affective activity. Interviewers must also recognize the three principles of good probing: (1) balance freedom and control, (2) avoid loading probes, and (3) use the respondent's own words.

In addition to the aforementioned probes, there are several special forms of probes:

1. Recapitulating
2. Reflecting and accepting feelings
3. Paraphrasing
4. Interpreting
5. Confronting

All of these tools for probing will become more meaningful, and the conditions for their use will become clearer, with the experience provided in the following exercises and subsequent interviewing.

NOTES

1. The first few interviews on new, unfamiliar topics may generate certain questions in addition to the planned questions. Often it is useful to add these to the schedule (questionnaire) for subsequent interviews.

2. For a more detailed treatment of interpretation see William H. Cormier and L. Sherilyn Cormier, *Interviewing Strategies for Helpers*, 2nd ed. (Monterey, Calif.: Brooks/Cole Publishing, 1985), 124–30.

3. For a more detailed analysis of the use of confrontation in the counseling interview, refer to William H. Cormier and L. Sherilyn Cormier, *Interviewing Strategies for Helpers*, 2nd ed. (Monterey, Calif.: Brooks/Cole Publishing, 1985), 114–24.

EXERCISE 9-A
DETECTING AND CORRECTING PROBING ERRORS

PURPOSE OF THE EXERCISE

In this exercise you play the role of *observer* of an interview in preparation for the role of *interviewer* in the next exercise. Here your task is to analyze critically an interview dialogue to detect and correct errors made by the interviewer.

Although the interviewer in the dialogue has certain positive attributes, he also makes some common errors in probing. Note that in the script the length of silences is indicated in parentheses; thus (2) stands for a two-second silence. Your task is to consider each probe by the interviewer and ask whether it commits a common error; if it does, suggest a specific probe that would avoid this error.

PROCEDURE

1. Carefully review the section called Interview Situation before reading the dialogue. Pay attention to both the setting of the interview and the objectives to be achieved by the reporter.
2. After a careful analysis of the dialogue, write a report with two parts: interviewer's strengths and detecting and correcting probing errors.
3. Share your report with a partner and discuss some of the outstanding differences in your two reports.
4. Bring your revised report to the class discussion.

DETAILS OF THE REPORT

1. Interviewer's strengths: Write no more than a sentence about each of the interviewer's questions, statements, or probes that you think demonstrate some positive skill or attribute of the interviewer. Just identify the probe, for example I-2, and say why it is good.

2. Detecting and correcting probing errors: For this purpose consider only probes I-3 through I-10. Look for common errors such as interrupting the respondent, changing the topic prematurely (too much topic control), using loaded or biased probes, and using questions or probes that are too broad or too narrow.

When suggesting each correction, assume that the interview up to that point has not been changed by any of your previous suggested corrections.

In each case where there is an error, give the probe number, and the nature of the error in a word, phrase, or sentence; then put in quotes your substitute probe which would correct the error. If there is nothing wrong with a probe except that it interrupts, then the correction is "Wait a couple of seconds to see what the respondent will say." Each correction should be done in the following format:

I-14 (a) This is a loaded question.
(b) "What did you do then?"

DISCUSSION WITH PARTNER

First, discuss points of difference in the first part of the report dealing with the interviewer's strengths. Try to understand each other's reasons for including or omitting a particular point.

Second, discuss the errors and corrections one at a time. Try to understand the extent to which you agree with your partner about *which* probes were in error, *what* was wrong with them, and *how* the error could be corrected. Try not to be defensive about the points at which you disagree, but try to reevaluate your own position in light of your partner's point of view. Where you feel it is justified, make corrections or additions in your initial report.

INTERVIEW SITUATION

A local motel-nightclub has just burned to the ground. Some of the motel guests were injured while escaping; many more nightclub patrons were injured and three died in the fire. The reporter from the local newspaper arrived on the scene after hearing the alarm over the CB scanner. He arrived only two minutes after the first fire engine and found the whole building in solid flames; parts had collapsed as if the building had been burning at least a half hour. Some of the cars in the parking lot nearest the building were aflame. Rumors were circulating about why it took so long for the fire department to arrive when the station is only three minutes away.

The reporter approaches one of the motel guests who is draped in a blanket, wearing slippers, and gazing at the fire in fascination.

The reporter's objectives are to get the facts about the fire such as where it was, when it started, what caused it, how much damage was caused, and who was to blame; the reporter is also to obtain human interest quotes from eyewitnesses, victims, the motel management, fire officials, and police officials.

THE SCRIPT

I-1:   Hello, I'm Jack Riley of the *Daily News*. Did all of your friends get out safely?

R-1:   Yes, we got out alive and with just a few scratches, but we left all of our baggage in there, and most of our clothes. (2)

I-2:   Is there anything I can do for you?

R-2:   Thanks, but we have already called some friends who are bringing some clothes and picking us up. We didn't have any change for the pay phone, but Arby's across the street let us use their business phone. Our car was too close to the building and caught fire and blew up. Lucky the insurance is paid up. (2)

I-3:   That must have been frightening! I'd like very much to get your story of what happened. When did you first realize something was wrong?

R-3:   We had just gone to bed and I was already asleep when my wife poked me and said, "I think there is something wrong. Listen!"

I-4:   What time was that?

R-4:   It was somewhere between 11:30 and midnight because we went to bed about 11:30 and told the desk we wanted a 7:30 wake-up call. I went to sleep pretty quick since I had been driving all day. (2)

I-5:   How did you get out? I know you were in a hurry since you left your baggage and clothes.

R-5:   We opened the door to the hall and saw that it was already full of smoke, so I shut that quickly and told Teresa that we would have to got out the window. That's when I was really glad we were on the ground floor.

I-6:   You were glad to be on the ground floor!

R-6:   Right! I'd hate to shinny down a rope made of sheets that was too short to reach the ground and Teresa wouldn't like it either, but she could do it if she had to. She kept her head through the whole thing. (2)

I-7:   But since you were on the ground floor you had no problem getting out the window and away from the building?

R-7:   Yeah. You could say that. (2)

I-8:   What did you do after you got out the window?

R-8:   We saw that the upper floor was on fire where it is attached to the nightclub, and people were shouting and running. Since we came out on the backside of the building we were near the parking lot, and I thought of our car so started walking toward the car, then realized we had left it near the part of the building that was on fire. As we got closer we could see that some of the cars were on fire. I was going to make a dash for mine to get it out of there but then I realized I didn't have the keys. I had left them in the room. Then I thought maybe we could push it away from the burning building, but it was locked and the brake was on and it was so hot near the fire that I couldn't try to break into the car. So we decided to get away from there. Something told me to get out quick, which was a good thing because as soon as we were about where we are now, a car two spaces away from mine blew up and flames shot about thirty feet into the air and then the next car caught fire. Ours blew up and is all burned up by now! (2)

I-9: Let's go back to when your wife said, "I think there is something wrong. Listen!" Did you hear sirens?

R-9: No, we didn't hear any sirens until after we had gotten out and had tried to save the car. Just after we ran away from where the car was we heard a siren, but it turned out to be a police car instead of a fire engine which is what we needed. (2)

I-10: Why did the management wait so long to call the fire department?

R-10: I have no idea. Maybe the person at the desk was sleeping on the job.

I-11: Thank you very much for your story. Could I have your name and telephone number in case we do a follow-up story?

R-11: Sure. Robert and Teresa Jansen. 878-0222.

I-12: Thanks again. I hope your friends get here soon!

Exercise 9-B
PROBING PRACTICE

OBJECTIVES

This role-playing exercise is designed to give you the feel of using a wider range of topic control than you would ordinarily use in sociable conversation, but at the same time to relieve you of the responsibility of selecting the right level of topic control at the right time as you would in a real interview. Since it is a role-playing game, and your partner is in the game with you, there is no need to worry about motivating the respondent to answer.

Although the level of topic control to be used is arbitrarily specified in advance, you still are responsible for using a probe that makes sense in view of the objectives of the interview and in the context of what has been said by the respondent to that point in the interview.

PROCEDURE

1. Choose a partner for the role-play.
2. You and your partner select different topics on which you would like to be interviewed. You may either select a topic from the list in this exercise or invent one of your own.
3. Plan a five-minute interview on the topic your partner has chosen. The plan should include four elements in the following sequence:
   a. Ask a broad opening question. Plan the wording to invite unrestricted comment.
   b. Use low topic-control probes to encourage the respondent to elaborate on the response to the opening question. These probes should be of the three lowest degrees of topic control: silence, encouragement, and immediate elaboration.
   c. After two or three minutes of low topic-control probes, abruptly change your style to high topic-control using only retrospective clarifications and mutations. Use these for one or two minutes. Of course the retrospective clarifications cannot be worded in advance since they need to refer to a specific word or phrase used earlier by your respondent. How-

ever, the mutations can be planned by simply making a list of points you want to cover in the interview and then using any that the respondent has not already talked about up to that point in the interview.

    d. End the interview by intentionally using a strongly loaded question. A couple of tentative loaded questions can be planned in advance; use whichever one seems to fit best at that point in the interview. Even if the respondent has already touched on the point of the question, you can still use the loaded question you planned, or you can improvise a loaded question on the spot.

4. Do the first role-play interview for five minutes as timed by the interviewer. The respondent should respond as spontaneously and frankly as possible.
5. Reverse roles and do the second interview on the new topic.
6. Discuss the two role-play interviews with your partner. Compare notes on the following points. (About 15 minutes should be sufficient.)
    a. Did each of us use all four types of questions according to plan?
    b. If not, why not?
    c. Which type was most difficult to use? Why?
    d. Would the most difficult type be easier or more difficult to use in a real interview?
7. Return to the class for a general discussion of the experience.

LIST OF TOPICS

1. Soviet-American relations
2. Serious social problems in America today
3. The dream vacation
4. Changing roles of women
5. Problems of pollution
6. The gun control controversy
7. Meaning of the "American way of life"
8. Images of France or some other nation
9. Intergenerational conflict
10. The problem of AIDS
11. Another topic of the respondent's choice

*Show me the golden nuggets of
relevant information you have
mined and sifted by your
questioning and probing!*

10

Recording and
Coding
Information

THE AMOUNT OF TIME and attention required for recording and coding information varies tremendously depending on the nature and purpose of the interview. If we are doing a public opinion poll to predict the outcome of a presidential election, all of the questions could have multiple-choice answers, even though the question is in open-ended form. For example, the interviewer asks, "Who are you going to vote for for president of the United States?" Then the interviewer puts a check by the appropriate name in the list of candidates. If each candidate's name is preceded by a letter or number, by simply checking, the interviewer has *recorded* the response and has *coded* it for input into a computer program.

In other professional settings the full range of possible answers cannot be known in advance. For example, when a client comes into a social agency, the social worker may not even know the general topic of conversation that will develop. This means that the interviewer does not know what questions are going to be needed before the interview begins. The interviewer may know only the first question in advance, "How can I help you?" In such a setting we can safely say that no recording or coding will be done by simply checking a blank on an interview form. In some situations none of the conversation is recorded. The only record might be a note about the *result* of the conversation such as a referral, a decision, or an action to be taken by either the interviewer or the respondent.

In professional settings like counseling, psychotherapy, journalism, or police interrogation, a detailed record of the exact words and phrases used by the respondent may be important. In some research settings a complete record of the interview is needed, including exactly how the interviewer questioned and probed. In such cases an audio or video tape captures the whole interaction process so that it can be analyzed and reanalyzed and coded according to different theoretical schemes for different purposes.

Studies done in a variety of interview settings show clearly that there is great danger of serious distortion and bias if the recording process is not accurate. For example, Fisher's classic experiment in public opinion polling[1] shows that if the respondent speaks too rapidly for the interviewer to take complete notes, there is a strong tendency for the interviewer to *selectively* record portions of the response that agree with his or her own attitudes on the topic of the interview. Trying to take verbatim notes under the wrong conditions could completely invalidate the results of an opinion poll.

Similarly, Wilkie[2] shows how in the helping professions distortions in recording the client's responses seriously limit the interviewer's understanding of the client's problems.

Once we recognize the importance of the recording operation in our efforts to obtain relevant, complete, and valid (unbiased) information, we will take greater care in selecting the most appropriate method of recording and in developing our own recording skills.

This chapter describes the full range of recording methods and emphasizes the one most fruitful for the purpose of learning interviewing skills.

RECORDING INFORMATION

There are two functions of recording information in the interview: to store relevant information for *future* use and to make probe notes to help the interviewer remember what responses need to be probed.

Recording to Store Information

Before we focus on the specific method of recording information that you will use in *learning* to interview, let us quickly review six recording tactics that you might use under different conditions.

Precode Response Categories. Recall the presidential election poll in which the recording operation consisted of making a single checkmark on a list to represent the relevant portion of the response. This is the most efficient recording method, but it is valid only in situations where the answer is simple and all of the possible relevant responses are known in advance.

Make Notes after the Interview. The interviewer using this method records no information during the progress of the interview, but waits until the respondent leaves and then makes notes from memory. This tactic is used when it is important—for the sake of the validity of the information obtained—that the respondent does not define the conversation as an interview. Therefore, the interviewer must have some other legitimate role in the situation in order to act as a participant-observer. Novelists, journalists, sociologists, law-enforcement officers, social reformers, and social psychologists often use the method of postinterview notes. It is effective when only a small portion of the conversation is relevant, when the participant-observer can recognize the relevant and valid information, and when the interviewer has a good memory and can frequently escape the scene to take notes while the memory is fresh. In some field settings, days may pass before relevant information is given. In other settings relevant information may come so rapidly and in such great quantities that the interviewer's dilemma is whether to leave and record the information obtained and miss what is happening while he or she is recording, or to stay and overload the memory so that much of the significant detail is lost. This dilemma can be solved by having a team of observers who rotate the roles of participant-observer and recorder.

Take Minimal Notes and Amplify Later. The interviewer may take sketchy notes during the formal interview and then amplify them as soon as possible after the interview. This method has the advantage of getting all the significant points while they are fresh, without burdening the interviewer with writing complete, verbatim sentences. Thus the interviewer can pay more attention to listening, observing, evaluating, and probing responses. In many types of interviews, a few key words and phrases in their original chronological order can help the interviewer recall relevant details. However, if the respondent speaks rapidly and a large portion of what is said is relevant, then there is a danger that important information will be lost with this method.

Take Verbatim Notes. Here taking verbatim notes means writing down relevant points in the exact words of the respondent during the progress of the interview. This method is used when it is important to know the vocabulary and phraseology with which the respondent expressed a relevant idea. It eliminates the danger of omitting or distorting the information. It has the additional advantage of eliminating the need for a tape recorder and subsequent transcription. But the method of verbatim notes also has many limitations. It cannot be used effectively if the interview is long; if the interviewer needs to concentrate on listening, observing, evaluating, and probing; if the respondent speaks too rapidly; or if the respondent must be asked to slow down, which dampens the respondent's enthusiasm and spontaneity, reduces the free-association possibilities, and lengthens the interview.

The limitations of verbatim notes do not apply to the method of tape-recording the interview.

Dictate Relevant Material from a Tape Recording. According to this method, the interview is first tape-recorded. Then the interviewer, or another person with a clear understanding of the objectives of the interview, listens to the tape and dictates onto another tape the relevant information. Whether this dictation must be in the exact words of the respondent or whether it can be paraphrased depends on the precise objectives of the interview.

Tape-recording the interview has many advantages. First, the method avoids the danger of omitting relevant points of the interview. Second, it preserves all of the audible nonverbal cues, which are helpful in interpreting the meaning and judging the validity of the responses. Third, it frees the interviewer from the distracting note-taking task so that full attention may be paid to listening, observing, evaluating, and probing. Fourth, the tape records not only the responses but also the interviewer's questions and probes complete with the audible nonverbal cues. (This point is very important in the process of learning to interview.)

The second phase of listening to the tape and dictating the relevant material onto another tape is particularly advantageous when the interview is long and only a small part of the information is relevant to the interview. No time is wasted in transcribing the total interview, including a large portion of irrelevant words. If the interviewers do the dictating, they will learn much about their own interviewing method; they will recognize their failures to probe for relevance, completeness, and validity.

The dictated material can be typed for a permanent record or for analysis. A variation of this method is to directly type the relevant information from the original tape rather than dictating it for another person to type.

Transcribe the Total Recording. In a few instances, a tape-recorded interview should be transcribed en toto. A total transcription is particularly useful when an interviewer is trying to understand the whole interaction process, including audible nonverbal cues such as tone of voice (of both participants), pacing, hesitations, false starts, confusions, and redundancies that are typical of unedited conversations. All of this information is particularly important to the listener who is learning to interview.

There are times, too, when the whole interview is needed for analysis. This need is characteristic of the initial exploratory study in a new problem area when we do not know precisely what might be relevant. What might seem irrelevant in the first interview may become very significant in the light of subsequent interviews. Any false starts, hesitations, confusions, and redundancies may be edited out in the transcribing process.

Selecting the best method of recording information depends on detailed knowledge of the purposes of the interview and how the information is to be used. Even with all of this knowledge, the final decision is usually one of judgment—to resolve the conflict between the desire for perfect relevance, completeness, and validity and the pressure to be economical in the expenditure of time, energy, and money.

When you do the skill-integrating interview assignment in the next chapter, you will use the system of tape-recording the interview and transcribing the total recording. There will be a slight variation in that you will edit out the false starts, repetitions, and meaningless utterances from the responses, but not from your questions, as you type.

Making Probe Notes

Probe notes, unlike notes to store information, are taken to remind the interviewer of specific points that need to be probed for elaboration and clarification. Instead of interrupting the respondent to probe every time a response needs upgrading, the interviewer makes a *probe note* that indicates what part of the response needs to be probed later. This method avoids the danger of dampening the respondent's spontaneity. Sometimes it is also more efficient than interrupting because in many cases the missing information is supplied spontaneously later without the probe, or the meaning of particular phrases becomes clear in the context of the unfolding story.

Conditions for Taking Probe Notes. The following remarks about taking probe notes assume that the interview is being tape-recorded; notes are not being taken to store relevant information. The use of the tape recorder frees the interviewer to pay more attention to what the respondent says, how it is said, and what needs to be probed.

The same conditions that make it important to use a tape recorder also make it important to take probe notes. For example, the longer, more complex, subtle, and exploratory the interview, the more important it is to allow the respondent to follow his or her own pattern of free association and to avoid interruptions. Therefore, it is important to both tape-record the interview and to take probe notes. Psychological interruptions can be avoided by allowing more silence, more encouragement probes, and less topic control. The probe notes allow the interviewer to postpone probes without forgetting to probe if the point is not covered spontaneously later in the interview.

Characteristics of Good Probe Notes. First, a good probe note springs directly from the ongoing process of *evaluating* the relevance, completeness, and validity of responses. The good probe note selects from the response the precise points that need to be clarified or elaborated.

Second, a good probe is *short*—no more than a word or phrase that can be written quickly without taking attention away from the ongoing interview. The note-taking activity should be minimally distracting for both the interviewer and the respondent.

Finally, the probe note should be in the *exact words* of the respondent. Later, when the interviewer uses the probe, it will be easier for the respondent to associate the idea with what he or she was thinking at that point in the interview. Use of exact words also helps the interviewer to recall the context of the interview at that moment and to remember more precisely what type of probe is needed.

Tactics of Using Probe Notes.   If the respondent does not already know what to expect, the interviewer should explain why he or she will be taking notes. A statement such as the following would suffice for this purpose:

> Even though the tape recorder will be picking up our whole conversation, I'll be taking a few notes to remind me of something that I need to know more about. Then I'll ask later, if you haven't already told me by then.

Without some explanation the respondent might feel that the interviewer has no need to take notes unless there is something incorrect in the response, and the respondent can be needlessly distracted by puzzling over the interviewer's note taking.

The interviewer will find it helpful to cross out each probe note as it is probed. Then at the end of the interview, the interviewer might declare a cleanup time to be sure all the indicated points have been clarified or elaborated. The interviewer can say something like this:

> You have been able to give me so much relevant information that I need to pause for just a moment to look over my notes to see if I have clarified all the points I wanted. If while I'm doing this you think of anything more you can tell me, let me know.

Whether the interviewer needs time for a review of the notes depends on the type of interview and the context of the interview situation. In training interviewers I have found that they tend to panic for fear they will terminate the interview only to discover later that some crucial information was omitted. The straightforward declaration of a cleanup period can avoid this anxiety.

An Illustration of Taking Probe Notes.   The following response is taken from an interview by a case manager in a multiservice center that emphasizes the coordination of combinations of social services needed to get families off welfare. A typical problem is to provide the necessary maintenance and support services so a mother can go to vocational school. The usual package of maintenance and support includes a monthly check for aid to dependent children, food stamps, day-care for the children, a rent subsidy, a utilities subsidy, and a transportation allowance. The respondent in the interview had all of these supports and had been attending vocational school for a few weeks when she dropped out. The case manager at the center called the client in to discuss her reasons for dropping out of school and to impress her with the idea that she is passing up an opportunity to get out of poverty. The interviewer hopes to discover the real reason for dropping out in order to remedy the situation before it is too late.

R: No, I haven't been sick exactly. I guess I look good enough but that's not say- ing how I feel. I'm tired! I have been doing this just three weeks but I'm plain tired. I hate to drive in traffic. I haven't had much experience. Traffic was nothing like this in Hamilton County and I was to Chattanooga only once. That's only part of the problem. I have been happier in the last three days since I quit school because I'm with my children like a mother should be! Maybe that Storybookland place is a good day-care center as far as they go, but they can't take the place of a mother. While I'm leaving them there, what am I doing? That Mrs. Dexter gives us nasty exams that trick you up plenty, and she asks questions anytime anyone misses a class. She harps on how our incentive allowance will be cut off if we don't come to class regularly. She thinks we are kids. And the Westside Skills Center isn't exactly in the best part of town! No, I wouldn't give up the chance of being a medical tech- nician just to avoid a drive in the traffic every day, but there are a lot better reasons not to take a chance like that. Who knows what's in the future? I know one thing right now, Mary Beth and Jaycee both need a mother now, not next year or the year after!

The interviewer hearing this response must evaluate it to determine whether it is relevant, complete, and valid. It seems relevant enough in that it is dealing with obstacles to attending vocational school, but is it valid or are some of the reasons just nice-sounding excuses? The case manager knows, for example, that the client had been complaining that she was "climbing the walls" having to stay at home with her two children all day. But now after three days at home again, she claims to be happy with the children. The case man- ager picks up some hints of what might be more powerful deterrents to the cli- ent's attendance at vocational school and jots these down for probe notes as follows: "mother should be," "nasty exams," "part of town," and "what's in future." These could be translated into the following probes used later in the interview:

I-1: You said that now you are with your children like a mother should be... could you tell me a little more about how you feel about that?

I-2: You mentioned that Mrs. Dexter gave you nasty exams. What do you mean by "nasty exams"?

I-3: You say that the Westside Skills Center is not in the best part of town—in what way, what did you have in mind?

I-4: I'm very interested in what you had in mind when you said, "who knows what's in the future?"

Probe I-1 might show that the client has guilt feelings about neglecting her children or that her husband complains about this. Probe I-2 might show that the client has a deep fear of failing the course which would make all her effort in vain. Maybe she assumes that she failed the last exam and does not want to return to school to find out. She may be wrong about this. Probe I-3 might discover that this white woman is particularly fearful of blacks in a slum area or is afraid of being mugged. Probe I-4 might unearth various fears about the future. Maybe she fears that she cannot pass the course and so will not be able to get a job as a medical technician. She might be pregnant or fear that she will be before she can finish two years of vocational school. Or she could fear that her husband will want to move back to Tennessee before she can finish vocational school. None of these possibilities could be either substantiated or ruled out with the incomplete information in the initial response.

CODING INTERVIEW RESPONSES

Interviews have some specific purpose, so it is necessary to store the responses in a relevant, usable, and accessible form to fulfill this purpose. For example, after interviewing and examining a patient, a physician often dictates the results into a tape recorder. Later, a transcription is made and filed in the patient's case history so it can be reviewed the next time the patient comes in. Human services workers often store information on clients in questionnaire forms or summary notes that cover the most important findings and results of an interview. Public opinion interviewers code much of the information during the interview by simply checking the nearest appropriate answer and leaving a few open-ended responses to be coded in the office; then the codes are fed into computers to obtain quantitative results. Everyone who uses the results of interviews, whether quantitative or not, needs some way to code the results so that they can be used without listening to the whole tape or reading the whole transcript.

Basic Steps in Coding

Regardless of the type of interview being coded or how the information is to be used, certain basic steps are essential in any reliable coding process. Difficulties in each of these steps arise depending on the type of information and the purpose for which it is to be used. The first step is to define the coding categories.

Defining the Coding Categories.   Some coding categories are so obvious and simple that no sophisticated definition is needed. For example, for a census-taker to classify respondents into male and female requires no refined definition. In contrast, other familiar concepts may present a difficult problem of definition. In Chapter 2 we saw how an apparently simple term like *family* requires a meticulous definition to have any reliability in counting the number of families in an urban neighborhood. The same need for careful definition exists in other seemingly simple terms like *employed, family conflict, child abuse, addiction*, and so forth.

Once a tentative set of coding categories is developed and defined, it should be pretested by having independent coders code the same interview material using the same definitions. If there is little agreement on the number of responses that fall into a given category, the definition of that category should be examined, discussed, and possibly revised.

Coding categories, especially for a large number of interviews, present two dangers: A definition may be too *concrete* so that it fits only a few examples from which it was derived, or it may be so *abstract* that the recognizable empirical characteristics are not specified and concrete cases cannot be identified. Nevertheless, coding categories must be more abstract than the concrete examples being classified in order to potentially include all of the relevant examples regardless of their superficial differences.

A useful set of coding categories has two basic logical characteristics: It is *all-inclusive* and *mutually exclusive*. To be all-inclusive, the set must include the entire range of relevant response categories in a particular dimension. Here's a simple example. If we want to classify people on the dimension of religious affiliation, the usual checklist of Protestant, Catholic, and Jewish is inadequate even in the United States where there are hundreds of thousands of Buddhists, atheists, humanists, and so on.

To be mutually exclusive, each category in the set making up the dimension must be defined clearly enough so that a concrete example could not logically fall into two categories at the same time.

Once we have a set of coding categories that is all-inclusive and mutually exclusive and that has been pretested for applicability, we can take the next step, which is relatively simple.

Assigning Category Symbols.   To perform the task of summarizing, condensing, and storing a concrete example that falls into a certain coding category, we assign an abstract symbol to represent any case in that category. Thus each category has its own symbolic label, or code. This label may be an abbreviation, a number, a letter, a color, a geometric shape, or anything else that is convenient for the process of summarizing, analyzing, storing, or retrieving the information. When information is going to be entered into a computer, labels are usually alphabetical, numeric, or some combination of the two. For some types of case history material that will not be entered into a computer, it may be convenient to use color codes.

The symbolic label must indicate both the question (dimension) and the answer (category). For example, the response "Unitarian" in answer to "What is your religion?" might be represented as 25-g. In this case it is answer "g" in the response categories for question 25.

Since it is often impossible to anticipate all of the possible categories of answers to a particular question, it is wise to include a final "other" category for all unanticipated responses. If we write in the response after checking "other," we then have an opportunity to develop additional coding categories by reviewing all of the "other" responses.

Thus the fully developed code includes a name and definition for the dimension and for each category in the dimension and a symbolic label for the dimension and each category it contains.

Classifying Relevant Information.   The concrete operational steps for coding relevant information depend on the nature of the information, the interviewing method used, the proportion of irrelevant information, the size of the verbal units (individual words, phrases, thoughts, feelings, themes, problems, and so on) being classified, and the level of abstraction of the coding categories. Rather than attempting to cover all of the possibilities, we will describe one good classifying process that can be used in learning to do effective depth interviews.

The physical act of classifying relevant information from the transcript could be done in three ways. First, the transcript could be cut up with scissors and the relevant words, phrases, or sentences put into little boxes labeled with the appropriate category symbols. However, this is completely impractical for several reasons: It is a time-consuming process, bits of material can be lost, the results of the whole analysis cannot be seen at a glance, fragments of information are removed from their context, and it is very difficult to compare the results of two independent coders and to calculate the reliability score.

A second approach would be to read through the transcript, underline each fragment of relevant information, and label each with the category symbol, thereby showing the category of relevant information into which it falls. This method has two advantages: We don't cut up the transcript and we keep each relevant fragment in its original context. However, it still has serious disadvantages: It does not allow the results of the whole analysis to be seen at a glance. It does not allow us to quickly compare the content of one interview with that of another or to compare one person's coding of an interview with another's. It does not allow us to summarize the results of a number of interviews on a topic by showing the frequency with which each type of answer was given. Finally, it does not provide a locating index to help find specific examples of a certain category of information in its original context in the transcript.

A third, and best, approach overcomes all of the shortcomings of the second approach. This method begins with the same first step—underlining the relevant words and phrases. Then, instead of labeling each fragment with the category symbol, we give each a unique identification number, sometimes called an "address," which indicates the fragment's precise location in the transcript. This number is simply the line number in the transcript plus a letter (a, b, c, or d) to indicate which fragment on that line is being located. The letter is needed only if there is more than one relevant fragment on the same line.

So far the relevant fragments are identified, but they are not classified into the categories of relevant information that have been defined. To carry out the classification process, we use a special coding sheet in which the column and row headings represent the categories of relevant information we have defined. Then, we put the identification number of each fragment of relevant information into the appropriate cells. This is the symbolic equivalent of the physical process, in the first approach, of cutting up the transcript and putting the relevant fragments into boxes.

The third approach has none of the disadvantages of either the first or second. The third approach allows the coder to compare the content of one interview with another on the same topic, and to compare the coding of the same interview by two independent coders. It allows us to summarize the results of a number of interviews on the same topic by showing the frequency with which each type of information is given. Finally, it provides a locating index to help us find specific examples of any category of information in its original context in the transcript.

This third system will be used in Exercise 10-B for a quick comparison between two independent coders' results, and the code sheet will act as a summary and index for the transcript. For example, you wish to know every negative olefactory image the respondent had in high school. The locations of all these types of images in the transcript are given by the identification numbers placed in the cell in the table where the "negative" column intersects with the "olefactory" row. This method will become perfectly clear as you do Exercise 10-B.

Testing the Reliability of Coding.   The reliability of the coding process asks whether two independent codings of material into categories relevant to the purposes of the interview would be the same or whether they would vary grossly. There are two ways of obtaining independent codings of the same material. In the test-retest method, a person codes the material once and without looking at the results re-codes the same material to see whether the first and second coding agree. In the independent-coder method, two different people code the same material independently. In both methods it is not possible to obtain a high degree of agreement unless the coders are *qualified*. Their qualifications will be discussed later.

Both methods assume that the two codings being compared are done *independently*. In the test-retest method it may be more difficult to achieve independence, because the coder who is coding the same material for the second time may be able to remember precisely how specific fragments of information were coded the first time. To guard against this, there must be a time lapse between the first and second coding. If the coder is coding many interviews on the same topic, less elapsed time is needed between the first and second codings. Even so, some people have a powerful memory for interview and case-study material and can remember a specific case for months. Perfect independence of the codings is easier to attain when two coders are used. To be independent, the coders cannot discuss or even know how the other person has coded any particular bit of information until both have completed the coding process. It is permissible, in fact advisable, for the coders to discuss the category definitions and even work together on a practice case *before* doing the coding to be used in testing reliability.

In either of the approaches, reliability is tested by doing some sort of systematic comparison of the two independent codings to discover the amount of agreement or disagreement between them. The comparison may be *qualitative*; that is, the two coders, for example, could compare and discuss their disagreements in order to improve their reliability in future codings of the same type of material. Alternatively, the comparison could be *quantitative*, resulting in some type of numerical score that expresses the degree of agreement.

For a valuable learning experience, do a qualitative comparison of your own coding of your own interview with another person's coding of that interview. Answers that you accepted as adequate and did not probe any further may prove to be vague and ambiguous, if not completely irrelevant. This discovery can come either when you are coding your own interview or when you compare your own coding with that of the independent coder. Usually there is a tendency to be over optimistic about relevance when coding one's own interview and to be shocked and amazed when one's coding partner does not agree about the meaning of some of the responses.

It is also useful to go beyond the qualitative discussion and to measure reliability *quantitatively*. A quantitative score allows you to answer such questions as: "Is my coding reliability improving?" "Is my evaluation and probing of responses in the interview improving?" "Do I have more reliability with one coding partner than with another?" "Do I obtain greater reliability on one interview topic than on another?" There are two basic methods of quantifying reliability.

Measuring Reliability.   Two general measures of reliability are the *percentage agreement* and the *reliability coefficient*.

The percentage agreement score is a crude measure of reliability. It is simply the percentage of information that was classified into the same category by two independent coders. This score is useful under certain conditions. It can be used to compare the reliability of one interview with another when both interviews are for the same purpose and use the same coding categories. It is also useful in discovering whether one pair of coders is more reliable than another in coding the same interview. It can be used to compare the reliability of a person's first and second interview on the same topic.

Despite these positive uses, there are two important things the percentage agreement score cannot do. First, it cannot give a valid comparison of the reliability of coding one interview with the reliability of another interview on a different topic with a different number of coding categories. Second, it does not give a valid clue to whether a particular percentage is acceptable or not.

Intuitively, it may seem that a percentage agreement of 80 percent is good or that 40 percent is bad, but this is not necessarily the case. Whether a particular percentage is good or bad depends on the number of categories in the coding scheme. For example, if coders are classifying information into two categories (relevant and irrelevant), there would be a 50 percent chance of agreement even if neither coder looked at the information but simply flipped a coin to classify it. In this case, a percentage agreement score of 50 percent would indicate zero (0.0) reliability. A 50 percent agreement score could be very good, however, when coding information into 100 categories. In this case, the probability of two coders putting a specific bit of information into the same category by pure chance is one in a hundred, or 1.0%. So 50 percent is fifty times the chance expectancy.

For these reasons, several different formulas have been developed to arrive at a *coefficient of reliability* that takes into account not only the number of categories in the coding system, but also how the information is distributed throughout the categories. For example, in one ten-category system, 90 percent of the information collected might fall into only two of the ten categories; while in another ten-category coding system, 90 percent of the information might fall into eight of the ten categories. This difference in distributions would also affect the probability of obtaining agreement by chance. Later in coding Exercise 10-B, you will be given a formula for the reliability coefficient which takes these important variables into account. The formula allows us to compare relative reliability even when the topic of the information is different and when the number of coding categories varies widely.

Locating Sources of Unreliability.   There are three general sources, or causes, of unreliability. Learning to reduce any or all of these will raise the reliability coefficient. First, the *coding categories* may be at fault either because they do not fit the information gathered or they are not clearly enough defined to be mutually exclusive and all-inclusive. Second, the *information* being coded may be ambiguous, vague, unclear, contradictory, or confusing. In this case, the interviewer may be at fault. Third, the *coders* may be at fault because they do not understand the definitions, cannot read well, are illogical, or not alert and motivated.

Therefore, reliability can be improved if we are careful in revising category definitions after pretesting them, if the interviewer clearly understands the purpose of the interview and is alert in evaluating and probing the responses, and if the coders understand the definitions of categories and are alert and logical in applying them. In my experience 100 percent reliability is rare and unreliability is due to some combination of these three causes.

SUMMARY

Six tactics should be considered when recording to store information:

1. Precode structured answers.
2. Make notes from memory after the interview.
3. Take minimal notes in the interview and amplify later.
4. Take verbatim notes during the interview.
5. Dictate only the relevant information from the tape-recorded interview.
6. Tape-record the interview and transcribe it all.

Probe notes, in contrast to notes for storing information, may be used later in the same interview. Follow these guidelines when using probe notes:

1. Take probe notes under appropriate conditions.
2. Know the characteristics of good probe notes.
3. Understand the tactics for using probe notes.

Regardless of the type of interview being coded, certain basic steps are essential to code information reliably:

1. Define the coding categories.
2. Assign code labels to the categories.

3. Classify relevant information into the categories.
4. Test the reliability of the coding.
5. Measure the reliability of the coding.
6. Locate the sources of unreliability in the coding.

Exercises 10-A and 10-B provide you an opportunity to practice taking probe notes and coding relevant information.

NOTES

1. Herbert Fisher, "Interviewer Bias in the Recording Operation," *International Journal of Opinion and Attitude Research* 4 (1950): 393.
2. Charlotte H. Wilkie, "A Study of Distortions in Recording Interviews," *Social Work* 8, no. 3 (July 1963): 31–36.

EXERCISE 10-A
TAKING PROBE NOTES

OBJECTIVES

To take probe notes, which means to note what should be probed, you must first clearly understand the *objectives* of the interview and *evaluate* each response in terms of its relevance, clarity, completeness, and validity in relation to these objectives. This exercise lets you practice making these evaluative decisions *instantaneously* in response to a live interview. At the same time, as an observer-listener you are relieved of the other responsibilities of the interviewer. If you practice making probe notes on someone else's interview, you will improve your chances of making good probe notes during your own interview.

PROCEDURE

1. A pair of students will do an interview in front of the class. The interview may or may not be tape-recorded depending on the decision of your instructor. The rest of the class members take the role of listener-observers.
2. The *interviewer* chooses a topic from the list in this exercise and informs the class of the choice so they also may study the objectives of the interview.
3. The *interviewer* studies the objectives of the interview and prepares three or four questions to start the interview.
4. The *observers* study the objectives so they can evaluate responses and note the points that need to be probed.
5. The *interviewer* begins the interview and continues for ten minutes.
6. The *respondent* cooperates by answering all questions spontaneously but with no particular effort to elaborate in great detail.
7. The *listener-observer* makes notes on points that need to be probed in view of the objectives of the interview. Remember that each note should be only a word or a phrase and a direct quote from the respondent.

8. The *listener-observer* crosses out a particular probe note if the respondent volunteers the information or the interviewer covers that point immediately or later.
9. When the interview is finished at the end of ten minutes, the listener-observers count how many probe notes they made and how many they crossed out because the items were covered by the respondent or interviewer. They also calculate the percentage of points that were covered by the interviewer. They then put these three figures at the top of the probe note sheet in the following form:

   Total probe notes   _____
   Number covered   _____
   Percent covered   _____

10. The instructor will decide at this point whether you should meet in pairs to compare notes and discuss your differences or go directly into a general discussion with the whole class.

POSSIBLE INTERVIEW TOPICS AND OBJECTIVES

You may have used one of the first two topics that follow in a previous exercise, and you will use one of the second two in Chapter 11. This need not determine your choice of topics for this exercise, because there are advantages both in dealing with a familiar topic and in becoming familiar with a new topic you might use in the future.

Select a topic (if you are the interviewer) and study the objectives carefully so you can use them as a guide to your probing for relevance, completeness, and validity.

Topic 1: *Plans for After College.* In general, try to cover three dimensions of this topic: images, feelings and actions.

1. Images: What does your respondent imagine about the period after college? What will he or she be doing, where, when, how, with whom, and why? How clear is the image? What are some of the alternative possibilities? What do these alternatives depend on?
2. Feelings: How does your respondent feel about these images? How sure does he or she feel that they will actually happen? Which points show some ambivalence of feeling? What is your respondent anxious or worried about? At which points does your respondent have confidence, pride, or faith in the future?
3. Actions: What actions has your respondent taken in preparation for the after-college period?

Topic 2: *Most Serious Social Problems in the United States.* There are several general objectives in this interview.

1. Discover which *problems* are seen as serious (a list).
2. Discover the *rank order* of seriousness of those on the list.
3. Find out what *criteria* your respondent uses in ranking one problem as more serious than another.
4. Find out how your respondent *feels* about the most serious problem. Is there hope for a solution? Will it probably get worse? Will it get better? How does your respondent feel about people who contribute to the problem? About those who do nothing to help solve the problem?
5. What *actions* does your respondent feel might help solve the problem? Is there anything he or she could do personally to help solve the problem? If so, what would that be? Has your respondent ever taken any action to solve any of these problems?

Topic 3: *The American Way of Life.* The objective is to discover your respondent's images, feelings, and knowledge regarding the American Way of Life.

1. What *images* come to your respondent's mind when he or she hears the phrase the American Way of Life? What are some of the positive images? Negative images? Neutral images? Who agrees with these images? Who promotes these images? (Try to get *concrete* images that you could see, hear, smell, and feel rather than abstract generalizations.)
2. Discover how your respondent *feels* about these images. How sure is he or she that they are correct or representative? What does he or she like most about the United States? Dislike most?
3. Discover if your respondent knows any *facts* to back up these feelings or images.

Topic 4: *Mexico.* The objectives are the same as those in topic 3—to discover your respondent's images, feelings, and knowledge about Mexico.

Exercise 10-B
CODING RELEVANT INFORMATION

This exercise covers only two of the four basic steps in coding outlined in this chapter. You will not have to define the coding categories or assign labels to these categories; these will be supplied. You will classify relevant information and do a crude test of the reliability of the coding.

PURPOSE OF THE EXERCISE

By dealing with the end-product of another person's interview, you will become aware of the need for the interviewer to keep the objectives of an interview firmly in mind and to pursue them relentlessly in order to increase the relevance, clarity, and completeness of the information. Similarly, when you are coding the interview transcript, you must constantly be aware of the same objectives so you can reliably classify the relevant information. Remember that even if you code the responses with logical precision, perfect reliability is not possible if the information is vague or incomplete. There is no way the coder can make up for deficiencies in the original interviewing.

This exercise will help prepare you for the field project in the final chapter by alerting you to the need to probe for relevance, clarity, and completeness and by familiarizing you with part of the coding process to be used there.

OVERVIEW OF THE PROCEDURE

1. Read the purposes of the interview and rapidly read through the transcript of the dialogue presented at the end of this exercise.
2. Re-read the dialogue and classify each underlined bit of information into one of the 18 cells (cross-categories) in the *coding sheet* furnished by your instructor. Note that the coding sheet requires you to simultaneously classify each underlined bit on two different dimensions: sense mode and feeling tone.

   You classify an underlined bit of information by putting only the *number* of the line of the interview transcript on which it appears into one of the 18 cells in the coding sheet. In cases where two or more bits are underlined on the same line, add an a, b, or c to the number to show whether it appears first, second, or third in order on the line. Before beginning this classification process, carefully read the section titled Classification Hints in this exercise.

    You must do your classification independently without discussion with another person in order to have a valid test of reliability when you compare your coding with your partner's.

3. When you have finished classifying the information, count the number of coded items in each row and column of the coding sheet and write in the row and column totals. Even though different coders may disagree on these totals, the *grand* total should equal 60 if you have not omitted any underlined bit of information. Also, if you have counted and added correctly, the sum of the row totals and the sum of the column totals should each equal the grand total of 60.

    When entering the numbers on the coding sheet, be sure to put the first number in any cell in the upper left corner of that cell. Other numbers entered later in that cell should appear in rank order from left to right with commas in between. This will greatly facilitate the comparison of coding sheets with your coding partner in the next step.

4. Choose a partner for the purposes of (1) comparing your coding, (2) discussing your disagreements on coding, (3) noting the sources of your disagreements (whether they are due to poorly defined coding categories, ambiguity in the responses to be coded, or faulty logic on the part of the coders), and (4) calculating the percentage-agreement score according to the procedure given later in this exercise.

5. Bring to the class discussion your percentage-agreement score and your ideas on the sources of your disagreements with your coding partner.

CLASSIFICATION HINTS

    Sense Mode.   The sense modes (the row heading on your coding sheet) need no special definitions because they are generally understood and directly experienced by all of us. It is enough to say that *visual* refers to the sense of sight, *auditory* refers to hearing, *olfactory* to smell, *gustatory* to taste, and *tactile* to touch.

    To obtain more agreement between you and your partner in classifying the relevant bits of information on this dimension, follow these rules:

1. If an underlined word or phrase is not clearly connected with any particular sensory mode in the context of the interview, classify it as *visual* if the person, object, or event named is described in such a manner that you could draw a picture of it. If no concrete picture comes to mind, classify it as "unclear" (row 6) in the sense mode dimension of your coding sheet.

2. In deciding on which sense mode is involved, take into consideration the context immediately preceding and following the underlined bit of information.
3. Classify each underlined fragment of information into *only one* category on the sense mode dimension and *only one* category on the feeling dimension, in other words, into *only one* of the 18 cells.

Feeling Tone. Feeling tone is defined broadly to include any emotional reactions, attitudes, or feelings associated with a remembered object, person, or event at the high school. Ideally, the objective is to find salient *positive* and *negative* memories and determine which end of the scale is predominant. The "neutral or undetermined" category of feeling tone actually contains two kinds of information. First are associations with images that are clearly emotionally *neutral*. In a sense, these might be considered irrelevant to the objectives of the interview because they would have relatively little influence on the student's attitudes toward college. Second are those objects, persons, or events that might have either a positive or a negative feeling association, but it is not clear from the context of the interview which it is. This should have been clarified at the time of the interview.

You must be careful when coding not to project your own values and attitudes by *assuming*, since you personally like or dislike something, that this respondent would also, even though there is no concrete evidence for this feeling. Of course there are times when it is safe to assume that a person does not like something, for example, a slap in the face; but if independent coders do not agree on what can be assumed in the particular context, then nothing should be assumed. Empathy is useful in both interviewing and coding, but it is not infallible.

In classifying information according to feeling tone, you should apply rules 2 and 3 for classifying according to sense mode.

CALCULATING THE PERCENTAGE AGREEMENT

Get together with your coding partner and compare your coding sheets using the following procedure, which should take no more than ten minutes.

1. One person calls off the numbers in cell number 1 of his or her own coding sheet. The caller should say "cell number one" and then call the numbers in rank order and wait for his or her partner to say "yes" or "no" to indicate that his coding sheet does or does not have the same number in that cell. Every time the partner says "yes," that number should be circled on *both* coding sheets to indicate agreement.
2. Repeat this process for all 18 cells in the coding sheet.
3. Calculate the percentage-agreement score by simply dividing the number of agreements (items circled on *one* of the coding sheets) by 60, which is the total number of items classified. Then multiply by 100 by moving the

decimal point two places to the right to get the percentage. Do not despair if you find that this percentage figure is low. Its real value is measured by comparing the percentage agreement with the probability of getting agreement purely by chance. In this case, since there are 18 categories, there is only one chance in 18 or a 5.5 percent probability of agreeing by chance. So an 11 percent agreement, for example, is twice as good as chance. In Chapter 11 you will be given a more sophisticated formula to calculate the coefficient of reliability.

INTERVIEW TO BE CODED

The interview in this exercise is part of a larger study of academic success and creativity in college. This particular interview aims at testing the hypothesis that one important factor in predicting students' success in college (other than the usual college entrance test scores and rank in high school class) would be their emotional experiences in high school. The kinds of pleasant and unpleasant feelings associated with high school might be important—whether they are associated with courses, teachers, students, physical plant, classroom procedures, or extracurricular activities. Conscious or unconscious associations with high school might color a student's attitude toward college. These images might be visual, auditory, olfactory, gustatory, or tactile, and they might carry a negative, positive, ambiguous, or neutral feeling tone.

The following transcript represents only the early part of one exploratory interview. Lines with relevant material are numbered for coding purposes.

INTERVIEW TRANSCRIPT

I-1: As you already know, this interview is part of a larger study to discover whether there is any connection between how well people do in college and the kinds of memories they have of their high school experiences. Would you start by telling me some of your most outstanding memories of your high school?

R-1: Well, its been two years—a long two years! But I can't forget certain things. I probably won't as long as I live.

(9) For example, I entered the <u>ninth grade</u> a year younger

(10) than average, so I <u>got bullied</u> around quite a bit by the

(11) other boys. . .got my <u>nose bloodied</u> in gym when I was paired with a guy with about six inches longer reach than I had. (5)

I-2: How did that make you feel about the school?

R-2: (15) Well, it was a <u>fearful place</u> at break time, before and after school before I caught the bus home, and in gym, but not in the classroom.

I-3:   What about lunchtime?

R-3:   That was a pleasant experience because I always took my
(20)   lunch in a <u>brown paper bag</u> and ate lunch with the same two
friends for a couple of years. Not only were the friends the
same but so was the lunch—always two sandwiches and some
(23)   good fruit like an <u>orange</u>,[a] <u>apple</u>,[b] or <u>banana</u>.[c] Same
(24)   sandwiches too. <u>Velveeta cheese</u> with lettuce and one
(25)   <u>peanut butter</u> and jelly on whole wheat. I loved that lunch. It
never occurred to me to get tired of it.

I-4:   Tell me a little more about what was pleasant about the lunch
period.

R-4:   Well, my two friends at lunch were Donald Cortez and Bernie
Johnson and we all felt like outcasts, Don because he was a
minority member and Bernie because he had just transferred
from Rancho Military Academy and felt lost, and I was
younger than most. I entered North Hollywood High School
before my thirteenth birthday. We shared experiences and
(35)   <u>made remarks</u> about what we were witnessing at the moment.
(36)   We nearly always ate on a bench <u>under a tree</u>
(37)   in the <u>large patio</u> and could watch the others. The patio had a
(38)   <u>large arcade</u> with Spanish arches and was about 200 feet long.
(39)   There was one <u>long row of benches</u> on the arcade where
some of the other students either ate their brown-bag lunch
or collected after eating in the cafeteria, which none of the
three of us could afford.

I-5:   Any other memorable experiences with students, either pleasant
or unpleasant?

R-5:   Since I lived in another town and had to catch the
(46)   <u>old yellow school bus</u> home every night, I could not
participate in extracurricular activities, so most of my association
with students was before school for about ten to fifteen
minutes or during lunchtime. My second two years I didn't eat
as often with Don and Bernie because I had joined the
(51)   orchestra, <u>playing violin</u>.[a] The <u>bass fiddle player</u>[b] was a good guy
and a year ahead of me. He asked if I would be interested in
playing with him and a guitarist friend during the lunch hour.
So for a year we met at lunchtime in the
(55)   <u>projection booth</u>[a] of the auditorium and <u>played pop</u>[b] and
(56)   <u>country-western music</u>. We got a few little jobs in North
Hollywood and West Los Angeles. That was a lot of fun!
On a couple of occasions we lost track of time, didn't hear the
bell, and were late to class after lunch.

I-6:   So far you haven't mentioned anything about courses, classes,
teachers, or administrators. Are there any pleasant or unpleasant
memories in any of these areas?

R-6:   I can remember every teacher I had in that four years.
There were 1300 students in the school and 43 teachers.
I remember I counted them in my annual, called *El Camino*. I
had about 15 of these teachers. I liked most of them and they
seemed to like me. There were some exceptions to that.

(68)   There was Miss Fink who taught algebra and looked like a
bulldog and had the same nasty disposition.

(70)   Then there was Mr. Soloman who taught geometry. He always
(71)   had a smile and a chuckle in his voice. He knew how to
(72)   explain things. I loved geometry and hated algebra so
(73)   didn't take trigonometry. I can still hear his voice as he
(74)   practically sang a theorem. Then there was Miss Hamilton. She
had a very pleasing figure and seemed to inspire rumors among
the male students.

I-7:   What sorts of rumors?

R-7:   Well . . . it was rumored that after biology class one of the
boys asked her what the tissue of the mammary gland was like
and she told him to gently press her bosom to note the
spongy quality. Probably wishful thinking on somebody's
part.

I-8:   In general how did you, personally, feel about Miss
Hamilton?

R-8:   (85)   I thought she was great and glamorous. She had a good sense of
humor and kept us interested in most of the course. She had a
little problem with some of the girls who did not want to dissect
frogs.

R-9:   Any other memorable teachers?

R-9:   There was Mr. Persons who taught physics. He was generally a
(91)   good guy with an easy-going manner. I liked him a lot until he
(92)   accused me of copying from other people in an exam when it
had been the other way around. I guess he assumed that since I
had opportunity by sitting next to the other student and since I
never talked much in class discussion and since I was younger, I
must have been the one who copied. Then there was
(97)   Mr. Corbin the chemistry teacher. He was my idol. He was a
Cal-Tech graduate, an Olympic fencing champion, and played
the violin. And to make him more glamorous, every Fourth of
July he acted as navigator on the yacht Monsoon in the race
from Los Angeles to Honolulu. Since I also played the violin
and had aspirations toward things nautical, I thought he was
great. I never thought of it before this moment, but he may be
the reason why I took fencing here at Richmond
State.

I-10:   Are there any other teachers that stand out in your mind at the
moment?

R-10:   Not really, none of the gym coaches stand out. None of the
(109)   English teachers stand out except <u>one that I hated</u>. And
(110)   I liked the orchestra teacher, <u>Miss Sheets</u>. Then there was
(111)   <u>Mr. Lynn</u> teaching Spanish—he was plain funny and fun.

I-11:   Tell me about the English teacher you hated.

R-11:   (113)   I'll never forget her. She was <u>Mrs. Kleinpeter</u> who taught World
             Literature. She stood in front of the class the first day, told us
             that we were to read sixteen books from a list and make a book
             report on each using the outline she would supply. We all
             went to the library, got our first book, sat down in class and
             read. That was the last we heard from her. She had her
(119)   <u>desk in the rear of the classroom</u> and was not in the classroom
             most of the time, but would drift in quietly to the
             rear once or twice during the hour. This went on for sixteen
             weeks.

I-12:   This may sound like an unusual question, but are there any
             sounds that you associate with your time at North Hollywood
             High School?

R-12:   (126)   Definitely! One <u>football cheer</u> of the rhythmic type comes back
             to me. It goes "Dot-dot, ski-watten-dotte, rah, rah, boom!" There
(128)   is the sound of violins <u>playing off key</u> in the
             orchestra rehearsal and the much better sound of our
(130)   <u>extracurricular trio</u>. Then once in awhile in geometry class
(131)   there was the squeaky <u>sound of chalk</u> on the blackboard. Then
(132)   in art metal class there was the <u>hammers pounding</u> on
             copper.

I-13:   Was the pounding of hammers a good or bad sound?

R-13:   It was definitely good—a sort of relief after having to be quiet in
             classes.

I-14:   Do you recall any smells associated with your high school?

R-14:   One unpleasant smell was when I had a student-aid job in
             the cafeteria when I was a senior. I had to wash these
(140)   <u>dirty garbage cans</u>. Then there was the time in chemistry
(141)   class when someone knocked over an <u>ammonia</u> bottle. It
             was a full gallon jug and the fumes were terrible. Then there
(143)   was the sickening smell of <u>liver of sulfur</u> in the art metal
             class. Oh yes, on Mondays there was always the smell of a
(145)   <u>cedar oiled sawdust</u> used by the janitors to sweep up the
             dust from the floors. That was pleasant. Of course there is
(147)   always the <u>gym lockers</u> and the <u>sweating bodies</u> before
             taking a shower. This is particularly unpleasant with the amount
             of crowding we had in gym.

I-15:   What are some of the most memorable visual images of your
             high school?

R-15:   First, I see the buildings and grounds. It was sort of
(153)   pseudo-Spanish architecture with Roman arches, arcade,
(154)   patios, et cetera. Then there were the red tile roofs too.
(155)   The lawn was always well manicured in front of the buildings
(156)   in the gym field. Then I picture the auditorium crammed
      with people during regular assemblies and on rainy-day gym
      periods. Some of the students were colorful. The fad was for the
(159)   boys to wear dirty corduroy pants with graffiti penciled about.
(160)   Most of the girls wore skirts and blouses or sweaters except
      for the girls from Italian and Mexican background who often
      wore dresses that showed them off to advantage but seemed a
      little like overkill to most of us.

I-16:   Any other outstanding visual images?

R-16:   Not really, except the things I have already mentioned.

I-17:   I forgot to ask you when we were talking about memorable
      smells whether there were any pleasant ones?

R-17:   Ah yes. There was Miss Hamilton. She always wore some brand
(169)   of delicious perfume.

I-18:   What can you remember about how anything felt to the sense of
      touch?

R-18:   Hmm . . . that's a hard one. I don't seem to recall anything
(173)   along that line. Except the gritty feel of the seats in the
      bleachers after a dust storm. Oh yes, and the
(175)   damp feel of the grass after a rain when we were doing
      push-ups in gym class.

Integrate your interviewing skills by keeping a steady focus on the prize (relevant, valid, and complete information) throughout the whole Skill Learning Cycle of planning, doing, and analyzing your interview. Then try again!

11

A Skill-Integrating Field Project

To THIS POINT we have practiced each interviewing skill separately. By taking them one at a time, we could focus more sharply and obtain a basic understanding and personal experience with each without being confused by attempting too many new concepts and skills at once. Now the time has come to integrate all the major skills by doing a real field interview.

PREVIEW OF THE SKILL LEARNING CYCLE

You cannot expect to be an expert interviewer as a result of reading ten short chapters and doing the exercises. Nevertheless, this final chapter and the guided interview practice in the field project will familiarize you with the basic *Skill Learning Cycle*, which you can repeat in the future to continue to improve your skills in interviewing.

To learn interviewing skills we must *do* interviews, but repeatedly doing interviews is not enough. What we do before and after an interview is equally important to the learning process. Before each interview there must be thoughtful planning of what to ask and how to ask it. After each interview there must be an objective analysis of the results in terms of both the interviewer's behavior and of the information obtained. To ensure that this analysis is objective, another person—in addition to the interviewer—should be involved in the analysis phase. To gain objectivity, we should not only hear ourselves on tape but allow another person to listen and evaluate the results. This guided field project will give you direct experience in using the whole Skill Learning Cycle which then can become your model for self-teaching in the future.

As a preview of what is to come, here are the specific steps you will take in carrying out the Skill Learning Cycle:

1. *Select* the interview topic and become familiar with the purposes of the interview.
2. *Select* an analysis partner from among your classmates.
3. *Plan* a fifteen-minute interview by formulating a few relevant questions and planning your approach to your respondent.
4. *Locate* a suitable respondent who is neither a friend nor a member of the class and make an appointment.
5. *Interview* your respondent on tape for fifteen minutes.
6. *Transcribe* all of your interview and make a copy.
7. *Do* the self-analysis of your own behavior. (The *self-analysis answer sheet* will be supplied by the instructor.)
8. *Code* your own and your partner's interview independently. (Forms will be supplied by the instructor.)
9. *Discuss* coding disagreements with your partner.
10. *Calculate* the coefficient of reliability. (Form will be supplied by the instructor.)
11. *Report* what you have learned and how you would proceed differently in another interview on the same topic.

Now that you have an overview of the steps in the cycle, we will consider each step in detail.

DETAILED STEPS IN THE FIELD PROJECT

Your instructor may decide to make some alterations or omissions in the procedures for this field project, but all of the steps, which have been classroom tested, are described in this chapter.

Select the Topic of the Interview

The two topics presented here have been carefully selected on the basis of three criteria. First, they both involve three general dimensions of information to be obtained: images, feelings, and facts. Second, all three dimensions can be covered in an interview of short duration, although they cannot be exhausted in a short interview. Third, they are topics anyone can talk on regardless of age, sex, role, ethnicity, or unique life history. The instructor will assign one of these topics for the whole class to use. Two topics are provided in case the class does two field interviews.

Images, Feelings, and Facts on Mexico.   Regardless of whether you have ever been to Mexico or ever intend to go there, you have images (accurate or inaccurate) and feelings (justified or unjustified) that come to mind when you hear the word *Mexico*. These images and feelings are probably quite different from those associated with our other neighbor, Canada. To understand the objectives of the interview, you must distinguish clearly between images, feelings, and facts.

For the purposes of this interview, an *image* will be broadly defined to include any memory or imagination of direct sensory experience—anything that is seen, heard, smelled, tasted, or touched, such as "brilliant sunsets," "the rumba," "essence of orange blossom," or "itchy mosquito bites." Whether the respondent has a positive or negative feeling about these images is to be *discovered* not assumed.

For the purposes of this interview, a *feeling* is some type of emotional experience associated with an image. Feelings are positive, neutral, or negative in tone; their essence is pleasantness or unpleasantness. The respondent may communicate feelings either verbally or nonverbally, but there are four reasons why you need to verify the nonverbal expression by probing for a *verbal* expression of feeling or attitude. First, unless you know the respondent well, it may be unreliable to judge his or her feeling purely on the basis of nonverbal expression. It is too easy for the interviewer to project his or her own feelings.

Here is an example of verifying the feeling associated with images of Mexico.

> R: The Sonora desert comes to mind with its vast expanse of sand, cactus, and heat.
> I: How do you, personally, feel about that sand, cactus, and heat?
> R: I love it. I'm an old desert rat from California. I was in the Sonora desert in Mexico for two weeks once. I can still smell the sage, and the desert air, and see the magnificent sunrises and sunsets.

To the interviewer who prefers sand on a beach edged by palm trees or by the cliffs of Maine, this Sonora desert scene may suggest a negative feeling. Without a verifying probe, the interviewer could wrongly assume that the respondent, also, places a negative value on "sand, cactus, and heat."

Second, you need verbal confirmation of the feeling to test the *reliability* of the coding by you and your coding partner, especially when only the typed transcript is used for coding, rather than the tape itself.

Third, by probing to verify apparent feelings, you can learn to what extent your initial hunches about the respondent's feelings, which were based on nonverbal cues, were accurate.

Fourth, showing interest in the respondent's feelings tends to motivate the respondent who feels the interviewer has a sympathetic interest.

For the *factual* dimension of the interview objectives, you are to discover whether your respondent knows certain objective facts about Mexico. Here is a list of specific facts ranging from one probably every American knows to one most Americans would not know. You are to formulate the questions needed to discover whether your respondent knows these facts:

1. The capital of Mexico is Mexico City.
2. The colors in the Mexican flag are red, white, and green.
3. Yucatan is part of Mexico.
4. Guatemala is on the southern border of Mexico.
5. Mexico's wars of independence from Spain began in 1810.
6. In 1963 the United States returned to Mexico the Chamizal section of El Paso, Texas.
7. The population of Mexico City is over 8.5 million.
8. American citizens do not need passports to enter Mexico as tourists.

Now you have the three dimensions of this interview: images, feelings, and facts. The image dimensions demand that the respondent be given total freedom to report *any* images. Feelings, for the purposes of this interview, must be linked to particular images. So if the respondent mentions an image but does not specify the associated feeling, it is your job to find that feeling and identify it as positive, neutral, or negative. If the respondent mentions a feeling about Mexico but gives no specific associated image, you should probe to discover the associated images.

The factual dimension is more restricted in scope. Your objective is not to discover all the facts the respondent knows about Mexico, but only to verify whether he or she knows eight specific facts that you have been given in advance. There is no need to identify the feelings associated with these facts.

Images, Feelings, and Facts about the American Way of Life.   The relationship between the three dimensions (images, feelings, and facts) are the same for this topic as they are described for the interview about Mexico. Therefore, we will simply supply the specific facts about the American Way of Life that you are to verify as known or unknown by your respondent.

1. The first ten amendments in the Bill of Rights were added to the U.S. Constitution in 1791.
2. The U.S. Constitution does not give the federal government any responsibility for public or private education.
3. About 20 percent of the U.S. population changes residence each year.
4. More than 600 foreign-language newspapers and periodicals in forty languages are printed and distributed in the United States.
5. About 35 percent of the U.S. population is affiliated with some religion.
6. Rock'n'roll music was introduced in America as "rhythm and blues" about 1910.
7. There are over fifty professional symphony orchestras in the United States.
8. About 70 percent of the average American's leisure time is spent at home.

Once the instructor has assigned one of the topics (Mexico or American Way of Life), you are ready to choose a partner.

Select a Partner

Your partner will cooperate with you in several ways. As a minimum, you will code each other's interview, calculate the coefficient of reliability, and discuss disagreements in the coding process. In addition you may work together on planning your interviews. In any case, your learning partner should be a person who was assigned the same interview topic you have.

Meet with your partner and decide together what pattern of cooperation you want to follow. There are several possible patterns that require only one planning meeting. First, you could decide to do no cooperative planning before the interview, but to only work together afterwards to *code* each other's interview, to *calculate* the coefficient of reliability, and to *discuss* the results. Second, you might agree to make up your own interview guide separately and give each other a copy; then, without any discussion, each could use whatever ideas from the other's guide that seem useful. Third, you could meet after doing your interview guide separately and then hammer out a revised interview guide to be used by both. If you start with this third plan in mind and find that you cannot agree on details, fall back on one of the other plans.

In my experience it is usually wise to follow a plan that does not require more than one meeting of the partners before the interview is done. If the instructor finds it feasible to use regular class time for this purpose, then more than one planning meeting of each pair becomes more practical.

Plan a Fifteen-Minute Interview

The end-product of your interview planning should be a one- or two-page *interview guide* with your questions arranged by topic in their most appropriate sequence. Study the next section on general objectives carefully so that your interview guide can achieve all the objectives.

General Objectives of the Interview. There are five general objectives of the interview. First, discover your respondent's most *salient* images and feelings regarding Mexico or the American Way of Life. It is impossible to discover all images and feelings! The most salient *images* are those that are the strongest, most outstanding, and easiest to recall. The most salient *feelings* are those that are strongest and, therefore, most clearly positive or negative.

Second, to the extent permitted by the fifteen-minute limit, probe the salient *images* to obtain enough *concrete* detail to be able to reliably classify them according to sense modality—sight, sound, smell, taste, or touch. Furthermore, probe the image to discover whether the associated feeling is positive, negative, or neutral.

Third, to the extent permitted by the fifteen-minute time limit, probe the *feelings* to clarify the associated images and make them concrete enough to be classified according to their sense modality. For example, to know that the respondent has a negative feeling about snakes does not tell us whether the respondent's image is the *sound* of the rattlesnake or the *sight* of a snake eating a gopher.

Fourth, discover the respondent's degree of knowledge regarding the eight specific points about Mexico or the American Way of Life. In this portion of the interview, neither salience or feelings are relevant. The point is to discover whether the respondent knows the specific facts.

Fifth, make sure you conduct questioning and probing on all the topics without forcing the respondent to fabricate responses and without suggesting any images or feelings.

Fifteen-Minute Time Limit.   Keep in mind that you should be able to cover all of the questions in less than fifteen minutes. If there is time left after discovering the most salient images and feelings, you should go back to clean up any ambiguities that exist and to probe for more concreteness of images and feelings. Your interview guide should not be more than two pages with topic headings, questions, and possible probes. The format should be laid out so that it can be seen at a glance. You do not have to leave any space on the page for answers or probe notes; the answers are on tape, and the probe notes should be written on a separate sheet.

Sequence of Topics.   In effect the interview has three topics; on your interview guide show them as images and associated feelings, factual knowledge, and feelings and associated images. Develop the topics in that order. The first and the third topics are similar except that in the first topic you ask directly about images and then probe for the feelings associated with each image as you go along. In the third topic you ask directly for positive and negative feelings and then probe for the images associated with each feeling as you go along. Under each topic you should have from two to ten questions and a plan for probing where needed. Now let's look at some guidelines that should be helpful for each of the three topics.

Images and Associated Feelings.   Since this topic opens the interview, you must design an *opening question* that is so broad that it in no way restricts the respondent to certain kinds of images or feelings or suggests any images or feelings. At the same time, the question should be a nonthreatening, open invitation to free association; the nonverbal accompaniment should motivate the respondent to plunge into his or her imagination.

This one broad opening question may be followed by a few other questions designed to stimulate the free-association process without suggesting any particular images or associated feelings. As you listen to the respondent's images and associated feelings, you must be ready to probe as you go along. You may be probing to obtain elaboration and clarification of the images so they can be classified by sense modality. Or you may be trying to clarify and verify the associated feelings so they can be reliably coded as to whether the images carry a positive, neutral, or negative feeling.

In all of your questioning and probing, keep in mind that an *image* must be as concrete as possible. An image is not a generalization, a principle, or abstraction. For example, a statement such as "Mexico is beautiful!" does not give you a clue about whether the *concrete* image in the respondent's mind is a white sand beach, a black sand beach, a snow-capped mountain, or a coyote howling in the desert. To probe for concreteness you could ask: "How is it beautiful?" or "What is beautiful about it?" or "What comes to your mind when you say 'Mexico is beautiful'?" The concrete image is one's imagination of a sensory experience such as a visual scene, a sound, a smell, a taste, or a tactile feeling.

It is crucially important that your probes do not suggest answers. After all, we want the respondent's images and feelings, not the interviewer's. To avoid biasing the response, use probes that are as neutral as possible and that exert as little topic control as possible. Have a plan in mind to first use a silent probe and then an encouragement probe before using immediate elaboration or immediate clarification probes. Probes of a particular point should be tried in that order—whether probing for images or for associated feelings. So you should never use the following kind of probe for images: "Is the campesino wearing a sombrero?" Instead, you should ask, "You mentioned the campesino in the field, how is he dressed?" "What sort of hat?" Similarly, in probing for feelings you should never ask, "Does that scene make you feel sad?" Instead, ask, "How does that make you feel?" If the least active probe, silence, is successful in getting the respondent to elaborate and clarify the images and feelings, there is no need to go on to more active probes.

Factual Knowledge.   The specific points of factual knowledge that you are to test in your interview were given earlier in this chapter and appear on the coding form to be supplied by your instructor. Most of the eight factual points can be verified by a single, straightforward question without any follow-up probes. Some of the bits of knowledge require two or more questions to verify the respondent's knowledge without giving away part of the answer by the question itself. In any case, avoid the multiple-choice question including the form that logically implies a yes-no answer. For example, the simple question "Is Yucatan part of Mexico?" implies a simple yes-no answer structure. Respondents would have a 50 percent chance of getting the correct answer, even if they had never heard of Yucatan and did not know whether it is a beach, city, state, or territory.

When you look at a particular point of knowledge, do not think of it as a simple, single-dimensioned question. Instead, analyze it to see how many different parts or levels of knowledge it contains. For example, to prove that your respondent knows that "Mexico's wars of independence from Spain began in 1810" you need to show that he or she knows (1) that Mexico was once a colony, (2) that it was a colony of Spain, (3) that it is no longer a colony, (4) that it gained its independence by war with Spain, and (5) that war began in 1810. This knowledge could never be shown by asking, for example, "Did Mexico's wars of independence from Spain begin in 1810?" This question supplies four of the five points of knowledge and leaves only the *date* of the event in question.

The process of using multiple questions to ascertain your respondent's knowledge should be used in facts 3, 5, and 6 about Mexico and in facts 1, 2, 4, and 6 about the American Way of Life. The extent to which we break down a knowledge point into its component parts depends on how thoroughly we want to test a person's knowledge, how much time there is for the interview, and how we are going to use the information. To save you time in this assignment, the number of knowledge points you are to break down into components by your questioning has been limited.

Feelings and Associated Images.   Of course this topic requires questions and probes similar to those used in the first topic—images and associated feelings. There are, however, two main differences. First, you are to discover only those images that are associated with a clearly *positive* or *negative* feeling. You have no interest in *neutral* images. Second, you must first specify whether you want to hear about the negative or the positive images. You do not just ask for an image but for a positive or negative image. In this case your follow-up probing must make the image clear enough to be able to classify it according to sense modality.

The wording of your questioning and probing on this topic should indicate two facts: You recognize that the respondent has already given you some positive and/or negative images in the first part of the interview, and you are looking for any additional images he or she might have that are clearly positive or negative.

A third probable difference is that, since you are looking for only the *salient* images and feelings and since you have already talked once about images and feelings, the respondent will have less that is new to say this time around. Don't try to "squeeze blood from a turnip" by probing for information that is not there, perhaps forcing your respondent to fabricate new images. You want only the salient, spontaneous images.

Contact a Suitable Respondent

Do not make the mistake of selecting a friend or member of the class for the interview. A friend may find your switch from the role of friend to interviewer a bit puzzling or may wonder why you are asking about things you should already know as a friend. Members of the class are also unsuitable because they know the interview is an artificial exercise; they know the questions to be asked and the techniques to be used. Also, it is more realistic for you to have to persuade an outsider to cooperate with you.

In explaining the purpose of the interview, emphasize that this is an assignment you must complete and that you cannot do it alone. Explain that its main purpose is to give *you* practice and to test *your* interviewing skills. Do *not* mention the topic now because your goal is to find the most salient images and feelings expressed *spontaneously* without forethought. Assure your respondent that the topic is an easy one and will take only fifteen minutes. At this time do *not* mention that the interview is to be tape-recorded. You will explain that at the time of the interview.

Make an appointment for an appropriate time and place for the interview. The interviewing must be done in a place where there is privacy and quiet. Interviewing may be done in some central location where the tape recorder is already set up and will be shared by others in the class (versus having your own tape recorder and finding you own interviewing space). In that case there will be a sign-up sheet at the location so the room can be reserved in half-hour intervals to allow time for one pair to get out and the other to get in, set up, and still have at least fifteen minutes for the interview itself. If a central location is used, take your respondent with you when you sign up to be sure you find a half-hour period when you, your respondent, and the room are all free. Once the time is selected, be sure both you and your respondent write it down. If the time is more than a day in the future, you might remind the person of the appointment the day preceding it.

Be sure to thank your respondent cordially for his or her willingness to help you and express your willingness to do a favor in return.

After you have selected an interview time, also sign up for a three-hour block of time to use the transcribing room, unless you have your own computer or typewriter, cassette recorder, and place to work.

Interview Your Respondent

Before you go to keep your appointment, be sure that you (1) have your own blank tape, (2) know how to use the particular tape recorder, (3) have your interview guide, and (4) have paper and pencil for probe notes.

Some, but not all, of the physical and social-psychological factors dealt with in Chapter 4 on establishing a communicative atmosphere should be applied in this case. Be sure to remove physical barriers between yourself and your respondent, ensure visual and auditory privacy, have certain facilities to attend to your respondent's potential needs, define the objectives of the interview, and explain the note taking and the tape-recording. Under these circumstances there is no need to give particular attention to dress and grooming if you are fellow students, to an explanation of who you are or when the respondent can expect to see you again, to assure the respondent of anonymity, or to explain why certain kinds of personal information are required.

Most of the needed explanation will already have been given in contacting and making an appointment with the respondent, but it is usually advisable to repeat these same points and thank the person again for coming.

One additional point. Before the interview begins, *explain* why you need to tape-record the interview. Do not ask for the respondent's permission to tape-record because your question might raise doubts in the respondent's mind. Instead, explain why you need to do it and how the tape is to be used. If the respondent objects, explain that given the objection you won't waste his or her time; instead you'll find someone else to interview. In my experience in decades of teaching interviewing, no respondent has ever objected when students were interviewing fellow students. However, in cases where the interviewer never mentioned that a tape recorder was going to be used, suspicion and resistance were registered by the respondent during or after the interview.

One of the most common problems in doing tape-recorded interviews is that either the interviewer's or the respondent's words are not always audible. Before the interview begins, test both your voice and the respondent's while sitting in the exact positions you will be in and with the microphone in place. Fortunately, words that may be unintelligible to an outside listener may be intelligible to the interviewer, who in this case will also be the transcriber. Try to avoid the exasperating experience of having to do an interview over again simply because it is not audible enough to transcribe accurately. Should this happen, do *not* reinterview the same person.

Remember that this type of interview is nonthreatening to the respondent and usually is thought of as fun. You want to establish an atmosphere of relaxed spontaneity. So you must avoid the feeling of time pressure, even though you have only fifteen minutes. This is plenty of time to cover all three subtopics; you should not worry about not being able to exhaust each topic or to go as deeply as possible into each one. Remember, you are trying to find only the *most salient* images, feelings, and knowledge. With a half-hour period in which to do a fifteen-minute interview, time is sufficient to get set up properly, give the appropriate explanations, have a little rapport-building conversation before the interview, and thank the person again afterwards.

It is important that you do not run over your fifteen-minute limit, so you must accurately time the interview in one of two ways. One way is to either have a watch in front of you or a clock where the respondent cannot see it. Just before you ask the first question in the interview proper, write down the time at which you must stop. When that time comes, wait until the respondent finishes the sentence and then say, "Our fifteen minutes are up, but . . ." and then add anything you feel is appropriate. Try to show that you realize the respondent has more to offer, but you have to stop because someone else has an appointment in the room. If there is time and you feel that the respondent would be greatly disappointed to terminate the interview so abruptly, you could continue for a few minutes. It is still important however, that your statement "our fifteen minutes are up" is on the tape, so that when you transcribe the tape you can stop typing at that point.

Transcribe Your Interview

Format of the Typescript. You need not be a skilled typist to transcribe your own interview because there is no need to produce finished copy. You may strike over, X out errors, and misspell without correcting. (If you are using a word processor, you can easily make a clean copy.) Use double spacing. Indicate your own words by the letter *I* for interviewer and your respondent's words by the letter *R*. When you give encouraging noises and words that are not really questions and don't interrupt the respondent, put them in parentheses in with *R*'s response rather than on a separate line.

Put your name, not the respondent's, and the topic of your interview at the top of the transcription. When you finish transcribing fifteen minutes of your interview, go back and type or write in the line numbers in the left margin. Number every fifth line beginning with number 5. If you follow these specifications, the format of your transcription will look like that in Figure 11.1.

Equipment for Transcribing. Ideally, to facilitate the transcribing process, it would be desirable to have a cassette tape recorder that is used only for transcribing and that is equipped with earphones and a foot pedal to start and stop the machine. Earphones are helpful when parts of the tape are marginally audible; they also allow you to avoid disturbing others and prevent others from disturbing you while transcribing. The foot pedal is useful because your hands can remain on the keyboard instead of reaching to turn the machine off and on. Nevertheless, I have found that it is perfectly possible to transcribe without earphones or a foot pedal. In this case the transcribing should be done in a room where it will not disturb others.

Principles of Transcribing. The beginning transcriber should be aware of several important principles. First, do not try to listen and type at the same time. Only a highly skilled typist can do this without making many errors and omissions. Listen only to the amount you can remember *accurately*; then stop the machine and type. The amount may not be a whole sentence; that's okay because if you wait too long to stop the machine, you may forget part of the response before you have finished typing what you heard. If this happens, you will have to back up the tape a bit and listen again, and you will waste more time than you saved by trying to remember long passages. With a little practice, you will discover how often you need to stop the machine. The faster your typing and the better your aural memory, the fewer times you will have to stop.

A second principle to observe for the purpose of learning to interview is to transcribe the *interviewer's* words *exactly* with any false starts, rewording, hesitations, and so forth. Such a record is important for analysis of the interviewer's verbal techniques. Do not be surprised to see that you do not speak with the unhesitating authority of a television anchorperson. For example, a typical bit

Figure 11.1   Sample transcription

Topic: _____   Interviewer: _____

I: What comes to your mind when you think of the American Way of Life?

R: Well...I hesitate because I get two very different sorts of reactions in

my mind. (I see!)

I: What sorts of reactions?

5 *R:*   Some good things and some bad things. (Uh-huh)

I: For example?

R: Well on the good side there's apple pie, baseball, democracy, high

standard of living and that sort of thing...(Uh-huh)..., then there's

things like crime, drugs, pollution, and general wasteful exploitation of

10   the nonrenewable resources, and other things on the bad side of the

American Way of Life. (Really!)

I: What specific examples of "democracy" fit in with the idea of the

American Way of Life?

R: Things like goining to the polls to vote, writing to your congressman,

15   and having freedom of expression. (I see. Good!)

I: Now could you tell me a little more about the "high standard of living"

you mentioned in connection with the American Way of Life?

of interviewer groping may look like this in print:

> *I:* Is that...I should say what do you think...or maybe feel is a better word,
> when you uh...picture the Mexican desert?

On the other hand, for the purpose of this assignment it *is* permissible and desirable to edit out false starts and hesitations on the part of the *respondent*. This will save you some typing time as illustrated in the following example:

> *On tape R:* Well...that is uh...usually I would think of something...or a
> scene that is...you might say desert with, you know like cactus,
> sand, jackrabbits and prairie dogs...that sort of thing.
> *Typed R:* Usually I would think of desert with cactus, sand, jackrabbits, and
> prairie dogs.

Of course, when you are listening to only short bursts before stopping the machine and typing, it is difficult to know how to edit out all of the meaningless "noise" from the sentence. As you start listening to a sentence, if you find that the first part has no clue to relevant material (as in the previous example), you can listen to a bit more before stopping and typing to see what, if anything, is relevant. In any case, do the amount of editing that your typing speed and aural memory will allow, but do *not* lose any relevant material in the process. It is better to err in the direction of including irrelevancies rather than to exclude relevancies. Remember that any word or phrase that is worth probing for elaboration or clarification must be included in the response.

The process of transcribing a fifteen-minute interview according to the foregoing specifications takes from 1$^1/_2$ to 2$^1/_2$ hours, depending on the speed of the respondent's speech, the audibility of the tape, and the skill of the transcriber. To be safe, reserve a tape recorder and typewriter for a three-hour period.

Analyze Your Interviewing Behavior

Two types of analyses are involved for the interview. First, you will analyze your own interview to note the skills you demonstrated. The purpose of this self-analysis is not to grade yourself but to heighten your awareness of your own behavior and your ability to improve it in the future. In the second type of analysis, which we will discuss in the next section, you will code the relevant content of both your own and your coding partner's interview. Your partner will also code his or her interview as well as yours. This allows a comparison of two independent coders' analyses of relevant information obtained in the interviews.

In analyzing your behavior, apply all that you have learned in Chapters 2 through 9; include the following skills: formulating relevant and motivating questions, establishing a communicative atmosphere, delivering the questions, listening to the respondent, observing the respondent, evaluating the responses, and probing the responses. Not all of the suggestions offered in these chapters can be expected to apply to all interview situations, but many do apply to this interview.

Figure 11.2 is a copy of the self-analysis questionnaire to be used in analyzing your own behavior. Put your answers on the self-analysis answer sheet supplied by your instructor. Note that the questionnaire and answer sheet are divided into sections corresponding to the topics of Chapters 2 through 9. The method for discovering the answers to the questions varies from one topic to another. For example, you can complete the first seven questions on formulating questions by analyzing your *interview guide* only. Fill in the second section on establishing a communicative atmosphere directly from your memory. Do the third section on delivering the question by listening carefully to the first three to four minutes of your tape. For the fourth section on listening to the respondent, read the typescript of your interview. Answer the fifth section, observing

Figure 11.2   Questionnaire for analyzing interviewer's behavior

---

SELF-ANALYSIS QUESTIONNAIRE

A. FORMULATING QUESTIONS (Chapters 2–3): Answer by analyzing your interview guide. Put the answers on the *answer sheet* supplied by the instructor.

---

1. Was your opening question in your interview guide broad enough to invite all possible images and associated feelings?
       a) yes   b) not sure   c) no

2. For which of the following imagery modalities did you have separate questions in your interview guide?
       a) sight   b) sound   c) smell   d) taste   e) touch

3. What is the total number of questions in your interview guide?

4. How many of these questions are in a form that implies a "yes" or "no" answer?

5. In retrospect, how many of the questions in your interview guide are *loaded* in some way?

6. In retrospect, how do you feel your questions on factual knowledge worked?
       a) no problems   b) some problems   c) many problems

7. Were you able to word the factual knowledge questions so that you did not give away part of the knowledge in the questions?
       a) yes always   b) most of the time   c) not usually

B. ESTABLISHING A COMMUNICATIVE ATMOSPHERE (Chapter 4): Answer from memory.

---

8. In retrospect, do you see any improvements that could have been made in the physical arrangements in the interview setting? If so, what?

9. Which of the following did you remember to do in the interview?
       a) explain the purpose of the interview
       b) explain your use of the tape recorder
       c) explain your note taking
       d) thank your respondent for coming at the beginning of the interview
       e) thank your respondent at the end of the interview

C. DELIVERING THE QUESTION (Chapter 5): Answer by listening to your tape.

---

10. Listen to the beginning portion of your tape up to the end of your *first page of typescript*. This will probably be about three to four minutes, depending on the pace of the interview. Listen to the tape as you scan the typescript and each time a silence of two or more seconds occurs, indicate its length and insert it in parentheses where it occurs in the typescript. Since you may have edited out some of the meaningless "noise" in the transcript, some of the silences will not be precisely locatable, but it is very important to measure all the silences of two or more seconds. (You can become your own human stopwatch with a little practice by looking at a watch with a sweep second hand and counting "one thousand, two thousand," and so on and adjusting your pace so that you come close to sixty per minute; then use this pace for counting the length of silences.)

When all the silences of two seconds or longer have been inserted in the typescript, count the number of silences of each length and fill in the blanks on the answer sheet.

2 seconds   3 seconds   4 seconds   5 seconds or more

11. After listening to the first portion of your tape, do you feel that your pacing (rate of speech and timing of pauses) was generally too fast or too slow?

a) much too fast   b) a little fast   c) just right
d) a little slow   e) much too slow

12. How would you rate your tone of voice in the early portion of the interview?

a) showed a lively interest in the topic and respondent
b) showed some interest most of the time
c) usually rather neutral in tone
d) sometimes a bit dull and uninterested
e) sometimes impatient or ego threatening

D. LISTENING TO THE RESPONDENT (Chapter 6): Answer by reading transcript.

13. Read the transcription of your interview to detect points that could have been probed that you did not notice at the time. How many such points did you find?

14. To what extent would you say you remembered to *show* your respondent that you were listening by each of the following ways? Use the following key:

0 = never   1 = rarely   2 = sometimes   3 = frequently

a) by my facial expression and eye contact
b) by encouraging sounds like "uh-huh," "I see," "really!" and so forth
c) by directly praising the respondent's efforts
d) by wording probes to show recognition of what has been said

15. What were some of the things that made it difficult for you to listen as closely and accurately as you would like?

E. OBSERVING THE RESPONDENT (Chapter 7): Answer from memory of the interview.

16. Do you recall any points in the interview where your respondent's nonverbal behavior gave you *visual* clues to any of the following? Check any that apply.

a) turn-taking desires.
b) validity of a verbal statement
c) feelings associated with images given
d) energy level or mood of the respondent

17. Did you notice any times that the respondent's body language seemed to be at odds with the verbal message given?

a) never noticed any   b) once or twice   c) more frequently

continued on page 214

Figure 11.2 continued

F. EVALUATING THE RESPONSES (Chapter 8): Answer by analyzing your transcript.

---

18. How many times did you mistakenly accept a generality as a concrete image?
     a) never   b) once or twice   c) three or more times
19. How many times did you *assume* you knew your respondent's feeling toward an image rather than probing for verbal confirmation of the feeling?
     a) never   b) once or twice   c) three or more times
20. How many apparent contradictions between facts and/or generalizations did you find in reading the transcript that you didn't notice while doing the interview?
     a) none   b) one or two   c) three or more
21. Do you recall any times that your respondent's nonverbal responses were incongruent with his or her verbal responses?
     a) none   b) one or two   c) three or more

G. PROBING (Chapter 9): Answer by analyzing your transcript.

---

22. How many probes did you use in your whole interview?
     (Do not count the basic questions in your interview guide but do include all of your probes whether a simple "uh-huh" or whole questions used to probe a previous response.)
23. In how many of the probes aimed at obtaining elaboration or clarification of a previous response did you forget to use the respondent's own words in indicating what you wanted elaborated or clarified?
24. How many of your elaboration or clarification probes were worded to imply that a dichotomus "yes" or "no" answer was wanted?
25. How many times did you probe for more concreteness of an image?
26. How many times did you probe for the *feeling* associated with a particular image?
27. How many times did you probe for elaboration or clarification of a *feeling*?
28. How many times did your probe simply *reflect* and *accept* a feeling?
29. How many simple *encouragement* probes did you use?

---

the respondent, by recalling the interview from your memory. Analyze your typescript to complete the sixth and seventh sections on evaluating the response and probing. Read through the whole questionnaire before you begin to obtain the answers one section at a time.

This analysis of your own behavior will probably take from two to three hours once you have transcribed your interview. When your analysis is complete, your instructor will discuss with you how to use the results.

Coding the Interview Content

You will code both your own and your coding partner's interview transcript. Remember *coding* means to classify the information in the respondent's answers into categories relevant to the intent of the interview. The first logical step in any coding process is to decide which of the content items are *relevant*. Do not assess the proportion of relevant and irrelevant information. Often an interviewer must tolerate a considerable amount of irrelevant information, but no good interviewer fails to obtain the necessary relevant information; so code only relevant information.

Several objectives are accomplished by coding the content of your own interview—objectives that cannot be accomplished any other way. First, winnowing out the irrelevant makes you aware of the need to keep the objectives of the interview clearly in mind at all times, whether interviewing or coding. Second, awareness of the amount of irrelevant talk raises the question of whether you allowed the respondent to wander too far from the objectives or whether your tolerance of the irrelevancies contributed positively to the spontaneity and validity of the interview. Third, in trying to classify the relevant materials, you will become acutely aware of any failures to probe for needed concreteness, clarity, or completeness, because it is extremely difficult to *reliably* classify material if the meaning is fuzzy or too abstract. Finally, coding the material in both your own interview and your coding partner's provides the information needed for mathematically calculating the degree of reliability of the coding process.

Identifying Relevant Material.   To begin the coding operation you need a copy of your interview transcript, a copy of your coding partner's transcript, and two copies of the one-page coding forms. (The forms will be supplied by your instructor.) Start coding your own interview first. Take the following steps for topics A and C of the interview—images with associated feelings and feelings with associated images.

1. *Review the objectives of the interview.* This can be done by reviewing the section in this chapter on selecting the interview topic and by studying the coding form for your particular topic.

2. *Underline relevant material.* Read your own transcript and underline only the relevant words and phrases; keep the objectives of the interview and the categories of the coding form in mind. Never underline a whole sentence if you can avoid it because often different parts of a sentence might be coded into different categories. The meaning of an underlined word or phrase should be interpreted in the larger context of the whole sentence or paragraph.

If an image is not concrete enough to be classified according to one of the five sense modes, do *not* underline it as relevant. But if the feeling tone is not clearly classifiable into positive or negative, the image may be classified in the "neutral or undetermined" column—provided that the image is clearly classifiable on the sense mode dimension.

Figure 11.3   Transcript with relevant material indicated by location

>   **20**
> *R:*   Part of the American Way of Life is the <u>noisy traffic,</u>
>   **21a**   **21b**
> the <u>exhaust fumes,</u> and <u>black smoke</u> from factories. On
>   **22a**   **22b**
> the other hand, you've got <u>microwave ovens,</u> <u>gritty seats</u>
>   **23a**   **23b**
> at the <u>baseball game,</u> and the <u>taste of hot dogs.</u>

    3. Identify the location of relevant material. Each relevant bit of information must be identified so that you can verify whether you and your coding partner put the same bit of information in the same cell in the coding form. Each bit will be identified by its location. If there is only one relevant image or feeling on a line, then it is identified by the line number. If there are more than one on a line, then we add an a, b, c, and so on to show which item on that line is being coded. Write the identification number above each underlined bit as in Figure 11.3. Remember that you have numbered every fifth line on your transcript to facilitate this location process.

    Classifying Relevant Material.   First, classify the relevant material for topics A and C, which use the same two-dimensional system (sense mode and feeling tone) for classifying images. Then code topic B, which deals with knowledge of facts coded on a single dimension.

    Topics A and C (images and feelings): Follow these steps to classify the relevant material on your coding form:

1. Make your entries on your coding form in *pencil* so you can make changes easily if you change your mind after discussion with your partner.
2. Place the identification number (location) of each underlined bit into the appropriate cell in your coding form so that you are correctly classifying it on both dimensions at once.
3. If on second though you feel that a particular bit of information is not classifiable according to the sense mode (sight, sound, smell, taste, or touch), do not code it.
4. Write in the identification numbers neatly and small enough to get two rows in the cell.
5. Put the identification numbers in each cell in the order they appear in the transcript. Begin in the upper left corner of the cell; separate each

Figure 11.4   Entries in hypothetical cell number 7

> **7**
> 3, 27, 32a, 33, 41,
> 42c, 89

number with a comma as shown in Figure 11.4. These format details are important for comparing the two coding forms, discussing the differences, and calculating the coefficient of reliability.

Topic B (factual knowledge): Coding factual knowledge differs in several ways from coding images and feelings. First, you do not underline specific bits of information to be coded. Instead, you simply review everything the respondent said in response to the one or more questions dealing with a particular factual point; then you make a judgment as to whether the respondent had all, some, or none of the knowledge. A second difference in this coding is that you classify each case on only one dimension, which might be called "completeness of knowledge." Thus the operation is simplified considerably because you have only three possible categories (columns) rather that the fifteen possible categories (cells) used in coding topics A and C.

To determine whether the respondent had complete knowledge of a given point, you must review the interview's questions and probes to determine whether they inadvertently supply any of the information. If they do supply the information, you cannot classify the response as knowledgeable on that detail. Your judgment of the completeness of the respondent's knowledge on a particular point does not have to be precise since the coding form supplies only the three degrees of knowledge (all, some, or none). It would be more difficult to obtain agreement between coders if there were more quantitative categories.

The process of coding responses to questions of factual knowledge can be summarized in the following steps.

1. Review the eight knowledge statements on your coding form and note which ones must be broken down into separate knowledge components.
2. Read the respondent's *whole* response to each of the eight factual knowledge items and determine whether it contains all, some, or none of the components.
3. Put one check in the appropriate column in your coding form for each of the eight topics.

After you complete coding your own interview, repeat the process for your partner's interview. The process will be the same. Simply trade transcriptions with your partner, use a second coding form, and proceed. The only difference in this second case is that your partner has done the underlining and identifying of relevant material. Even though you might not have underlined precisely the same words, you should accept your partner's underlining and identification numbers. This does not mean, however, that you must agree that all of the underlined fragments are relevant. If you think a particular item does not pass the relevance test, simply omit it from the coding. When you have finished the two coding forms, put the appropriate names in the blanks for interviewer and coder at the top of each. Now you are ready to meet with your coding partner to compare codings, to discuss differences, to make any changes in your own coding that you feel are justified, and to calculate the coefficient of reliability.

Compare Codings with Your Partner

First, compare and discuss the two codings of one interview and make any justifiable changes in the coding; then do the same with the second interview. Let's look at the comparison process in enough detail to allow you and your partner to lay the foundation successfully for mathematically calculating the coefficient of reliability.

Comparing the Two Coding Forms.   To compare your and your partner's coding of the same interview, get together and take the following steps for topics A and C on the coding sheet.

1. Each of you bring the interview transcripts as well as your two completed coding forms.
2. While each of you looks at your coding form for the same person's interview, one person calls off his or her own entries in one cell while the other person checks to note which of the same items he or she entered in that same cell. When the listener has the same item, he or she says "yes" and circles that number on his or her coding sheet, and the caller also circles that number on his or her own sheet. If the listener does *not* have the number, he or she says "no" and the caller goes on to the next number.
3. In doing step 2, be sure that the caller first identifies which cell's contents are going to be called off. Otherwise confusion will reign! Give the cell number from the coding form *before* you start calling off the statements it contains.

This procedure should not take more than five minutes because many of the cells might be empty or have only two or three items entered. When all of the agreements have been circled on both coding forms for one interview, you are ready to discuss the comparison.

To compare your coding for topic B, factual knowledge, use the same procedure; circle the checkmarks which both coders have placed in the same column for each of the eight items.

Discussing Disagreements.   Begin the discussion by each of you looking at your own coding form for either your own or your partner's interview. Look for the first disagreement (uncircled number) on your form. If you have a number in the first cell that your partner does not, find out where your partner put that number. Your partner may have put in a different cell or may not have entered it in any cell. If your partner did not enter it in any cell, perhaps he or she considered it irrelevant or simply overlooked it.

In cases where the same number is in different cells or one of you considered the item irrelevant, try to ascertain the source of the disagreement. There are three basic reasons why two coders can disagree:

1. Clarity of purpose and definitions: One person might consider an item irrelevant because of a different understanding of the purposes of the interview. Or, the same item might be placed in different cells because the two of you have a different understanding of the definitions of the categories in one or both dimensions.

2. Clarity of response: An item may be considered irrelevant or appear in different cells because the response is ambiguous, incomplete, and confusing and thus difficult to interpret for the intended meaning. This could have been remedied by further probing for completeness and clarity in the interview.

3. Clarity of thought: Disagreements may arise in the placement of an item simply because one (or both) of the coders was not alert and logical in the coding.

In discussing the sources of disagreement, one or both of you might recognize that you made an error and want to change your initial coding. If you are not convinced by your partner that you made an error in coding a particular item, stick to your decision and do not change. In effect, you agree to disagree. When you have finished discussing your disagreements in coding one interview, enter in the blank provided at the top of your coding form the number of changes in all three topics you made in your own coding as a result of the discussion.

When you have completed the discussion of one interview, go on to the discussion of the second interview and repeat the process.

Calculate the Coefficient of Reliability

In the formula you are going to use to calculate the degree of reliability shown by your and your partner's coding of your two interviews, the reliability measure will range between 0 and 1. Zero indicates complete disagreement and 1.0 indicates perfect agreement.

Advantages of Measuring Reliability   After comparing codings and discussing disagreements with your partner, you will have a rough idea of how much you disagreed, but you need a more precise measure of reliability (amount of agreement) to compare the reliability in the coding of your own interview versus your partner's interview. Since both interviews will have been coded by the same two people and since the same coding categories are used, most of the variation in reliability will be due to differences in the clarity of the responses in the two interviews. This clarity, in turn, is a function of both the skill of the interviewer and the articulateness of the respondent. At least part of any lack of clarity could have been corrected by more careful listening, more critical evaluation of the responses, and more diligent probing by the interviewer. So this precise coefficient of reliability is useful in alerting interviewers to the need for more effective interviewing.

Another advantage of the precise measure is that it allows you to compare this performance with a similar interview in the future, thus measuring the amount of gain in the reliability of the interviewing.

Procedure for Calculating.   The formula given here for calculating the coefficient of reliability was developed by Scott[1] and has two basic advantages over other formulas. First, it has a maximum range from 0.0 to 1.0 (like any statistical correlation) regardless of the number of coding categories or how the cases are distributed in those categories. This makes comparison of the reliability in two different situations valid. A second advantage, which does not immediately concern us here, is that it lends itself to a precise test of statistical significance of the difference between two coefficients of reliability.

A calculation form (labeled 11-C) will be provided by your instructor for you to use in calculating the coefficient of reliability of your and your partner's coding.

Note that you calculate a separate coefficient of reliability for each of the three topics in the interview. The *calculation form (11-C)* provides for all three. The formula is:

$$C = \frac{Po - Pe}{1 - Pe}$$

where C = coefficient of reliability

Po = proportion of agreements actually observed

$Po = \dfrac{A}{T}$ where A is the number of agreements (items circled on *both* coding sheets for that interview)

where T is the total number of items (circled and uncircled) appearing on *both* coding sheets

Pe = proportion of agreements expected by chance

$Pe = \Sigma pi^2$ where Σ is the sum for all the cells in the coding system

where pi is the proportion of *all* the items classified that appear in a particular cell (Then this decimal fraction is squared.)

The operational meaning of this formula will become clear as you follow the calculation steps described next. Before the calculations begin, you and your partner must have finished coding both interviews. Partners should exchange coding sheets so that you each have both coding sheets for your own interview. When you have the two codings of your *own* interview and one calculation form (11-C), you are ready to calculate the coefficient of reliability.

Steps in calculating.   First we will consider the steps in calculating the coefficient of reliability for topics A and C of *your* interview; then we'll look at the simpler steps for calculating the coefficient for topic B.

1. Calculate *Po* for topics A and C. The term *Po* in the formula on the calculation form 11-C is the *proportion* of agreements actually *observed* in comparing the two coding forms. Sometimes this is called the percentage agreement score. To calculate *Po* simply count the number of circled items on *both* coding sheets or multiply the number of circled items on one sheet by two. This gives you *A*, which represents the total number of *agreements*. Now count the total number of items (circled and uncircled) on both coding sheets; this gives you the *T* value in the formula for *Po*. Now divide *A* by *T* and put the resulting decimal fraction in place of *Po* in the basic formula.

2. Calculate *Pe* for topics A and C. *Pe* is the *proportion* of agreements that would be *expected* by chance in view of the number of cells and the distribution of items in these cells. To calculate *Pe*, you must use calculation form 11-C and take the following steps:

    a. Using *your* coding of your *own* interview, count the number of items you entered in cell 1 in your coding form and enter this figure in the first row (cell 1) of column (a) in calculation form 11-C. Continue this process for the remaining 14 cells to complete column (a). Don't be surprised if the count in several cells is zero!

    b. Complete column (b) by counting the number of items in each cell of your *partner's* coding of *your* interview. Now you have the basic data to complete the other columns in the calculation form without further reference to the coding forms.

    c. For each cell (row), add the figures in columns (a) and (b) and put the sum in column (c). Now total the figures in column (c).

    d. Divide each cell in column (c) by the total of column (c) and enter the results in column (d).

    e. Square each figure in column (d) and enter the product in column (e) as a decimal fraction. Sum the figures in column (e) and you have the value for *Pe* in your basic formula. Since you have already obtained *Po* in step 1, you have all you need to calculate *C*, which is the coefficient of reliability.

    f. Calculate *C* and enter the result in the appropriate blank on your calculation Form 11-C.

3. Calculating *Po* for Topic B. To calculate *C* for topic B (factual knowledge), follow the directions on the calculation form where *Pe* and (1 − *Pe*) have already been calculated for you. Enter the resulting *C* value in the appropriate blank.

Cross-Checking the Calculations. After completing all of the steps for calculating the coefficient of reliability, both you and your partner have completed the calculation for your *own* interviews. To check on the accuracy of the calculations, trade coding forms and calculation forms and check the figures in all of the five columns for topics A and C as well as the final calculation of the formula. Also cross-check the calculation of *Po* and *C* for topic B. Now you should have an accurate measure of the reliability of the coding of each of your interviews!

Reporting the Coefficient of Reliability.   Your instructor will provide a form called Coefficient of Reliability Team Report to use in reporting the coefficients obtained for the interviews done by you and your coding partner. From these reports, the instructor will make a summary to use in class discussion.

Report Your Experience

The philosophy behind the Skill Learning Cycle assumes that to learn the high-order skills needed for good depth interviewing, we must *know* what we want to accomplish in the interview, *plan* how we are going to achieve those objectives, and *do* the interview by properly delivering the question, by listening and observing to evaluate the response, and by probing to obtain the information needed to meet the objectives of the interview. Once the interview is completed, we need to *analyze* it to evaluate our own interviewing behavior and to evaluate the interview's effectiveness in terms of the quantity and quality of the information obtained. All this you have done.

In order to maximize the learning value of this activity, you need to take one final step: *Reflect* on your experiences. Your reflection will maximize the way you learn from experience and will make you ready to do a better job in future interviews. To stimulate the reflection process, you should write an *experiential report*.

Your reflections should take the form of an internal conversation in which you ask yourself questions and search your experiences for the answers. Your questions might be similar to these: What surprised me about the experience? What would I do differently in the future? How did the experience make certain ideas and concepts more meaningful, more understandable? What did I learn about myself in the process? What part of the experience did I enjoy most and least? What was most difficult? In general, what did I learn?

In going to your experiences for the answers, be sure to include all phases of the experience: planning, doing, and analyzing. Do not forget to review the results of your self-analysis as well as the results of the content analysis and the discussion of the coding disagreements.

Try to keep your experiential report short and succinct—a *distillation* of the high points of your experience. Most of your time should be spent reviewing the experience rather than writing a detailed experiential odyssey. The report should not exceed one typed page.

Your instructor may want to use these experiential reports as a basis of analysis and discussion or in planning future interviewing experiences. In any case, writing the experiential report and the required reflection will be of great value in maximizing your learning.

SUMMARY

The interview field project in this chapter is conducted by completing the major steps in the Skill Learning Cycle:

1. Select the topic for your interview. (For the field project in this chapter, the instructor selects the topic.)
2. Select a partner to work with.
3. Plan a fifteen-minute interview.
4. Contact a suitable respondent.
5. Interview your respondent on tape.
6. Transcribe the tape.
7. Analyze your own interviewing behavior.
8. Code the relevant content of the interview.
9. Compare codings with your partner.
10. Calculate the coefficient of coding reliability.
11. Write a report on your experiences.

NOTE

1. W. A. Scott, "Reliability of Content Analysis," *Public Opinion Quarterly* 19 (1955): 321–25.

Epilogue

YEARS OF EXPERIENCE in doing interviews, doing research on interviewing, and teaching people to interview have convinced me that learning to be an effective interviewer requires experience guided by a learning strategy. It is not the *quantity* of experience but the *quality* that is the important factor. Any amount of blind repetition and unexamined interviewing experience may merely fix bad habits into a rigid pattern. To avoid this danger, our initial interviewing behavior must be planned, performed, objectively observed, analyzed, evaluated, and reflected on before we do repeated interviews.

The Skill Learning Cycle provides a strategy for achieving a high-quality experience. It presents a conceptual scheme and a specific plan of action that we can repeat to improve our interviewing in the future.

Now that you have experienced the full Skill Learning Cycle here in the final chapter, you will likely have a greater insight, appreciation, and understanding of the vital functional relationships among the various phases of the cycle. For example, perhaps now you can see clearly the integral relationship between understanding objectives, formulating questions, and evaluating responses; between listening, observing, evaluating responses, and probing; and between understanding objectives, coding responses, and testing reliability. This interrelatedness constitutes a powerful gestalt that is the essence of understanding how to interview.

The Skill Learning Cycle is a self-teaching process that you can successfully apply in the future. For example, tape-record a few of your interviews

225

done as part of your job, analyze the results, and plan your next interview in light of your analysis. You can do all of the cycle without a partner except the discussion and the measurement of reliability.

Your direct experience with the Skill Learning Cycle in this text will allow you to improve your basic interviewing skills in any setting. If you take the initiative and repeat the cycle, either on your own or with the help of another interested learner, your skills will grow and you will constantly improve as an interviewer.

Nothing would please me more than to have helped launch you into this self-improvement phase in interviewing.

Annotated Bibliography

THIS ANNOTATED LIST of books is presented to be a bridge between the basic skills dealt with in this book and the application of these skills in a variety of professional settings.

Specific interviewing objectives, strategies, techniques, and tactics, as well as potential legal and ethical problems, are illustrated for the professional settings of journalism (print, radio, and television), social work, counseling, management, criminal interrogation, courtroom cross-examination, and medicine for nurses, physicians, and psychiatrists.

Brady, John. *The Craft of Interviewing*. New York: Vintage Books, 1976.

> A paperback whose major focus is the steps in doing interviews for and writing up feature stories as opposed to news stories. Gives practical suggestions—illustrated by amusing examples—for locating and contacting respondents, getting their cooperation, doing background research in preparation for the interview, questioning techniques, and writing up the interview for publication.

Broughton, Irv. *The Art of Interviewing for Television, Radio and Film*. Blue Ridge Summit, Pa.: TAB Books, 1981.

> Deals with how to prepare for an interview, types of questions to be asked, types of respondents, legal aspects, and technical problems of the interview. Distinguishes between live and videotaped interviews for broadcast. Gives specific techniques for handling the sound aspects of the interview. One hundred pages of transcripts of actual interviews are a special feature.

Cormier, William H., and Cormier, L. Sherilyn. *Interviewing Strategies for Helpers*. Boston: Jones and Bartlett Publications, 1987.

One of the most comprehensive treatments of helping strategies for counseling and social work. Describes tactics for helping clients assess problems and define goals, then goes on to give guidelines for selecting and applying such intervention strategies as symbolic modeling, emotive imagery, cognitive restructuring, stress inoculation, meditation, muscle relaxation, desensitization, and self-management. There is an extensive bibliography of over 800 books and articles on the interviewing process.

Couleman, John L., and Block, Marian R. *The Medical Interview: A Primer for Students of the Art*. Philadelphia: F. A. Davis Co., 1987.

Describes interviewing mainly as a diagnostic tool for physicians. Gives many short doctor-patient dialogues to illustrate techniques. Discusses special problem topics and types of problem patients and gives suggestions for dealing with these problems. An appendix has a nine-page medical history interview transcribed from a real taped interview. There is also an excellent bibliography on the medical interview.

Drake, J. D. *Interviewing for Managers*. rev. ed. New York: American Management Association, 1982.

Chapters 9 through 15 deal with interviewing for specific management objectives such as conducting evaluation interviews, selling the candidate, matching the candidate to the job, interviewing college graduates, and abiding by the rules of fair employment practices in the interview.

Edwards, B. J., and Brilhart, John K. *Communication in Nursing Practice*. St. Louis: C. V. Mosby, 1981.

Considers such topics as nursing as communicating, interpersonal communication in the therapeutic process, nonverbal cues in nursing, beliefs and values of the effective nurse-communicator, and the nurse as interviewer as well as the nurse as problem solver, public speaker, and member of the complex hierarchical organization called the hospital.

Enelow, Allen J., and Swisher, Scott. *Interviewing and Patient Care*. 3rd ed. Fairlawn, N. J.: Oxford University Press, 1986.

Covers mainly interviewing for physicians. Gives suggestions for the initial diagnostic interview and shows how to obtain certain types of problem information. Has chapters on interviewing the deaf and the blind and other special types of respondents such as children, parents, family groups, and the elderly.

Ferber, Robert, ed. *Readings in Survey Research*. Chicago: American Marketing Association, 1978.

Deals with sample design, question design, mail surveys, telephone surveys, personal interview surveys, panels, and other survey strategies.

Gorden, Raymond L. *Interviewing: Strategy, Techniques and Tactics*. 4th ed. Chicago: Dorsey Press, 1987.

Considers the information-gathering interview as a form of communication in social contexts. Perhaps the most relevant portion for the purposes of this bibliography is Part IV, which gives sample dialogues of good and bad interviews in 8 professional settings: social work, employee appraisal, parent-teacher conferences, mass-media impact evaluation, nursing, counseling, journalism, and police interrogation.

Higginbotham, James B., and Cox, Keith K. *Focus Group Interviews: A Reader*. Chicago: American Marketing Association, 1979.

A small book (129 p.) that presents the interviewer as a discussion leader of a small group in order to obtain information about the discussants' beliefs, knowledge, attitudes, and feelings regarding a product or service. It contains twenty-four articles under four headings: (1) what is focus-group interviewing, (2) preparing and planning for focus-group interviews, (3) marketing applications, and (4) advantages and limitations of group focus interviews.

Hoopes, James. *Oral History: An Introduction for Students*. Chapel Hill: University of North Carolina Press, 1979.

Part I discusses nature and objectives of oral history. Part II deals with the influence of society, culture, and personality on the oral history process. Part III describes the field work process of arranging, preparing, and conducting the interview. Part IV covers writing the report, legal and ethical problems, and oral history collections and sources.

Inbau, Fred E., and Reid, John E. *Criminal Interrogations and Confessions*. 3rd ed. Baltimore: Williams and Wilkins, 1985.

An excellent distillation of the most effective strategies, techniques, and tactics that can be legally used in attempting to establish the innocence or guilt of a suspect. Written by Fred Inbau, law professor at Northwestern University and former director of the Chicago Police Scientific Crime Detection Laboratory, with the help of John Reid, staff member of the same laboratory.

Schwartz, Louis E. *Proof, Persuasion, and Cross-Examination: A Winning New Approach in the Courtroom*. Englewood Cliffs, N. J.: Executive Reports, 1973.

Deals mainly with cross-examining witnesses in the courtroom to obtain testimony to determine a witness's basis for evidence: personal knowledge, recollection, direct perception, actions, state of mind, or operations of the mind.

Shea, Shawn C. *Psychiatric Interviewing: The Art of Understanding*. Philadelphia: W. B. Saunders, 1988.

Begins with the fundamentals of interviewing in Part I. Part II covers exploring psychoses and affective disorders as well as eliciting social histories. Part III deals with suicidal and homicidal ideation. Transcribed interview dialogues are used to illustrate many of the concepts.

Stricklin, David, and Sharpless, Rebecca. *The Past Meets the Present: Essays on Oral History*. New York: University Press of America, 1988.

A small book in which eight writers cover such basic issues as the nature of oral history, the current state of the craft, case studies in oral history, and the future of oral history.

Author Index

231

Subject Index

THE BOOK'S MANUFACTURE

Basic Interviewing Skills
was typeset by Point West, Inc.
Carol Stream, Illinois.
The typefaces are Baskerville and Omega.
Printing and binding were done by
Braun-Brumfield, Inc., Ann Arbor, Michigan.
Cover design by Lucy Lesiak Design, Chicago.
Internal design by John B. Goetz,
Design & Production Services Co., Chicago.